M000034996

UNREASONABLE

Also by Devon W. Carbado

Acting White?: Rethinking Race in "Post-Racial" America

The Long Walk to Freedom: Runaway Slave Narratives

UNREASONABLE

BLACK LIVES, POLICE POWER, AND THE FOURTH AMENDMENT

DEVON W. CARBADO

THE
NEW
PRESS

NEW YORK
LONDON

Requests for permission to reproduce selections from this book should be made through
our website: https://thenewpress.com/contact.

Published in the United States by The New Press, New York, 2022
Distributed by Two Rivers Distribution

ISBN 978-1-62097-424-7 (hc)
ISBN 978-1-62097-425-4 (ebook)
CIP data is available

The New Press publishes books that promote and enrich public discussion and
understanding of the issues vital to our democracy and to a more equitable world. These
books are made possible by the enthusiasm of our readers; the support of a committed
group of donors, large and small; the collaboration of our many partners in the
independent media and the not-for-profit sector; booksellers, who often hand-sell New
Press books; librarians; and above all by our authors.

www.thenewpress.com

Book design and composition by Bookbright Media
This book was set in Minion Pro and Fort

Printed in the United States of America

10 9 8 7 6 5 4 3 2 1

For my parents Bela Silvera Carbado and George Carbado

Contents

UNREASONABLE

Prologue

I still remember the day I became a Black American. I wasn't born one—to borrow from a point Simone de Beauvoir made about women. Indeed, I wasn't born American at all, but immigrated here from my birthplace of the United Kingdom.

But I became a Black American anyway. Before I freely embraced that identity, others ascribed it to me. That ascription meant that I was strictly scrutinized from the moment I left home—in elevators, walking the streets, at department stores, in parks, at restaurants, at work, at the movies—to the moment I returned.

Resisting this scrutiny was virtually impossible. Blackness per se triggered it. There was nothing I could do to prevent myself from becoming a Black American—and, more specifically, the historical figure of the Black American man.

Day after day, I would have some interaction, some episode, some moment, that facilitated my racial naturalization into Black American life. None of these naturalization ceremonies involved judges in government buildings in the middle of the afternoon.

And far too many involved police officers on public streets in the middle of the night.

One of my earliest racial naturalization ceremonies occurred shortly after I had purchased my first car: a $1,500 yellow Triumph Spitfire convertible. It took me a little over a year of saving almost every cent of my roughly four-dollars-an-hour wage to raise enough money to buy that car. For a very long time it was the most expensive thing I had ever purchased and the most valuable thing I owned.

I still remember driving the Spitfire off the lot home—South on La Brea. East on Olympic. South on Arlington. To 23rd Street. I was on cloud nine, convinced that I was living a piece of the American Dream. I had a car. I had a job. And, I was getting an education. I was miles ahead of where I would have been had I stayed in London.

Only a few months later, my sense of living the American Dream was deferred. One of my brothers and I were in the Spitfire, driving to a friend's house around nine in the evening.

Our trip was interrupted by the blare of a siren (if you're Black, you can probably hear it—that classic American sound rings in the ears of every Black American with piercing familiarity).[1]

On the one hand, I doubt that I'm going to get every detail of what I'm about to describe exactly right. On the other hand, the episode has for me been utterly and completely unforgettable.

My brother and I were on our way to Inglewood, a predominantly Black neighborhood south of Los Angeles; a police car had signaled us to pull over. One officer stationed himself beside the passenger door, the other approached my window. He directed his flashlight into the interior of the car, locating its beam, alternately, on our faces.

"Anything wrong, officers?" I asked, attempting to discern the face behind the flashlight. Neither officer responded. Things had already become decidedly unfriendly. I inquired again as to whether we had done anything wrong. Again, cold silence. Then, out of nowhere, one of the officers instructed, "Step outside the car with your hands on your heads." We did as he asked. He then told us to sit on the side of the curb. Grudgingly, we complied.

We sat on the pavement, our feet in the road, our backs to the officers, our faces to the public.

We were racially exposed.

I asked a third time whether we had done anything wrong. One officer responded, rather curtly, that we should shut up and not make any trouble. Perhaps foolishly, I insisted on knowing why we were being stopped. "We have a right to know, don't we?

Today I might have acted differently, less defiantly. But my strange career with race in the United States had only just begun. I had not yet lived in this country long enough to learn the ways of the police, the racial conventions of Black and Blue encounters, the so-called rules of the game: "Don't move. Don't turn around. Don't give some rookie an excuse to shoot you." No one had explained to me that "[i]f you get pulled over, you just keep your mouth shut. . . . Don't get into arguments, and don't be stupid. It doesn't make a difference [that you did nothing wrong]. Just do what they tell you to do."[2]

No one ever sat me down to have "the talk," to explain to me that *Black + Male + Non-Compliance* = "Contempt of cop,"[3] a peculiar type of state crime for which police officers themselves serve as judge, jury, and—sometimes—executioner. It had not occurred to me that the stop was potentially life threatening. I was in a dangerous place—behind a veil of ignorance[4]—with no knowledge of what it meant to be a part of the social problem America labeled "Black."

Making matters worse, English racism had not taught me these lessons. To begin, I was barely a teenager during the 1981 "riots" in Brixton, a relatively Black part of South London. Racially naïve, I had not felt implicated in or triggered by the racialized backdrop of police violence that preceded that moment of civil unrest. Moreover, I was eighteen when I left London for Los Angeles, around the age at which I would have become particularly vulnerable to the so-called "sus laws," or repeated instances of "stop-and-search," the U.K. equivalent of stop-and-frisk.

I am not saying, to be clear, that back then, Black adolescents under the age of eighteen were safe from encounters with the police. They were not. Then as now, Black British children—as young as ten years old—have had to negotiate their relationship to law enforcement. The point is that, at eighteen, precisely the age at which I would have begun more freely to traverse the neighborhoods of London, encounters with the police almost certainly would have become a composing arrangement of my social life.

The short of it is that when I left London in the mid-1980s I had no consciousness about race and policing from which I could draw to temper my very undisciplined interactions with the officers. Whatever England had done to me, she had not taken away my racial innocence (or so I thought). I was a free person, to paraphrase my mother, who often described herself as a "free women," despite her encounters with racism. I had the right to assert rights. Thus, I insisted in knowing what we had done to them—or anyone else—to deserve what they were doing to us.

The officers discerned that I was not from the United States. Presumably, my accent provided a clue, although my lack of racial etiquette—mouthing off to white police officers in a "high crime area" in the middle of the night—might alone have suggested that I was an outsider to the usual racial dynamics of police encounters. Refusing to stay silent, asserting my rights, confronting authority (each a function of my pre-American Blackness), all signaled that I was not from here, and that I had not been racially socialized into nor internalized the racial survival strategy of performing obedience for the police.

One of the officers looked at my brother and me, seemingly puzzled. While there was no disjuncture between how we looked and the phenotypic cues for Black identity, our performance of Blackness could have created a racial ambiguity problem that the officers had to sort out. In other words, to the extent that the officers were racially committed to viewing us as criminals, or thugs, or troublemakers, our English accents might have challenged that perception.

But not for very long. The officers presumed that we had the souls of Black folk.[5] Just a little more information would clear everything up and the officers' adjudication of our Blackness would be complete.

> "Where are you guys from?"
> "The U.K.," my brother responded.
> "The what?"

"England."

"England?"

"Yes, England."

"You were born in England?"

"Yes."

"What part?"

"Birmingham."

"Uhmm . . . Where are your parents from?"

"The West Indies."

We now made sense, racially speaking. Our accents no longer racially covered us. In their eyes, our English identity had been dislocated, falsified—enveloped by our diasporic roots. The officers now had every reason to make us feel the way we looked: like Black Americans.

"How long has he been in America?" the officer wanted to know, pointing at me.

"About a year," my brother responded.

"Well, tell him that if he doesn't want to find himself in jail, he should shut the fuck up."

The history of racial violence in his words existentially moved us. We were now squarely within a subregion of the borders of American Blackness. Our rite of passage had begun. My brother nudged me several times with his elbows. "Cool it," he muttered under his breath. The intense look in his eyes inflected his words. "Don't provoke them."

By this time, my brother needn't have said anything. I was beginning to see the picture. I had the right to do whatever *they* wanted me to do, a reasonable expectation of uncertainty. With that awareness, I sat there. Quietly. In a state of rights without rights.

Although I didn't know it at the time, I was unwittingly participating in a naturalization ceremony, in which the administered oath was a submission to authority. I was being "pushed" and "pulled" through the racial body of America to be born again. A new Motherland awaited me. Eventually I would belong to her. Her racial project was transforming me into a very specific naturalized son: a new Black American.

None of this is to say that Black Americans are vulnerable to the police in precisely the same way. Gender, including gender identity, age, location, sexual orientation, immigrant status, and economic background, among other social factors, mediate Black people's exposure to police contact and violence. At the same time, none of those factors undoes the historical ways in which the Black body—in all of its configurations—has been the site on which the United States has worked out its "law and order" commitments.

Nor do I mean to say that Black Americans' encounters with the police are marked entirely by submission and acquiescence. Black people have always resisted police incursions into the sanctity and dignity of their lives. The Black Lives Matter Movement and various other movements for Black lives are recent examples of what I mean. It is also true, however, that many Black Americans—at too early an age—learn exactly how to submit to police authority to quite literally save their lives. If, paraphrasing W. E. B. Du Bois, riding Jim Crow was sign of Blackness in 1930s America, learning to be what Nikki Jones calls a "professional suspect" is a formative part of the Black experience today.[6]

On any given day, countless Black Americans perform choreographed-submission to police authority, even before an officer commands it. As I explain elsewhere, "'Hands-up-don't-shoot' is a part of much broader set of self-governance practices in which Black America regularly engages: Empty your pockets and purse; place your hands on the dashboard; keep your hands on the steering-wheel; lift up your shirt; spread your legs; yes sir; no sir.; fold your arms behind your back; lace your fingers behind your head. All part of a social script Black Americans must commit to memory without specific law enforcement guidance or direction."[7] My problem was that, as a recent immigrant, I had missed my dress rehearsals.

Nor did I know that there were ways for me to *work my identity*, to narrowly tailor my Blackness and present myself as racially palatable, reducing the likelihood that the officers would perceive me as criminally suspect.[8] It never dawned on me, for example, to do what Black Jamaican immigrant Garnette Cadogan regularly did to ward off the police: assemble "a cop-proof wardrobe. Light-colored oxford shirt. V-neck sweater. Khaki pants. Chukkas. Sweatshirt or T-shirt with my university insignia."[9] When these strategies failed to work, Cadogan deployed additional safeguards, such as thickening his Jamaican accent, mentioning the college at which he was enrolled, and "accidentally" displaying his college identification card when police officers asked for his driver's license.[10]

Cadogan's efforts were a way of signaling that he was Black but not a criminal and a way of managing the daily burden of getting "out of the shower with the police in . . . my head." Within a year, almost all of Cadogan's strategies would be a part of my racial repertoire. But back then, sitting on the curb, none of the strategies had occurred to me. The police had not yet taken up permanent residence in my head.

Without our consent, one officer rummaged through the car—no doubt in search of *ex post* probable cause, meaning a reason to justify pulling us over after-the-fact. The search yielded nothing.

One of the officers asked for my driver's license, which I provided. My brother was then asked for his. He explained that he didn't yet have one because he had only recently arrived in the country.

"Do you have any identification?"

"No. My passport is at home."

We both knew that this was the wrong response.

With something less than racial animus but more than professional detachment, we were instructed to stand up, which we did. Within seconds, I was pressed against the side of the patrol car. My brother was in a similar state of confinement. Neither of us knew that we were in the middle of a stop-and-frisk choreography.

As a general matter, the stop-and-frisk choreography includes at least the following three moves:

> *The Spread-Eagle*: Hands on the car, multiple kicks at our ankles, to the right, to the left—each one spreading the legs further and further apart;
>
> *The Pat-Down*: Unwelcome hands moving up and down our bodies, in-between our legs . . . ; and then
>
> *The Full Search*: In and out of every pocket (at least twice) with surgical precision.

Our stop-and-frisk encounter ended when one of the officers muttered through the back of his head, "You're free to go."

"Pardon?"

"I said you can go now."

And that was that. I wanted to say something like, "Are you absolutely certain, Officer? We really don't mind the intrusion, Officer. Honest." But those thoughts were simultaneously articulable and unspeakable. I said absolutely nothing. Standing my ground, as best I could, in a noisy state of silence.

The encounter left us more racially aware and less racially intact. Still, the officers did not physically abuse us, we did not "kiss concrete," and we managed to escape jail. Relative to some Black and Blue encounters—and considering my initial racial faux pas of questioning their authority and asserting our rights—we got off easy.

We had no idea that our encounter was part of a much larger story about race and policing in Los Angeles: a story about the militarization of the police to manage the "war on crime" and the "war on drugs"; a story about the programmatic targeting of Black people inside and outside of Black communities as a necessary entailment of those "wars"; a story about the chokehold as a law enforcement tool to discipline particularly young African American men[11]; a story about the deployment of the criminal justice apparatus into various domains of the welfare state, including to police Black women's access to public benefits and healthcare[12]; and a story about the carceralization of Los Angeles as a particular location for the mass incarceration of Black and Brown people.[13]

After that experience, I had several other encounters with the police. Though they varied in time, place, and manner, each one pushed me further into my Black American identity. I shall recount only one more here with the same caveat as before.

Two of my brothers and my brother-in-law, who is also Black, had just arrived from England. On our way from the airport, we stopped at my sister's apartment, which was in a predominantly white neighborhood. After letting us in, my sister left to perform errands. It was about two o'clock in the afternoon, and my brothers wanted some tea. I showed one of them to the kitchen.

After about five minutes, we heard the kettle whistling.

"Get the kettle, will you," I called to my brother.

There was no answer. My other brother went to see what was going on. Finally, the kettle stopped whistling, but he never returned.

My brother-in-law and I were convinced that my brothers were engaged in some sort of prank. "What are they doing in there?" Together, we went into the kitchen. At the door were two police officers. Guns drawn, they instructed us to exit the apartment. With our hands in the air, we did so.

Outside, both of my brothers were pinned against the wall at gunpoint. There were several officers. Each was visibly edgy, nervous, and apprehensive.

White passersby engaged in conspicuous racial consumption. Their eyes all over our bodies. The racial product was a familiar public spectacle: white police officers enforcing law and order against Black men. The currency of their stares purchased for them precisely what it took away from us: a sense of racial comfort and safety.

No doubt our policed bodies confirmed what the white onlookers already suspected: that we were criminals.

Whether Black people witnessed the spectacle as well, I simply do not recall. To extent that they did, at least some of them would have been right there, existentially with us, in a state of "vicarious marginalization."[14]

The officers wanted to know whether there was anyone else inside. "No. What's going on?" my brother-in-law inquired. The officer responded that they had received a call from a neighbor that several men had entered an apartment with guns. "Rubbish, we're just coming in from the airport."

"Do you have any drugs?" Again, my brother-in-law answered in the negative, and with all the veracity he could signal.

"May we look inside the apartment?" We "consented."

Two officers entered the apartment. After about two minutes, they came out shaking their heads, presumably signaling that they were not at a crime scene. In fact, we were not criminals. Based on "bad" information—but information that was presumed to be good—they had made an "error." "Sometimes these things happen." At least, they were willing to apologize.

"Look, we're really sorry about this, but when we get a call that there are men [read: *Black men*] with guns, we take it seriously. Again, we really are sorry for the inconvenience."

With that apology, the officers departed. We were racially profiled. Held at gunpoint. And we might have been killed. None of that seemed to *really* matter. Our sense of precarity was the neighbors' sense of security; our vulnerability, their safety; our rightlessness and marginalization, their entitlement and power.

My eyes followed the officers into their cars. As they drove off, one of them turned his head in our direction: Black men, standing, in the almost-gunned-down position in which they had left us. Our eyes met for a couple of seconds, and then the officer looked away. Another Black and Blue encounter awaited all us. Whether we realized it or not, our bodies were keeping score.[15]

We went inside, drank our tea, and didn't much talk about what had transpired—perhaps we didn't know how. Perhaps we were too shocked, or wanted to put the episode behind us—to move on, to start forgetting. Perhaps we needed more time, more distance. Perhaps we needed to recover our dignity and repossess our bodies.

By the time my sister got home, however, we were ready to talk. We told her what those officers had done to us. She was furious. "Bloody bastards!" She lodged a complaint with the local police department. She called the local paper. She contacted the NAACP.

"No, nobody was shot."

"No, they were not physically abused."

"Yes, I suppose everyone is alright."

It would take me years to make sense my encounters with the police, including but not limited to the episodes you just read. It was only after graduating law school, subsequently getting a job as a law professor, and teaching courses on constitutional criminal procedure that I came to understand that my experiences with the police was not fundamentally an individual "bad cop" problem.

The truth is that many forms of policing that people find troubling are perfectly legal under a particular body of constitutional law—Fourth Amendment doctrine. Over the past five decades, the Supreme Court has interpreted the Fourth Amendment to allocate enormous power to the police: to surveil, to racially profile, to stop-and-frisk, and to kill.

This book describes that power.

INTRODUCTION

I begin this book detailing two of my own encounters with the police to emphasize a dimension of the race and police violence problem that contemporary debates too often obscure: Black people's constant exposure to police contact means that they are constantly exposed to the possibility of their own death. Put more provocatively, Black people's exposure to the police is quite literally killing us—one police encounter at a time.

Not every encounter between Black Americans and law enforcement culminates in physical violence or death. Indeed, my own interactions left me alive to tell the tale, though things could have ended quite differently. With their weapons drawn and tensions high, there was a real risk that I might be killed or seriously wounded.

And therein lies a critical point: For Black people, ordinary police interactions often *do* result in a range of violence. In that sense, simply limiting the frequency with which police interact with Black people could save Black lives. If the police have fewer opportunities to stop and question Black people, they have fewer opportunities to kill us.

As part of the Bill of Rights (the original ten amendments added to the United States Constitution in 1791), the Fourth Amendment is arguably the most significant constitutional provision for regulating police conduct—more important than the Fifth Amendment[1] *Miranda* warnings ("You have the right to remain silent. . . ."), more important that the Sixth Amendment right to counsel,[2] and more important than the Fourteenth Amendment's equal protection and due process rights.³ The Fourth Amendment is ground zero for understanding the constitutional constraints on the investigation powers of the police.

While scholars continue to debate whether the other nine Bill of Rights amendments sufficiently protect and empower "we the people," this book contends that Fourth Amendment law overly protects and empowers "we the police." For decades, the police-centric nature of Fourth Amendment law has forced Black people to live their lives in a state of anticipatory mourning and trauma. Which is to say, Black people long have had to confront the reality that they or someone they know will inevitably experience vulnerability, uncertainty, degradation, or physical violence at the hands of law enforcement. At the same time, they are faced with both public displays of dead Black bodies—and the conspicuous consumption of that racialized necrology—and the ensuing debates regarding whether a particular officer's particular act of violence against a particular Black person was justifiable. Individualized assessments of state violence that ask whether *individual* police officers are "good" or "bad" cops—and whether the *individual* Black Americans they kill were "good" or "bad" Black people—obscures the structural dimensions of the problem.

"Structural police violence" sounds academic, I know. And, indeed, academics have long had drawn-out fights about whether some particular account of a social phenomenon—like racism or air pollution or animal abuse—is or isn't structural. I promise not to rehearse those debates.

Nevertheless, you might still be concerned about the "structural police violence" frame given ongoing contestations over "structural racism." Against the backdrop of those controversies, any invocation of the term "structural" might be a conversation stopper. In that regard, I want to be clear that I'm not promising that you will agree with the description of police violence I will provide. Nor do I presume that you will share my view that my account of police violence reflects a structural sensibility. If you bear with me, however, my hope is that you will understand why I propose an understanding of police violence that transcends a focus on individual "bad cops."

The structure I have in mind consists of the following seven levels: (I) Vulnerability; (II) Frequency; (III) Police Culture & Training; (IV) Justification; (V) Immunity & Indemnification; (VI) Dissociation; and (VII) Discretion.

Level I – Vulnerability. Black people are vulnerable to police contact and surveillance through a variety of converging factors, including racial stereotyping, *de facto* racial segregation, and Fourth Amendment law—the subject of this book (stay tuned). Typically, this vulnerability takes the form of "proactive policing," which is predicated on the belief that police officers should rigorously enforce minor infractions and surveil communities for signs of disorder to deter future, more serious crime. Although evidence on proactive policing's efficacy is mixed at best,[4] what is clear is that it facilitates contact between Black people and the police.[5]

Racial stereotypes that Black people are criminally suspicious and dangerous also increases their vulnerability to police contact. They do so by making Black people the seemingly "reasonable"—indeed, "natural"—targets for proactive policing.[6] Likewise, the pervasive nature of *de facto* racial segregation concentrates Black people in economically depressed neighborhoods that are the greatest targets of proactive policing.

Racial segregation facilitates contact between Black people and the police in another way. It furthers longstanding racialized assumptions about who belongs—and does not belong—in any given area. So, while many Black people are criminalized in their own neighborhoods based upon assumptions about their criminality or the perceived need to police crimes of poverty and disorder, Black people's presence in predominantly white neighborhoods is also potentially criminalizing because their hypervisibility in those spaces marks them as presumptively "out of place."[7]

Level II – Frequency. Black people's vulnerability to police contact increases the frequency with which they can expect to experience such contact, and therefore the possibility of physical violence. The key insight here is intuitive: If one is outside of the zone of police contact, the chances of being killed by the police are virtually zero. Conversely, the more frequently one is exposed to the police, the greater one's exposure to the possibility of police violence.

Level III – Police Culture & Training. Law enforcement self-governance, culture, and training can also enable police violence. For example, for far too long police culture has, at least implicitly, and sometimes explicitly, encouraged police violence,[8] police trainings have either failed to stop that violence,[9] or encouraged violence,[10] and police unions have essentially defended or acquiesced in this violence.[11] In addition, many police departments' internal investigations and use-of-force review processes are often opaque, unaccountable to outside review, and rarely result in either formal or informal discipline against offending officers.[12]

Level IV – Justification. When police violence does occur, various actors in our legal systems (whether in the criminal or civil context) work to convert it into *justifiable force*. For example, prosecutors might refuse to bring charges against the assaulting officer, a grand jury might refuse to indict an officer, and judges and juries might refuse to find that an officer's use of violence was excessive. In each instance, there is no dispute that the officer used deadly force—the question is whether the use of force was *reasonable*. Prosecutors, grand juries, judges, and juries too often answer that question in the affirmative, transforming acts of police violence into justifiable force.

Level V – Immunity & Indemnification. The Supreme Court has ruled that police officers are generally immune from being sued for violating a person's constitutional rights unless the prohibition on the officer's violation was clearly established law, in what is known as "qualified immunity doctrine."[13] The problem, however, is that the Court's determination of whether the law was clearly established turns on "hairsplitting" factual distinctions between cases that "reaches absurd levels."[14]

My colleague Joanna Schwartz, a leading expert on qualified immunity, sometimes explains this absurdity with this real-world example: In Case A, the Sixth Circuit Court of Appeals ruled that releasing a dog on a person who had surrendered by lying down violated the Fourth Amendment. Therefore, the decision "clearly established" that engaging in such behavior is unconstitutional. Later on, the same court hears Case B, in which police officers released a dog on a burglary suspect "who had surrendered and was sitting with his hands raised," and was subsequently attacked by the dog.[15] Case closed, right?

You would think that Case A "clearly established" that police officers may not deploy a dog against a person who has already surrendered. Yet in Case B, the government argued—*successfully*—that there is a difference between surrendering to the police via lying down versus by sitting and raising one's hands in the air! In other words, even assuming that a police officer knew that it would violate the Constitution to release a dog on a person who surrendered by lying down, that knowledge did not "clearly establish" that it was unconstitutional for them to use a dog against a person who surrendered by sitting down and raising their hands. This kind of reasoning is not a peripheral part of the Supreme Court's qualified immunity doctrine. It is a core feature of that body of law.

Making matters worse, courts often avoid deciding whether an officer's actions violate the Constitution, focusing the entirety of their analysis on whether such actions were already a "clearly established" violation. This might seem like a technicality, but without ruling explicitly on whether the officer's conduct was unconstitutional, the law surrounding such conduct remains unsettled. The greater that uncertainty in the law, the greater the leeway for police officers to argue that their conduct did not violate "clearly established" rights.[16] You see the vicious cycle.

Given that qualified immunity cases turn on nitpicking factual differences, such as the ones discussed above, one might surmise that police departments regularly educate their officers about such differences. For the most part, they do not.[17] On the one hand, then, when police officers defend themselves against excessive force claims they routinely argue that there were no "clearly established" laws that put them on notice that their behavior was unconstitutional. On the other hand, departments' various training initiatives fail to make officers aware of cases that could inform those officers of "clearly established" laws.[18]

One last point worth making about qualified immunity is this: It further perpetuates the good cop/bad cop dynamic but with a twist. Undergirding qualified immunity is the idea that even "bad cops" can get away with police violence. By that I mean, in adjudicating qualified immunity cases, courts are not concerned with holding "bad cops" accountable, in the sense that their behaviors violate the Constitution. Instead, courts are only concerned with "*really* bad cops," in the sense that their violations were "clearly established." On this point, the Supreme Court has been especially clear: Qualified immunity protects "all but the plainly incompetent or those who knowingly violate the law,"[19] which is to say, all but the "really bad" police officers.[20]

Finally, even where a plaintiff does clear the qualified immunity hurdle and goes on to win their case, local governments almost always indemnify the police officers involved. This indemnification takes shape by providing legal representation for the officers, as well as paying any monetary damages on the officers' behalf. Thus, taxpayers routinely pay more for an officer's knowing constitutional violations than the officer responsible, who often pay nothing and face no additional consequences.[21]

Level VI – Dissociation. Holding police departments, cities, or municipalities liable for the violence inflicted by its individual officers is no easy task. Under constitutional law, a plaintiff must establish a link between the officer's particular act of violence at issue and the department or city's "policy or custom."[22] Though demonstrating that link is not impossible, it is exceedingly difficult.[23] The law effectively dissociates the officer's conduct from the police department in which they officer works.

Level VII – Discretion. By converting police violence into justifiable force, offering qualified immunity to officers sued for their behavior, indemnifying officers against liability, and allowing departments and municipalities to avoid accountability for the actions of their officers, the legal system sends a message of unaccountability not only to the supposed "bad cops," but to the entirety of law enforcement. The core of that message is distressing: We have your back. Thus, the decision about where, when, how, and who you should use deadly force against is entirely up to you. You have discretion to decide who to kill when.

One can argue that this message of unaccountability and discretion is not as strong as I've described. But even I was surprised by the degree to which police officers are allowed to define the scope of their own powers. In an impressive examination of excessive force cases, Osagie Obasogie and Zachary Newman demonstrated that courts routinely rely on police policies and training materials to determine whether an officer's use of force is reasonable.[24] That reliance suggests that Fourth Amendment law is being defined not just from the "top" (that is, by courts), but also from the "bottom" (that is, by police departments). Put another way, police policies—not just court opinions—are defining the *constitutional* boundaries of police power. At least to some extent, police departments write the rules which courts apply when holding them "accountable."

Am I saying that police departments have completely "captured" the Court? No. But their policies and procedures do seem to be shaping the regulatory boundaries of Fourth Amendment law. When one combines that problem with the overall message of unaccountability and discretion Fourth Amendment law sends, police departments (and individual police officers) end up having broad latitude to define the bounds of acceptable behavior. That kind of discretionary power creates strong disincentives for police departments to establish protocols reining in whether, when, and how police force may be deployed. The absence of such protocols may cause police officers to view violent force an as ordinary feature of law enforcement that they may use at will, rather than as an extraordinary exercise of state power that they should wield as a last resort.

The preceding seven levels might be understood as a structure,[25] thus the notion of police violence as a structural phenomenon. This structure would be virtually undisturbed by identifying and punishing individual "bad cops."

The problem is even worse if one considers that the structure I've outlined is incomplete: It does not purport to tell the whole story of police violence against Black people. Nor does it describe the complex historical relationship between policing and racial subordination writ large. At bottom, my hope is that even if you think my argument does not go far enough, or goes too far, you'll agree that limiting the debate to arguments about "good" or "bad" cops misses the mark.

For the most part, this book focuses on Level I: Black people's vulnerability to police surveillance and contact. It details the specific ways in which Fourth Amendment law permits the police to interact with Black people with little to no basis. These interactions are worrisome not only because they can create pathways to excessive force, but also because their frequency normalizes police presence as a natural part of the Black experience and further devalues our lives.

Although I have said "Black lives matter" so many times as to be numbed to this aspirational mantra, the hard truth is that under Fourth Amendment law, Black life is undervalued. That devaluation is manifested in the legally sanctioned ways in which the police may not only kill Black people, but also routinely stage public scenes of interactional violence through which Black people are scrutinized, interrogated, disciplined, and violated—in short, routinely subject to what Patricia Williams calls "spirit murder,"[26] a form of killing whose violence presupposes an afterlife of further racial injury.

Consider for a moment the kinds of police contact about which Black people have long complained, all with no justification other than our Black bodies: being watched, approached, questioned, asked for identification, made to feel violent and dangerous, treated as suspect, stopped and frisked, searched and stripped. Enduring warrantless intrusions into our homes, no-knock warrants executed in the middle of the night, targeted at airports, sexually violated at the border, socially controlled on the streets. Experiencing *driving while Black, walking while Black, working while Black, parenting while Black*—simply *living while Black*. These recurring scripts of Black life, enacted and re-enacted in police scene after scene, are all staged according to directions of Fourth Amendment law. To better under these points, view the following image. As you do so, pay attention to the different sources of police power it depicts:

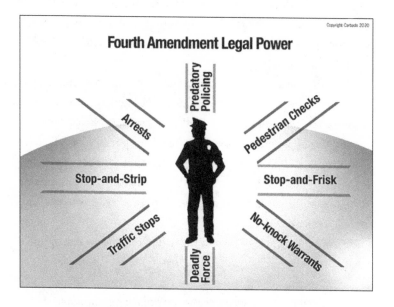

Even the most cursory review of the image reveals that police officers need not go rogue—that is, break the law—to wield an enormous array of powers. Whether the image depicts a "good" or "bad" officer is beside the point: the law empowers him to stop-and-frisk, effectuate arrests, conduct traffic stops, employ no-knock warrants, and deploy deadly force, While these powers are not absolute, they are strong enough to protect officers from far too many claims of wrongdoing. More worrisome still, when an officer's conduct does violate the Constitution, that officer may still benefit from the shield of qualified immunity.

To repeat: The police power problem I am describing is not principally about lawlessness. Available to "good" and "bad" cops alike, the powers the image depicts are a window on the ways in which Fourth Amendment law effectively decriminalizes coercive and violent forms of police conduct.

The image is revealing in another sense: It suggests that police officers are not born. They are made, socially constructed through their access to and deployment of numerous sources of power, including those Fourth Amendment law confers. In that regard, stripping away these powers may result in something unfamiliar with respect to policing, even if there remains a profession tasked with "public safety" and "upholding the law."

More than any other time in United States history, community organizers, activists, and academics are advancing arguments in favor of police abolitionism.[27] Whether one subscribes to those arguments, thinks they are reasonable—or even possible—at the very least they should get us collectively thinking about police *power* abolitionism or minimalism,[28] which is to say abolishing or minimizing racially subordinating forms of power Fourth Amendment law allocates to police officers.

This is a good place to turn to the text of the Fourth Amendment itself. It reads:

> *The right of the people to be secure in their persons, hous-*
> *es, papers, and effects, against unreasonable searches and*
> *seizures, shall not be violated, and no Warrants shall*
> *issue, but upon probable cause, supported by Oath or*

affirmation, and particularly describing the place to be searched, and the persons or things to be seized.[29]

It's not obvious why the text of the Fourth Amendment—which speaks of "the right of the people"—would end up creating a body of law that protects "the right of the police." Without getting bogged down into the history of the Fourth Amendment, the basic idea behind the provision is that the government should not be permitted to invade our privacy, compromise our sense of security, or restrict our freedom of movement without some prior justification, for example, probable cause or a warrant.

But "the right of the people" was never intended to include "the right of *Black people*." For one thing, the Bill of Rights was part of a Constitution that presupposed, protected, and indeed legitimized chattel slavery. To appreciate the degree to which this is true, it is helpful to discuss slave patrols—what scholars are increasingly describing as precursors to early police forces.[30]

The founders anticipated the use of slave patrols in the Constitution, in a section commonly referred to as the Fugitive Slave Clause, which provided that: "No person held to Service or Labour in one State, under the Laws thereof, escaping into another, shall, in Consequence of any Law or Regulation therein, be discharged from such Service or Labour, but shall be delivered up on Claim of the Party to whom such Service or Labour may be due." This provision did not expressly mention slavery, using the euphemism "person held to Service or Labour." As such, it is an early example of how *not* explicitly referencing race—or colorblindness—can be a strategy through which to constitutionalize racial subordination.

Congress also anticipated that slave patrols would comprise part of the governing regime of slavery, and passed the *Fugitive Slave Act* less than a decade after the Fourth Amendment took effect. Predicated on the right of slaveowners to repossess Black people, the Act *facilitated* rather than *regulated* slave patrols. As such, the Act (and its successor legislation) was part of the broader economy of slavery that, to borrow from Saidiya Hartman, shored up the idea that Black people were "in need of discipline rather than protection."[31]

Some states, however, pushed back and attempted to undermine the Fugitive Slave Act by passing "personal liberty" laws, which afforded African Americans some procedural protections (for example, requiring slave catchers to obtain a warrant from a judicial officer before seizing alleged runaway slaves) and imposed criminal penalties on slave catchers who illegally removed African Americans from the state.[32]

In *Prigg v. Pennsylvania*, however, the Supreme Court expressly ruled that the states' "personal liberty" laws protecting Black Americans were unconstitutional. According to the Court, "The right to seize and retake fugitive slaves . . . is, under the Constitution, recognized as an absolute positive right . . . uncontrolled and uncontrollable by state sovereignty or state legislation."[33] As Ronald Sullivan puts it, the Court's decision maintained that "states had no authority to regulate the practices of slave catchers within their borders" and that slaveowners had an "unqualified common law right to reclaim runaway slaves—a right that was not subject to any regulatory authority or any other form of process."[34] Central to the Court's thinking was the idea that very formation of the Union was predicated on the right of slaveowners to their "property":

> The full recognition of this right and title was indispensable to the security of this species of property in all the slave-holding States, and indeed was so vital to the preservation of their domestic interests and institutions that it cannot be doubted that it constituted a fundamental article without the adoption of which the Union could not have been formed. Its true design was to guard against the doctrines and principles prevalent in the non-slave-holding States, by preventing them from intermeddling with, or obstructing, or abolishing the rights of the owners of slaves.[35]

Indeed, as Chief Justice Taney argued in his concurring opinion, nothing in the Constitution prevented states from helping slaveowners recapture their slaves. Just the opposite. According to Taney, the states had a *duty* to help: "The States are not prohibited, and that, on the contrary, it is enjoined upon them as a duty to protect and support the owner when he is endeavoring to obtain possession of his property found within their respective territories."[36]

Accordingly, both the majority and concurrence opinion expansively defined the scope of the slave owner's rights, effectively permitting slave catchers to not only search and seize Black people, but to move them from the condition of freedom to one of bondage without a warrant—indeed with virtually no procedural protections at all. In this way, because Blackness carried with it the mark of slavery, every Black person was potentially if not presumptively a runaway slave—that is, a person available for capture. Even Blacks "with papers" were subject to intense scrutiny and had to rebut the presumption that there were not illegally trafficking in their own freedom.

I should be clear to note that *Prigg* is not formally a Fourth Amendment case. For one, by the time it was decided the Court had taken the view that the Fourth Amendment (and the Bill of Rights more generally) only limited the federal government's power—not state power. Unsurprisingly then, at no point in *Prigg* does the Court even explore whether Black people alleged to be runaways could benefit from the Fourth Amendment's prescription against "unreasonable searches and seizures." Instead, it focused its analysis almost entirely on the right of the slaveowner to recapture runaway slaves, "a positive, unqualified right . . . which no state law or regulation can in any way qualify, regulate, control, or restrain."[37]

But the problem for Black people in antebellum America was not simply that the Fourth Amendment did not protect them against local and state actors, including those who organized or were a part of slave patrols. The problem was more fundamental. About fifteen years after his concurring opinion in *Prigg*, in which he argued that the states had an affirmative duty to help slave catchers, Chief Justice

Taney penned the infamous Supreme Court decision, *Dred Scott v. Sandford*. There, Taney further instantiated not only the relationship between Blackness and slavery, but also the relationship between slavery and the Constitution.

Getting to what he perceived to be the heart of the matter, Justice Taney described the central question *Dred Scott* presented this way: "Can a negro whose ancestors were imported into this country and sold as slaves, become a member of the political community formed and brought into existence by the Constitution of the United States and as such become entitled to all the rights, and privileges, and immunities, guarantied by that instrument to the citizen [including] *the privilege of suing in a court of the United States*."[38] With little difficulty, Justice Taney answered that question in the negative. More than that, he did so on terms that reveal how principles of United States constitutionalism can create fields of violence and domination for Black people.[39] Which is to say, almost six decades after the Constitution was amended to include the Bill of Rights, including the Fourth Amendment, Taney concluded that Black people *were not* and *could never* become citizens of the United States. The implication of that conclusion was that Black people could be reduced to a state of bondage *forever.*

Taney's reasoning explicitly drew on the Fugitive Slave Clause. He maintained that the presence of that clause in the United States Constitution, and the fact that it presupposed that people of African descent could be reduced to chattel slavery, was a clear indication that Black people were viewed (originally) as "a separate class of persons . . . not regarded as . . . citizens."[40] Elaborating on the point, Taney observed that:

> [Black people] had for more than a century before been regarded as beings of an inferior order, and altogether unfit to associate with the white race, either in social or political relations; and so far inferior, that they had no rights which the white man was bound to respect; and

that the negro might justly and lawfully be reduced to slavery for his benefit. He was bought and sold, and treated as an ordinary article of merchandise and traffic, whenever a profit could be made by it.[41]

Taney's analysis along the preceding lines is a window on one of the shortcomings of approaches to constitutional law that privilege "originalism," roughly, the idea that judges should interpret the United States Constitution consistent with the constitutional and democratic arrangements our "Founding Forefathers" intended.

To the extent that Black people existed outside of the parameters of citizenship, with "no rights which the white man was bound to respect," and lacked "the privilege of suing in a court of the United States," they were constitutionally displaced people, beyond the reach of the protections of the United States Constitution, including those the Fourth Amendment afforded. In other words, Chief Justice Taney's ruling in *Dred Scott* was a way of saying that Black people were not, and could not be, part of "the people" who had the right under the Fourth Amendment "to be secure in their persons, houses, papers, and effects, against unreasonable searches and seizures." Accordingly, their bodies could be searched and seized, captured, and violated—all without triggering Fourth Amendment protections.

Fast forward to Reconstruction, which shifted the constitutional landscape in the United States radically though incompletely. The Thirteenth Amendment abolished slavery ("except as punishment for a crime").[42] The Fourteenth Amendment guaranteed equal protection and due process rights and expressly repudiated *Dred Scott* by declaring that "all persons born . . . in the United States . . . are citizens of the United States."[43] And the Fifteenth Amendment prohibited the government from restricting the right to vote on the basis of race.[44] Each was a significant constitutional development.

But marking the nonlinear progress of civil rights in the United

States,[45] those developments were soon met with racial retrenchment. The Supreme Court began rolling back these advancements
almost immediately, with the classic example being *Plessy v. Ferguson*. There, the Court ruled that the Jim Crow regime of "separate but
equal" did not violate either the promise of equal protection under
the Fourteenth Amendment nor the Thirteenth Amendment's prohibition against slavery.[46]

Plessy's legalized racism lasted more than half a century. It was not
until 1954, against the background of massive civil rights and social
movement resistance to racial segregation, that the Supreme Court
issued one of the most celebrated cases in United States constitutional
history—*Brown v. Board of Education*. That case declared that "in the
field of public education the doctrine of 'separate but equal' has no
place."[47] Writing for a unanimous Court, Chief Justice Warren maintained that "Separate educational facilities are inherently unequal."[48]
Though the *Brown* decision focused squarely on K–12 education, the
Court would subsequently rely on the case to repudiate other manifestations of Jim Crow, culminating in 1967 with *Loving v. Virginia*,
which ruled that bans against interracial marriages violated the constitutional requirements of due process and equal protection.[49]

The 1960s witnessed other important antiracist developments as
well. By the middle of that decade, the "Second Reconstruction" was
well underway with the passage of historic civil rights legislation,
including a voting rights act and antidiscrimination laws that prohibited employment and housing discrimination. Moreover, by that
time, and specifically with respect to policing, the Supreme Court
had made much of the Bill of Rights, including the Fourth Amendment, applicable to the states, including city and local officials.

The result was that by the end of the 1960s, and during a civil rights
and social movement context in which Black people were decrying
and resisting various forms of police repression, every police department in the United States became subjected to the "unreasonable
search and seizure" constraints imposed by the Fourth Amendment. Importantly, those constraints were not expressly predicated

on whether they operated as racially exclusive safeguards for "whites only." At least as a formal matter, Black people were part of "the people" whose privacy and security the Fourth Amendment was supposed to protect.

Although one can debate the degree to which Fourth Amendment law meaningfully curtailed police power to the benefit of Black people in the 1960s, today that body of doctrine is not much of a constraint on racialized policing at all. Indeed, the central claim of this book is that, over the past five decades, the Supreme Court has effectively legalized racially targeted policing by interpreting the Fourth Amendment to protect police officers at the expense of Black Americans. This may sound like hyperbole—but it is not. The Court has stated explicitly that an officer's reliance on race as a basis for suspicion does not necessarily violate the Fourth Amendment,[50] and has applied the Fourth Amendment in ways that make it easy for police officers to incorporate race into their decision-making but hard to challenge when officers do so.

There's a line in criminal law that goes something like: Better that ten guilty people go free than one innocent person is convicted. With respect to Black people, Fourth Amendment law reflects a very different sentiment: Better that the police stop thousands of innocent Black people than one guilty Black person go free. That is to say: Fourth Amendment law makes it easy for police officers to stamp Black people—in police interaction after police interaction—as presumptively guilty of something. The end result is that, in the racialized and police-dominated world Fourth Amendment law has helped to create and sustain, every Black person is potentially a runaway criminal.

Before I wade deeper into the troubled waters of Fourth Amendment doctrine, a word about my approach to that body of law is in order. Although this book focuses on legal cases, it presupposes neither legal training nor familiarity with the Fourth Amendment. I've made the legal analysis accessible by building on the time-honored law school technique of using hypothetical situations based on real cases. This contextual approach will bring the Fourth Amendment to life, crystallize the everyday consequences of that area of law, and drive home the point that the Court's interpretations of the Fourth Amendment routinely privilege police power over Black lives.

To bring you along further, I will also on occasion ask you to pause your reading and "think like a lawyer." When I do so, I will describe the relevant law, present the relevant facts, and then ask questions like: "How would you argue this case on behalf of the police?" "On behalf of the person challenging the police conduct?" "On behalf of African Americans?" That active engagement will help you see that Black people were not predestined to occupy a peripheral place in Fourth Amendment law. The Supreme Court put them there, one case at a time.

As this book goes to print, the nation continues to struggle through moments of "racial reckoning." As we do so, everyone should understand the relationship between Fourth Amendment law and police power, not just those who are privileged with a legal education. Democratizing legal knowledge in this way has the potential to expose people from all walks of life to the ways in which Fourth Amendment law empowers the police to dominate the lives of Black people.

For those of you who have attended law school, you may wonder why, after reading this book, your law school coursework did not include this account of the Fourth Amendment. Although it would be putting the point too strongly to say that the law school curriculum routinely covers up the racial dimensions of Fourth Amendment law, for the most part the relevant Fourth Amendment texts racially sanitize the doctrine. The truth is that many of the scholars writing on and teaching about the Fourth Amendment have only ever experienced its protections—not its violence—which is then reflected in the literature.

I am not saying the minimalization of race in law school courses on the Fourth Amendment derives from some racially invidious strategy. Instead, it merely reflects the "ordinary" way in which the

law school curriculum obfuscates the central role law has played
in shaping the racially hierarchical dimensions of social life. With
respect to Fourth Amendment specifically, that obfuscation means
that law students may leave their Constitutional Criminal Procedure
classes without discussing the fact that many (not all) of the litigants
in the cases that reach the Supreme Court are Black, many (not all) of
the police officers whose conduct Black litigants are challenging are
white, and many (not all) of the places in which the police interaction occurred are communities of color, particularly predominantly
Black neighborhoods.

As a prelude to describing the specific areas of Fourth Amendment
law this book will cover, it's helpful to remember that at its core the
Fourth Amendment prohibits unreasonable searches and seizures.[51]
The Court determines whether the government violates this prohibition by asking two questions:

1. Was the police officer's conduct a *search* or *seizure* under the
    Fourth Amendment? (You should think of this as the *trigger*
    question—is the Fourth Amendment "triggered" by way of a
    search or seizure?); and
2. If the police conduct was a search or seizure, was it *rea-
    sonable*? (You should consider this the *justification*
    question—assuming the government engaged in a search or
    seizure, was it justified in doing so?)

By persistently answering "no" to the first question (the Fourth
Amendment was not triggered) and "yes" to the second (a search or
seizure was reasonable) when deciding Fourth Amendment cases,
the Supreme Court has eliminated, or at least substantially reduced,
the barriers the police need to force interactions with Black people.
The absence or reduction of those barriers exposes Black people to
police contact, leaves them less secure in their "persons, papers,
houses, and effects," and has gotten them killed. Put another way,
Fourth Amendment law has effectively turned Black people into a

criminalized corporeal complex over which police officers can exercise enormous power. This book describes the contours of that power and illustrates how, when deployed, Black people experience the Fourth Amendment as a system of surveillance, social control, and violence, rather than as a constitutional safeguard that protects them from unreasonable searches and seizures.[52]

Chapter 1, "Pedestrian Checks," focuses on the "Is there a seizure?" question. I show how, by answering "no" in a number of critical cases, the Supreme Court has allowed police officers to target Black people without any justification. Every time the Court concludes that a given police practice is *not* a seizure, it confers upon police officers the freedom and power to engage in that practice without further justification. That space of law enforcement freedom and power is, for Black people, a space of captivity and powerlessness. To make this point concrete, I highlight twelve racially motivated decisions police officers can make to disrupt pedestrians' freedom of movement without triggering Fourth Amendment protections.

Chapter 2, "Traffic Stops," foregrounds another troubling context in which police officers can focus their attention on Black people—traffic stops. Many of you are familiar with the pithy-if-demoralizing expression "Driving While Black."[53] What you may not know is that the problem of race-based traffic stops transcends the initial decision to pull someone over.

An officer's decision to stop a car is only the first of a range of legal options police officers are empowered to exercise. Others include questioning the driver, demanding they exit the car, and even arrest. The existence of these powers makes traffic stops a gateway to more intrusive and violent—yet constitutionally "reasonable"—encounters with the police. Chapter 2 describes the forms those encounters can take and the precarity they create for Black people.

Chapter 3, "Stop-and-Frisk," discusses two police practices that every police department in the United States likely employs—"stops" and "frisks." It begins by noting that the initial battle over whether these practices were constitutional raised questions both about whether stops and frisks triggered the Fourth Amendment (Were stops *seizures* and were frisks *searches?*) and whether the Court would deem each *reasonable* (Do stops and frisks require probable cause?).

Chief Justice Warren answered both questions in the landmark case, *Terry v. Ohio*. Writing for the majority of the Court, he ruled that stops *are* seizures and frisks *are* searches, but that *neither* require probable cause as justification. Instead, he announced that "specific and articulable facts,"[54] what we now call "reasonable suspicion," are enough. It is fair to say that reasonable suspicion is more than nothing, more than a hunch, but less than probable cause, and that the standard operates more like a license than a barrier for the police to employ stops and frisks.

Chapter 4, "Stop-and-Strip," demonstrates some of the insidious ways in which police officers use the license of "reasonable suspicion" to violate Black people, restrict their freedom of movement, and occupy the streets of their communities. Although the "reasonable suspicion" standard announced in *Terry v. Ohio* was intended to address a very limited type of dangerous police encounter, it has since metastasized like a cancer across broad swaths of Fourth Amendment law. It now justifies a range of governmental intrusions into Black people's privacy and sense of security, including at the United States border. There, customs officials may invoke reasonable suspicion to subject Black women not only to stop-and-frisk, but to a more invasive form of detention that I refer to as stop-and-strip.

Chapter 5, "Predatory Policing," emphasizes a form of policing about which many Americans likely know very little: law enforcement's use of routine policing mechanisms—such as warrants, arrests, and citations—to prey on the economic and social vulnerability of Black Americans. Police officers can employ predatory policing to generate revenue for municipalities and police departments, and even to facilitate their own pay increases and promotions. For example, an officer might target economically and racially disadvantaged communities for "fines and fees" (issuing multiple citations for low-level infractions, each of which carries a fine) or use the threat of arrest to seize property (jewelry, cash, and cars), the proceeds of which add to the department's coffers. An officer might also deploy the police powers of arrest predatorily in a very different way: to force economically, racially, and politically marginalized women—particularly Black women—to "consent" to sexual violence.

By now, you will not be surprised to read that Fourth Amendment law does little to prevent the preceding examples of predatory policing. Indeed, the regime often legitimizes such practices. The end result is that Black people across the United States sometimes find themselves paying for and going into debt through forms of policing that leave them violated, economically exploited, and incarcerated.

If your sense is that the story this book tells is distressing, you would be right. The Supreme Court's jurisprudence on the Fourth Amendment likely will continue to empower police officers, rather than protect the privacy and security of Black Americans. All of this *is* distressing, so what can we do?

Too many books end with a chapter that purports to solve the problems described in their previous chapters. Not here. For the truth is: Not only is there is no easy Fourth Amendment fix, but also that the Fourth Amendment is only one of the structural forces that is shaping the excessive presence of the police in Black people's lives. It is also true, however, that arguments that were once considered political landmines—for example, advocating some version of defund/divest/invest (roughly, shifting resources from policing to other parts of the welfare state, such as education)—are now emerging as a meaningful part of discussions about policing. I do not intend to present a solution that presumes to settle these ongoing debates.

My hope is that this book will make people aware of some of the previously overlooked racial dimensions of Fourth Amendment law. That awareness can serve not only as a kind of "know-your-rightslessness" campaign, but can also to mobilize readers, activists, lawyers, policy-makers, and others to stage various interventions to curb the scope of police authority across multiple domains of power, including through state courts; through state and federal government legislative action (including on what counts and doesn't count as a crime); and through law enforcement administrative regulations and self-governance accountability mechanisms. More broadly, the arguments this book advances can be deployed more radically to fundamentally reimagine the necessity for and/or the role of policing in the United States.

At the same time, I want to be clear to state that my critique of the Supreme Court's Fourth Amendment decisions does not criticize the desire to seek justice within the Court's arena. In different ways, legal scholars Patricia Williams, Kimberlé Crenshaw, and Dorothy Roberts—African American women whose scholarship and advocacy have been at the forefront of racial justice interventions in law—have made similar points. Speaking specifically about why Black people might have profound commitment to asserting rights, Professor Williams notes:

> To say that blacks never fully believed in rights is true. Yet it is also true that blacks believed in them so much and so hard that we gave them life where there was none before; we held onto them, put the hope of them into our wombs, mothered them and not the notion of them. And this was not the dry process of reification, from which life is drained and reality fades as the cement of conceptual determinism hardens round—but its opposite. This was the resurrection of life from ashes four hundred years old. The making of something out of nothing took immense alchemical fire—the fusion of a whole nation and the kindling of several generations.[55]

Kimberlé Crenshaw, too, insists on using law to effect social change, even as she is clear-eyed about the very real costs of doing do. According to Professor Crenshaw:

The civil rights community, however, must come to terms with the fact that antidiscrimination discourse is fundamentally ambiguous and can accommodate conservative as well as liberal views of race and equality. This dilemma suggests that the civil rights constituency cannot afford to view antidiscrimination doctrine as a permanent pronouncement of society's commitment to ending racial subordination. Rather, antidiscrimination law represents an ongoing ideological struggle in which the occasional winners harness the moral, coercive, consensual power of law.[56]

More recently, Professor Dorothy Roberts has articulated her views about law and social change in the context of considering whether constitutional law can reflect an abolitionist orientation: "Despite my disgust with the perpetual defense of oppression in the name of constitutional principles, I am inspired by the possibility of an abolition constitutionalism emerging from the struggle to demolish prisons and create a society where they are obsolete."[57]

Part of the reason it might make sense for Black people to negotiate their relationship to law as *one* venue for change, rather than abandoning it altogether, is that the long history of race and racism in this country is not simply a product of unlawful acts, but of lawful *compliance*. Slavery was legal, as was Jim Crow. Where slavery was legal, freedom was "theft"; where Jim Crow was legal, Black presence was "trespass."

The legalization of racism is not an historical relic but a contemporary social practice. The death penalty is legal. Mass incarceration is legal. And most of the police practices this book describes are legal. The role law plays in creating a racially subordinating policing landscape invites us to consider whether advocates can employ law to disrupt at least pieces of that landscape.

Needless to say, legal disruption—particularly in the form of Fourth Amendment litigation—might very well produce civil rights losses. But fear of losses alone is not an argument to abandon litiga-tion as *one* avenue for pursuing social change. First, consider legal scholar Doug NeJaime's pithy expression "winning through losing."[58] The basic idea is that civil rights losses at the Supreme Court can serve as a galvanizing call to action. Take, for example, how conservatives mobilized around their "loss" in *Roe v. Wade* to build a right-to-life social movement over the past half-century. Yet progressives seeking racial justice tend not to employ Supreme Court losses in this way. There's no good reason why they shouldn't. I'm not saying that doing so would be easy or uncontroversial. My colleague Scott Cummings has foregrounded some of the concerns people have raised about law reform efforts for social change, including the degree to which liti-gation in particular can overdetermine the content and trajectory of social movement organizing and advocacy.[59] However, taking those concerns seriously doesn't mean backing away from legal interven-tions altogether. Nor does it mean that racial justice advocates should refrain from employing Supreme Court losses as a galvanizing tool.

Second, Supreme Court opinions embed crucial and compelling stories about how we imagine our constitutional democracy—and those stories are articulated not only in majority opinions, but also in *dissenting* ones. Dissents have a way of making the unspeakable speakable, including by speaking truth to power. They can also vin-dicate a losing litigant's (and those in similar positions) sense of how the world should—and can—be. From that perspective, it matters both *whether* a Supreme Court justice dissents and *how* she does so.

Consider, for example, the following quote from Justice Sotomay-or's dissent in a Fourth Amendment case: "For generations, black and brown parents have given their children "the talk"—instructing them never to run down the street; always keep your hands where they can be seen; do not even think of talking back to a stranger—all out of fear of how an officer with a gun will react to them. See, e.g., W. E. B. Du Bois, *The Souls of Black Folk* (1903); J. Baldwin, *The Fire Next Time* (1963); T. Coates, *Between the World and Me* (2015)."[60] The race conscious sensibility reflected in Sotomayor's dissent affirms not only a salient dimension of Black life, but also progressive articulations of Black consciousness.

Dissents can be powerful in another sense: By underscoring that our constitutional norms are not preordained from on high, but deeply contested territory. A single justice can call into question the legitimacy and motivations of the majority view. The questioning of the majority opinion *inside* the boundaries of the case can serve to mobilize resistance *outside* the boundaries of courts. This destabilizing power is precisely why "some European nations have made it a crime for a judge to publish a dissent or even make it known, through conversations or private letters, that she has disagree with one of her court's decisions."[61] The role dissents can perform in that regard argues in favor of not only employing constitutional litigation in pursuit of racial justice, but also in making expansive and unabashed arguments that articulate a progressive vision for the country that—even if losing—can shape the way justices on the Court articulate their dissents.

Finally, federal trial courts and courts of appeal are tasked with interpreting the Fourth Amendment—not just the Supreme Court. Many of those lower court judges will be more willing than Supreme Court justices to incorporate concerns about race into their jurisprudence, either explicitly or implicitly. By bringing progressive cases and making progressive arguments, we make it easier for sympathetic judges to interpret the Constitution in a way that protects the dignity and sanctity of Black lives. Of course, their rulings could be reversed on appeal, but many won't even be appealed, making this a worthwhile antiracist endeavor.

This brings us to the last two chapters of the book. They focus our attention on precisely how a judge might interpret the Fourth Amendment to attend to the racialized dimensions of policing. Chapter 6, "Unreasonable," presents an unedited version of the Supreme Court's decision in *Whren v. United States*, a case discussed in Chapter 2 that all but ensured that Black people would continue to experience "Driving While Black" as a criminalized act. As Supreme Court opinions go, this one is relatively short. And, given what you will have learned about Fourth Amendment law by the time you read the case, you will have no difficulty understanding the Court's analysis.

Do not be surprised if, while reading *Whren*, you are seduced into thinking that the Court reached the right conclusion. After all, *Whren* was a unanimous opinion. Even the liberal justices signed on, including the late civil rights icon Justice Ginsburg. That unanimity might lead you to think that there was no way out of the racialized outcome the case produced.

Chapter 7, "Reasonable," argues otherwise. It presents a reimagined version of *Whren* that reaches a very different result. This rewritten *Whren* concludes that, although a police officer may have probable cause to believe that a person has committed a traffic infraction, the officer's decision to stop that particular person solely because of their race is not, under Fourth Amendment law, constitutional.

Even in an age of divided racial politics, the claim that Black people should not experience "Driving While Black" as a crime ought to generate consensus, not controversy. The very fact that I need to argue that racial profiling of any sort should be *unreasonable* under Fourth Amendment law is an indication of just how much current interpretations of the Fourth Amendment have tipped the scales in favor of police officers and against the interests of Black people.

I offer my rewritten opinion not as an antiracist cure-all, but as an effort to expose and undermine one slice of Fourth Amendment law,[62] understanding that no single legal intervention can fully disrupt the police-dominated dimensions of Black life. Likewise, *Unreasonable* as a book is not a "how to" manual, but an acknowledgement that mapping the contours of one's cage is the first step to plotting an escape or dismantling the cage altogether. As such, the purpose of this book is to raise our individual and collective consciousness about the racially-subordinating dimensions of Fourth Amendment law, and to motivate all of us to incorporate that knowledge into our thinking, advocacy, and organizing.

Chapter One

Pedestrian Checks

Across the United States, many Black Americans believe that police officers regularly approach and question Black people with no evidence of wrongdoing. We hold this view either because of direct experience with such *baseless police interactions*, or because we live it vicariously through the experiences of our mothers and fathers, aunts and uncles, siblings and cousins, and friends and neighbors. Baseless police interactions with people on the street (what I call "pedestrian checks") are part of the collective consciousness of Black Americans, helping to constitute what Michael Dawson refers to as our "linked fate."[1]

What many Americans might not know is the longstanding role that the Supreme Court has played in pushing pedestrian checks beyond the reach of the Fourth Amendment. That Fourth Amendment law is not a barrier to pedestrian checks provides at least a partial explanation for why pedestrian checks figure so prominently in the lives of Black people.

Some of you may have read the Department of Justice Report on Ferguson, Missouri, which was published in the aftermath of social upheaval and protest in Ferguson following the police shooting death of Michael Brown, a Black teenager. To those of you who have not read the Ferguson Report, you should. It is a sobering look at a regional criminal justice system in which racism and classism were bureaucratized as normal features of governance. Here, I reference the report for a very narrow reason: it includes a discussion of what

Ferguson police officers regularly referred to as "ped checks." Here's the relevant passage from the report:

> This incident [involving a police officer seizing an African American man and running a warrant check without any evidence that the man had engaged in any wrongdoing] is also consistent with a pattern of suspicionless, legally unsupportable stops we found documented in FPD's [Ferguson Police Department's] records, described by FPD as "ped checks" or "pedestrian checks." Though at times officers use the term to refer to reasonable-suspicion-based pedestrian stops, or "*Terry* stops," they often use it when stopping a person with no objective, articulable suspicion. For example, one night in December 2013, officers went out and "ped. checked those wandering around" in Ferguson's apartment complexes. In another case, officers responded to a call about a man selling drugs by stopping a group of six African-American youths who, due to their numbers, did not match the facts of the call. The youths were "detained and ped checked." Officers invoke the term "ped check" as though it has some unique constitutional legitimacy. It does not. Officers may not detain a person, even briefly, without articulable reasonable suspicion.

As such, when the Ferguson Report speaks of pedestrian checks it refers to instances in which Ferguson police officers seized people without any evidence of wrongdoing, in violation of the Fourth Amendment.

Recall from the Introduction that the Fourth Amendment protects us from "unreasonable searches and seizures." That means that only when police officers engage in a *search* or *seizure* does the Fourth Amendment require them to justify it. If the government fails to offer an appropriate justification, the search or seizure is deemed *unreasonable* and therefore *unconstitutional.*

The Ferguson Report describes how the Ferguson Police Department "ped checks" included seizures, and sometimes searches of Black Americans without any justification. This made both practices unreasonable, and therefore unconstitutional. Although the unconstitutional pedestrian checks described in the Ferguson Report should be highlighted and condemned, I would like to focus on pedestrian checks of an altogether different sort: baseless police interactions that do not qualify as either a search or a seizure, *do not trigger* the Fourth Amendment, and therefore do not need to be supported by any evidence of wrongdoing.

Remember: Every time the Court determines that a certain police practice does not qualify as a search or seizure, it ducks the question of whether that practice is *reasonable*, meaning justified. To put that point slightly differently, when the Supreme Court concludes that a pedestrian check is not a search or a seizure, it gives police officers the green light to perform that pedestrian check without any basis— that is to say, without a warrant, without probable cause, and without reasonable suspicion. Without any justification whatsoever. Accordingly, far from being unconstitutional, pedestrian checks that are neither searches nor seizures do not implicate the Fourth Amendment *at all.*

The problem runs deeper. By concluding that a pedestrian check is neither a search nor a seizure, the Court avoids the question of whether that check was racially motivated, as they never ask the police to justify their actions. Pause for a moment and think about what this means: If a pedestrian check does not trigger the Fourth Amendment, police officers have discretion not only to initiate that pedestrian check without any basis, but to select the people they wish to subject to pedestrian checks based on race alone.

You might think that some other constitutional provision—such as the Equal Protection Clause of the Fourteenth Amendment—solves this problem. After all, the Equal Protection Clause provides that all persons are entitled to equal protection of the law. Presumably, racially selective policing runs afoul of that mandate. As a technical matter, that is certainly true. But the Equal Protection Clause is— realistically speaking—of limited utility to challenge racially selective policing. The Supreme Court has repeatedly ruled that to sustain an equal protection challenge against the government, plaintiffs must demonstrate discriminatory intent.[2] A showing of disparate impact is not enough. How many plaintiffs will succeed in proving that a particular police officer during a particular encounter intentionally discriminated against them? None, unless the officer's racism is captured on the officer's body camera or a witness's cellphone. And, even that kind of proof may not be enough.

At any rate, this chapter is not about the Fourteenth Amendment. It is about the Fourth. My goal is to illustrate with some specificity the discretion Fourth Amendment law gives to police officers to target and engage Black American pedestrians without any evidence of wrongdoing.

Decision 1: To Follow

Assume that Tanya, a Black woman, is walking home from work at nine in the evening. Two officers observe her. They have no reason to believe that Tanya has done anything wrong. They decide to follow her anyway. Indeed, they follow her all the way home to ensure that Tanya does not commit a crime (a sex crime, let's say) and to arrest her if she does.

Remember, the officers have no objective reason to believe that Tanya has done—or will do—anything wrong. There is no objective evidence, in other words, that Tanya has ever engaged in prostitution. Nevertheless, they follow her based solely on their gendered racial suspicion (*stereotype*) of Black women as sex workers.

The foregoing conduct would not trigger the Fourth Amendment.[3] The Supreme Court would conclude that Tanya has not been seized. Indeed, the officers haven't even approached her. That the officers decided to follow Tanya (from several blocks to several miles) only because she is a Black woman would not matter. The Fourth Amendment is silent as to this form of racialized surveillance.

Decision 2: To Approach

Let's say that now the officers decide to approach Tanya. They haven't yet determined whether or not they will question her. At this point, the officers want to see whether Tanya will act nervous in their presence or try to avoid her altogether. The officer's decision to approach Tanya would not trigger Fourth Amendment protections. The Court would still conclude that Tanya has not been seized.[4] Because approaching Tanya does not implicate the Fourth Amendment, the officers do not need a prior justification to do so. As with the previous example, the outcome remains the same even if Tanya's race influenced the officers' decision to approach her.

Decision 3: To Question About Whereabouts and Identity

But what if in the context of approaching Tanya, the officers decide to question her? Assume, more specifically, that they ask Tanya the following questions: "Do you live around here?" "What's your name?" "Where are you going?" "Where are you coming from?" "May I see your identification?" None of this would constitute a seizure.[5] As I will explain below, Tanya is supposed to know that she is not obligated to comply, and she is supposed to feel empowered to exercise that right by ignoring the officers, explicitly refusing their requests, or walking away.

Decision 4: To Question on a Bus

Assume that officers follow Tanya onto a bus. Indeed, stipulate that the police specifically followed Tanya on the bus to question her. Again, our assumption is that the officers have no objective reason to believe that Tanya has done anything wrong. Could Tanya now successfully argue that she has been seized? After all, she is now in a confined space, with the officers blocking the aisle, and her exit.

This is a good place to pause and describe how the Supreme Court has defined what constitutes a seizure with more precision. The legal standard is that a seizure has not taken place if the person feels free to decline officers' requests or otherwise terminate the encounter in the sense of ignoring the officer or walking away.[6] The Court has repeatedly stated that the mere fact that police officers question a person does not mean that that person is seized.[7] Under the Court's view, suspects whom the police question are "free to leave[.]"

One of the most striking articulations of this view appears in *Florida v. Bostick*.[8] In that case, officers observed Terrance Bostick sitting in the back of a bus and proceeded to question him.[9]

The government stipulated that the police officers had no reason to believe that Bostick had done anything wrong.[10] That concession required the government to argue that Bostick was *not* seized. Why? Because if Bostick was seized, and the government had no justification for conducting that seizure, the seizure would be baseless and therefore *unreasonable*. To avoid this problem, the government argued that the officers' conduct did not implicate the Fourth Amendment at all, because although they had followed Bostick onto a bus and questioned him, he was *not* seized.[11] Thus, the officers needed no justification—no evidence that Bostick had done anything wrong—to approach and engage him.[12]

Although the Court did not definitively decide the seizure question in *Bostick*, it made clear that "mere police questioning" does not constitute a seizure—even if it occurs in the confined space of a bus.[13] The Court maintained that although passengers on buses are constrained, it is because of their decision to travel by bus—not because of what the police officers do. According to the Court, the officers merely "walked up to Bostick . . . asked him a few questions, and asked if they could search his bags."[14] The Court intimated that that is not enough to transform a consensual bus encounter into a seizure.[15]

More than a decade later, in *United States v. Drayton*,[16] the Court made that point explicit: police officers may question people on buses without triggering the Fourth Amendment.[17] What makes the

Court's conclusion in *Drayton* particularly remarkable is that the record revealed that the officer in the case had boarded more than eight hundred buses in one year to question passengers. Fewer than ten passengers declined the request to search their luggage, suggesting that they did not feel free to leave.[18]

The Court's reasoning in both cases makes merely questioning someone on the street even less likely to qualify as a seizure. Indeed, the Court in *Bostick* expressly noted that had Bostick's encounter occurred off the bus, like the hypothetical I describe in Decision 3, it would be easy to conclude that he was not seized.[19]

Accordingly, not only could a police officer decide to approach and question Tanya on the street or on a bus without any justification, but even if his decision was racially motivated it would not trigger the Fourth Amendment's protections.

Decision 5: To Question About Immigration Status

Assume that the officers perceive Tanya to be a foreigner (based on her accent) and question her about her immigration status.[20] Notwithstanding what I have said so far, you might surmise that some forms of questioning—like those about immigration status—might be so intrusive or intimidating that an officer's decision to pursue them would automatically trigger the Fourth Amendment. You would be wrong.

Stipulate that the officers have no objective reason to believe that Tanya is undocumented. Nevertheless, one of them approaches Tanya and asks: "Where are you from?" "How long have you been in this country?" "Are you an illegal alien?" "May I see proof of citizenship?" None of these questions implicates the Fourth Amendment.[21]

The Court's decision in *INS v. Delgado* provides one of the most troubling examples of broad immigration questioning. The issue before the Court was whether so-called "factory sweeps"—the Immigration and Naturalization Service's (INS) practice of entering workplaces with the employer's consent to question workers about their immigration status—were constitutional.[22] Today, such practices are carried out by the Immigration Control Enforcement, or ICE.

Like the bus sweep in *Bostick*, the factory sweeps in *Delgado* were conducted without individualized suspicion. That is, in none of the sweeps did the INS have reason to believe that any particular worker was undocumented.[23] Thus, as in *Bostick*, the Court had to decide whether the law enforcement's activity constituted a seizure. Answering "yes" would have made the INS's conduct an unreasonable seizure, since it was not supported by evidence that any individual person was undocumented.

Justice Rehnquist, writing for the Court, asked two questions: (1) whether the individual workers whom the INS questioned were seized, and (2) whether the INS's conduct effectuated a seizure of the entire workforce. He answered both in the negative.

With respect to the first question, Justice Rehnquist stated that the interactions were brief, with the INS merely asking "one or two questions."[24] Moreover, the questions that the INS asked focused on place of birth, citizenship status, and proof of residency, and were "not particularly intrusive."[25] According to Justice Rehnquist, the INS's conduct "could hardly result in a reasonable fear that respondents were not free to continue working or to move about in the factory."[26] Thus, he concluded, the individual workers whom the INS questioned were not seized.

Justice Rehnquist's account sanitizes the episode, which involved between twenty and thirty INS agents. These agents wore their INS badges, carried handcuffs, and they were armed.[27] Some of the agents guarded the exits; others moved systematically through the factory, row by row, "in para-military formation."[28] Moreover, though the individual questioning may have been "brief," the entire episode lasted between one and two hours.

At no time during the sweep did the agents inform the workers that they were free to leave.[29] Presumably, the workers inferred just the opposite, especially since the INS arrested several of the workers who attempted to exit the factory.[30] Indeed, as one worker explained, "They see you leaving and they think I'm guilty."[31] Against this back-drop, Justice Brennan was right to suggest that Justice Rehnquist's analysis was "rooted . . . in fantasy"[32] and "striking . . . [in] its studied air of unreality."[33]

In addition to concluding that the individual workers whom the INS questioned were not seized, Justice Rehnquist also held that the workplace as a whole was not seized. He repeated his point that the mere questioning of individuals is not a seizure.[34] He then added that the fact that the questioning occurred in the work-place does not necessarily change the analysis. According to him, "[o]rdinarily, when people are at work their freedom to move about has been meaningfully restricted, not by the actions of law enforce-ment officials, but by the workers' voluntary obligations to their employers."[35] In other words, assuming the employees in *Delgado* felt constrained, that sense of constraint derived from their regular workplace responsibilities and not the INS's full-scale sweep.[36]

As legal scholar Tracey Maclin has observed, Justice Rehnquist's approach is tantamount to "blam[ing] the victim,"[37] The burden is placed not "on the government to show justification for the intru-sion, . . . [but] . . . on the citizen to challenge government author-ity."[38] Moreover, Rehnquist's analysis discounts the ways in which law enforcement presence alters how people experience social spaces. When, for example, the INS agents in *Delgado* entered the factory, they transformed that already confining space into a government-centered and more coercive environment: an INS raid.[39]

The bottom line for Tanya is that whether she is on the street as a pedestrian, on a bus as a passenger, or at her workplace as an employ-ee, the government may question her about her immigration status without triggering the Fourth Amendment. Moreover, were an offi-cer to say, "I questioned Tanya because she looked like a Nigerian immigrant in terms of her dress and appearance," that racial motiva-tion would not violate the Fourth Amendment. In a related context, the Supreme Court has said that "apparent Mexican ancestry" (whatever that means) can be a basis for determining whether someone is undocumented.

Decision 6: To Seek Permission to Search

What if after the officers approach Tanya—again without any objective reason to believe that she has done anything wrong—they ask to search her bag? Is Tanya now seized? Does the answer turn on whether the officer informs Tanya of her right to refuse consent?

The Supreme Court has held that police officers do not need inform people of their right to refuse a search.[40] Officers' failure to warn does not make a search invalid. Nor does the failure to warn people of their right to refuse consent turn an encounter into a seizure.[41]

Thus, consistent with Fourth Amendment law, police officers may approach individuals whom they have no reason to believe engaged in wrongdoing, and ask those individuals for permission to search their persons or effects. Under such circumstances, people are not seized because (ostensibly) they are free to say no and go about their business. That people may not know that they have this right to refuse consent—or would not feel empowered to exercise that right— is largely irrelevant for Fourth Amendment purposes.

The case in which the Supreme Court developed this doctrine is *Schneckloth v. Bustamonte.*[42] In that case, Officer James Rand stopped a car after observing two burned-out lights.[43] Robert Bustamonte was a passenger, and five other men were in the car. Only one of the men, passenger Joe Alcala, had identification.[44]

Officer Rand asked each man to exit the car.[45] By this time, two other officers had arrived (why other patrol cars were summoned to the scene when the basis for the stop was a burned-out light, the Court never addresses).[46] Officer Rand requested permission to search the car.[47] Alcala responded, "Sure, go ahead."[48]

Although there was no indication that Officer Rand or the other two officers used direct coercion to get Alcala to consent to the search, none of the officers informed Alcala that he had the right to refuse.[49] Upon searching the car, the officers found three stolen checks under one of the seats.[50] Bustamonte challenged the legality of the search, and lost.

The Court described two scenarios in which someone might consent to a search: one, where the officers did not already have probable cause to arrest the person, and another, where they did. The Court reasoned that in the second instance, consenting to a search might be the better alternative for someone possibly facing arrest. Central to this conclusion was the idea that "[i]f the search is conducted and proves fruitless, that itself may convince the police that an arrest with its possible stigma and embarrassment is unnecessary."[51] That logic seems reasonable enough.

But adding race to the picture exposes some limitations in the Court's analysis. If Black Americans believe that police officers are likely to perceive Black people as criminally suspect, they may feel extra pressure to say yes to consent to searches to disconfirm that stereotype. Black Americans might also feel pressured to say yes to consent searches on the view that saying no carries the risk of both prolonging the encounter and escalating the situation.

Of course, whites are also subject to pressures to comply with requests from the police. The point is that, because of racial stereotypes of Black criminality, Black people are subject to a kind of surplus compliance. Blacks, as a general matter, are going to be less trusting of the police, less comfortable in their presence, and more concerned about their physical safety than whites. Whether justified or not, these fears add pressure for Blacks to terminate police encounters by giving up their rights, consenting to searches, and otherwise being overly cooperative.

These racial concerns figure nowhere in the *Bustamonte* case. Instead, the Court focused its attention on the potential cost to law enforcement if people were informed of their right to refuse such searches. According to the Court:

In situations where the police have some evidence of illicit activity, but lack probable cause to arrest or search, a search authorized by a valid consent may be the only means of obtaining important and reliable evidence. In the present case for example, while the police had reason to stop the car for traffic violations, the State does not contend that there was probable cause to search the vehicle or that the search was incident to a valid arrest of any of the occupants. Yet, the search yielded tangible evidence that served as a basis for a prosecution, and provided some assurance that others, wholly innocent of the crime, were not mistakenly brought to trial. And in those cases where there is probable cause to arrest or search, but where the police lack a warrant, a consent search may still be valuable.

The passage is quite remarkable. It links the legitimacy of consent searches in which officers have no evidence of criminal wrongdoing to the fact that police officers in those instances have no evidence of wrongdoing! This turns Fourth Amendment protections upside down; it is precisely because consent searches do not require reasonable suspicion, probable cause, or a warrant that they ought to be scrutinized.

Nor is the Court right in assuming that consenting to a search will "convince the police that an arrest with its possible stigma and embarrassment is unnecessary." Although exposing the inside of one's bag to a police officer is one way of saying, "I am not carrying drugs," this strategy will not always be enough to dissipate an officer's suspicions. To understand why, let's bring Tanya back into the analysis.

Imagine that a police officer suspects, but has no objective reason to believe, that Tanya is a drug dealer. Assume that Tanya is carrying a bag and that the officer requests permission to search it. Tanya complies, and the officer searches the bag but does not find any drugs.

Tanya's consent to the search will not necessarily terminate the interaction—in fact, it may prolong it. Still suspicious, the officer may believe that Tanya granted permission to search her bag because she is carrying drugs elsewhere on her person. He may even assume that Tanya strategically consented to the search to conceal her criminality.

Alternatively, the officer may know that Tanya's race puts her in a vulnerable position: She might be eager to terminate the encounter because of her fear of the police, or overeager to prove her innocence because she's worried that the officer perceives her to be criminally suspect simply because she is Black.

If the officer believes that any of preceding concerns motivated Tanya's consent, he may feel emboldened to request permission to conduct another more intrusive search: a search of Tanya's clothing. If Tanya does not consent to this second search, the officer's suspicions would presumably intensify. Why would a person who is not carrying drugs grant permission to search her bag but not her person? Something like this hypothetical played itself out in a Supreme Court case I mentioned earlier, *United States v. Drayton*.[52]

In *Drayton*, three members of the Tallahassee police department—one Black and two white—boarded a bus just as it was about to depart. Working from the back of the bus forward, the officers asked passengers questions as to their travel destinations, their identity, and their personal belongings. The "[d]efendants Drayton and Brown were seated next to each other a few rows from the rear." One of the officers identified himself as a police officer, informed the defendants that he was part of a drug interdiction team, and asked whether they had any luggage. Both responded in the affirmative. The officer then asked for permission to search the bag, to which Brown responded, "Go ahead." An officer searched the bag but found nothing illegal.

If Brown's consent was a privacy-compromising tactic intended to disconfirm his assumed criminality, and to end the encounter quickly, it did not work. Indeed, it had the opposite effect. Upon learning that Brown's bag did not contain any illegal drugs, the officer requested permission to conduct another, more intrusive search of Brown's person: a pat down. His reason? He thought the defendants "were *overly cooperative* during the search [of the bag]." The Supreme Court concluded that this search was constitutional.[53]

Enter Tanya. With *Drayton* in mind, it is fair to say that Tanya is vulnerable to multiple requests for her consent to a search—not just one. Saying yes to an officer's first request to search her bag won't necessarily terminate the encounter, but could lead to another request to search her person. Without more, merely making a second search request would not make the encounter a seizure. Thus, the officer would not need any justification to seek that consent.

Nor does it matter that the officer failed to inform Tanya of her right to refuse consent. Police officers are free to exploit a person's lack of awareness about the scope of their Fourth Amendment rights.

Pause and think about that point. Is it really fair to say that a person consents to something if they do not know they have a right to refuse? And even if people know their rights, wouldn't a requirement that police officers inform them of that right increase the likelihood that the average person, and certainly the average Black person, would feel empowered to exercise it?

The Court was not oblivious to these questions and the concerns they raise. But far more important to the Court was the worry that requiring police officers to notify people of their right to refuse consent would impose too high a burden on law enforcement. The Court seemed to imagine that police officers would be required to employ something like the following script:

> You have a right to refuse to allow me to search your home, and if you decide to refuse, I will respect your refusal. If you do decide to let me search, you won't be able to change your mind later on, and during the search I'll be able to look in places and take things that I couldn't even if I could get a warrant. You have the right to a law-

yer before you decide, and if you can't afford a lawyer we will get you one and you won't have to pay for him. There are many different laws which are designed to protect you from my searching, but they are too complicated for me to explain or for you to understand, so if you think you would like to take advantage of this very important information, you will need a lawyer to help you before you tell me I can search.[54]

Many people would argue that requiring that kind of warning would be impractical.[55] Indeed, that is precisely what the government argued on appeal—"that the very complexity of such warnings proves its unworkability."[56]

But the choice is not between telling a person everything and telling her nothing. In other words, one might conclude that police officers should be required to warn people of their right to refuse consent and reject the idea that the warnings be extensive. There is a middle ground: Prior to conducting a consent search, police officers could be required to inform a person of nothing more than "you have a right to refuse consent." Full stop. At the time *Bustamonte* was litigated, federal law enforcement officials regularly offered warnings of that sort.[57] However, Tanya is unlikely to get them. Fourth Amendment law has created a fiction that people can exercise rights they do not know they have.

There are other ways the Court could restrain the power police officers have to conduct consent searches. The Court could require that police officers have some evidence of wrongdoing before they seek permission to search. Why should an officer be permitted to ask Tanya for permission to search when that officer has no objective reason to think that Tanya has done anything wrong? In other words, why not require police officers to justify consent searches? We could debate whether that justification should be in the form of probable cause or reasonable. (We will explore the difference these two standards in later chapters.) The point is that *some* showing of wrongdoing should be required.

None of what I've said means that police officers may actively coerce consent from Tanya. On that point, Fourth Amendment law is clear. So, for example, an officer may not instruct Tanya that, if she refuses to consent to a search, he will arrest her. That form of coercion would render Tanya's consent involuntary. But the officer may seek permission to search Tanya and her effects without knowledge that Tanya has done anything wrong—and knowing that Tanya may not know her rights or feel empowered to exercise them.

To summarize: The problem here, as with other pedestrian checks, concerns the utter and complete freedom police officers have to force an encounter with Tanya, Tanya's sense of powerlessness, or her relatively weak "bargaining power," with respect to how to navigate the encounter, and the fact that police officers might strategically target Tanya to exploit her vulnerability (in this instance, to exploit Tanya's sense that she is not free to decline the officer's request to search). Fourth Amendment law does not mention, let alone address, these problems.

Decision 7: To Conduct Voluntary Interviews

Having approached Tanya, the officers ask for her identification and discover that her last name is Mohammed. They also discover that Tanya's address indicates that she lives relatively close to a mosque that they know the FBI has had under surveillance for some time. The officers specifically ask Tanya whether she is a Muslim.

"Yes. Why does that matter?"

"Because it matters to us," the officer retorts before following up with another religious question.

"Do you attend the 5th Street Mosque?"

"Yes," she answers, this time more nervously and cooperatively than the first, hoping that her compliance will end the encounter.

"Would you mind accompanying us to the station. The FBI is investigating terrorist activity at the mosque you attend, and we just want to make sure that you are not involved in any way and that you don't know anyone who is. We, like lots of other police departments across the country, have been helping the FBI with its anti-terrorist initiatives. We know that you want to help us in these efforts."

At this point, Tanya feels that she cannot say no. She accompanies the officers to the police station, where they question her for three hours and then indicate that she is "free to leave but that we might follow up." Embarrassed, humiliated, and concerned that the FBI might seek to question her again, Tanya relays her experience to the American Civil Liberties Union (ACLU) to ascertain whether the agency violated her Fourth Amendment rights. She is surprised to learn that the answer is no, and that the FBI regularly employs what it refers to as "voluntary interviews."

That the FBI refers to investigatory engagements of the sort Tanya experienced as "voluntary interviews" is a window into how the Supreme Court might respond to the practice.[58] Likely, the Court would conclude that because Tanya "voluntarily" went to the FBI's office, she was not seized. Because the FBI agents did not use force or otherwise coerce Tanya into staying, she was "free to leave."

As with prior examples, the fact that Tanya did not know her rights or may have felt disempowered to exercise them during the FBI questioning does not change the outcome. "Mere questioning," even in the context of a police station, would not transform a voluntary encounter into a seizure.

Nor would it matter if, instead of encountering Tanya on the street, the officers showed up at her house, knocked on her door, and announced that they are police officers who are helping the FBI to combat terrorism.[59] The Court would still conclude that Tanya went to the police station and was interviewed of her own free will.

What if Tanya could demonstrate that, in fact, she exercised no such free will? Subjectively, she felt compelled both to accompany the police to the station and to answer their questions. If you recall the doctrinal test for determining whether a seizure has occurred, you will recognize that Tanya's subjective feelings are not important.[60]

The inquiry concerns not what Tanya felt, but what a "reasonable person" under similar circumstances would have felt.[61]

But that still leaves a central question: Upon what basis would the Court conclude that a reasonable person in Tanya's position would not feel free to leave a "voluntary interview"? After all, one could argue that no one would feel free to leave the FBI office under the circumstances I have described—and few, if any, of us would have felt free to decline the officers' invitation to accompany them in the first place. This sense of constraint would be all the more salient if Tanya is, or is perceived to be, a Muslim—and a Black one at that.[62]

Putting these points in more formal legal terms; even discounting Tanya's subjective feelings, and interpreting the "free to leave" test in more objective terms, the question may still be formulated in two ways: (1) Whether a reasonable person would feel free to leave; or— more specifically—(2) Whether a reasonable Black Muslim person would feel free to leave? One can see how defining the bounds of such a "reasonable person" might dramatically shift the outcome.

Regardless, the Court would conclude that Tanya has not been seized. Two features of the seizure analysis help to explain why. First, the free-to-leave framework is a normative or policy-driven inquiry rhetorically disguised as an empirical or factual one. Here's what I mean. Every time the Court asks "whether a reasonable person would feel free to leave or otherwise terminate the encounter," it is really asking whether certain police practices—even ones we may experience as intrusive—should be tolerated without any justification. When the Court thinks the answer to that question is "yes" (the police practice at issue should be tolerated, even without any evidence of wrongdoing), the Court rules that a reasonable person would *not* have felt seized. When the Court thinks the answer to that question is "no" (the police practice at issue should not be tolerated without some evidence of wrongdoing), it rules that a reasonable person would have felt seized.

Note, then, that when the Court conducts its seizure analysis, it is not trying to figure out how reasonable people would experience particular forms of police conduct. Instead, the Court is making judgments—normative and policy judgments—about the kinds of burdens people should put up with.

Applying the preceding insights to our voluntary interview hypothetical, the legal conclusion that a reasonable person is not seized in the context of a voluntary interview is a normative position that a reasonable person *should not* feel seized. Put more provocatively, a *reasonable Muslim* should not feel seized under the facts I described. Only *un*reasonable Muslims would not put up with "voluntary interviews" in the sense of experiencing them as seizures that the government must justify.

Something like that argument was at play in a very different context—the internment of Japanese Americans during World War II. There, the Supreme Court, in *Korematsu v. United States*, rationalized the internment of people of Japanese descent in part on the view that interment was their wartime burden.[63] According to the Court, "Citizenship has its responsibilities as well as its privileges, and in time of war the burden is always heavier."[64] The problem with that statement is that the specific burden at issue in the case (internment) was not "heavier" for everyone. It was heavier only for some (people of Japanese descent).

To repeat: internment is a very different context from the "voluntary interview" predicament in which Tanya finds herself, although it's worth noting that both implicate concerns about national security and the government routinely invoked *Korematsu* to defend and legitimize the "war on terror" and the specific targeting of Muslims it authorized.[65] I turned to *Korematsu* for a relatively narrow reason: namely, to reference a more explicit way in which the Supreme Court allocated the burdens of citizenship in the name national security and public safety. In the seizure context, the Court does something quite similar.

A second feature of the seizure doctrine that makes it difficult to argue that Tanya's "voluntary interview" constitutes a seizure is the Court's "colorblind" approach. After an early nod in the direction of factoring race into whether someone felt free to leave,[66] the Supreme Court has never again taken race into account in determining whether a person is seized.[67] This colorblind approach is particularly striking, because the determination for whether a police officer has seized a person is a supposed to be a "totality of the circumstances" inquiry, meaning that courts are to take all the relevant facts into account.[68]

One would think that because race is a profoundly salient dimension of social life which has a particularly fraught relationship to policing that the Court would include race in its "totality of the circumstances" analysis. But the Court's colorblind approach to this area of Fourth Amendment law proceeds as though race plays no role in shaping a person's sense of agency and freedom during interactions with the police.[69]

The marginalization of race in the Court's Fourth Amendment jurisprudence doesn't come from nowhere. Across broad bodies of constitutional law—in cases implicating voting rights, affirmative action, employment discrimination, voluntary integration programs, and indigenous sovereignty—the Court has invoked colorblindness not only to obscure some of the ways in which race continues to structure social life, but also to limit the degree to which the government may employ race conscious remedies to mitigate ongoing patterns of racial inequality.[70]

None of this means the invocation of colorblindness inside or outside of the law is per se problematic. What's problematic is the radicalization of colorblindness to delegitimize efforts to make the United States a more racially egalitarian society. While the Supreme Court's seizure analysis does not explicitly engage in debates about colorblindness, that body of law rarely centers concerns about race and racial inequality.

With respect to age, the Court's approach has been more nuanced. In 2011, in an opinion authored by Justice Sotomayor, the first and thus far only women of color or Latinx person to serve as a Supreme Court justice, the Court concluded that courts may properly consider age in their "totality of the circumstances" inquiry as to whether an officer's conduct amounts to a seizure. According to the Court:

> In some circumstances, a child's age "would have affected how a reasonable person" in the suspect's position "would perceive his or her freedom to leave." That is, a reasonable child subjected to police questioning will sometimes feel pressured to submit when a reasonable adult would feel free to go. We think it clear that courts can account for that reality without doing any damage to the objective nature of the custody analysis.[71]

The foregoing reasoning applies to race. To help me drive this point home, indulge the following thought experiment: With Black and white people in mind, substitute race for age throughout the passage above. Under this thought experiment, the quote now reads:

> In some circumstances, a person's *race* "would have affected how a reasonable person" in the suspect's position "would perceive his or her freedom to leave." That is, a reasonable *Black* person subjected to police questioning will sometimes feel pressured to submit when a reasonable *white* person would feel free to go. We think it clear that courts can account for that reality without doing any damage to the objective nature of the custody analysis.

In drawing this comparison, I do not mean to suggest that Blacks are to whites what children are to adults—such infantilization has a nasty racial history. I can't stress that point enough. I use the analogy here simply to note that even if one thinks that race is less relevant than age in determining whether an officer has seized a person, the claim that race is irrelevant to the analysis is difficult to sustain.

The Court's avoidance of race is troubling, not only because it furthers the Court's longstanding practice of pretending that race does not matter, but also because it takes off the table an important factor that could heighten a person's sense of constraint and powerlessness in the context of police encounters and could heighten their vulnerability to being policed in the first place. For example, because Black people are likely to experience a greater sense of constraint than white people in the context of police interactions, the Court's failure to consider race is not a race-neutral approach. Instead, it creates a *racial preference* in the seizure doctrine for people who are not racially vulnerable to interactions with the police, and who do not experience a sense of *racial constraint* in those interactions.

Black people, across all sorts of differences, are likely to feel seized earlier in a police interaction than whites, likely to feel "more" seized in any given moment, and less likely to know or feel empowered to exercise their rights. With reference to Black men, legal scholar Cynthia Lee puts the point this way:

> A young black male who has grown up in South Central Los Angeles knows that if he is stopped by a police officer, he should do whatever the officer says and not talk back unless he wants to kiss the ground. This young man may not feel free to leave or terminate the encounter with the officer, but if the reviewing court believes the average (white) person would have felt free to leave, then the encounter will not be considered a seizure and the young black male will not be able to complain that his Fourth Amendment rights have been violated.[72]

Lee's point pertains to Blacks more generally. The racial asymmetry she names is why Paul Butler describes the Fourth Amendment with more racial specificity as "the white Fourth Amendment."[73] The point is that the Supreme Court's colorblind interpretation of the Fourth Amendment ends up protecting white Americans more than it does Black Americans.

By avoiding race, the Supreme Court cannot adequately incorporate Black people's precarious experiences with the police into their Fourth Amendment jurisprudence. Nowhere in the Court's entire body of Fourth Amendment law will one find concerns about the sense of exposure, of anxiety, and of vulnerability too often incidental to Black people's encounters with the police. The racial harms police routinely commit—from trampling Black dignity, to snuffing out Black life—is simply not legible as concerns in Fourth Amendment law.[74]

I'm not saying that incorporating race into the seizure analysis would be easy. Many people would argue against replacing the generic reasonable person standard in favor of identity-specific standards—for example, a "reasonable Black person" standard when the suspect is Black or a "reasonable Latinx person" standard when the suspect is Latinx. That opposition could be based on the view not only that identity-specific standards are color-conscious and therefore run afoul of colorblindness, but also on the view that such standards would be unworkable.

But think back to our discussion of age. When the Court included age in the seizure analysis it did not adopt a sixteen-year-old standard or a fifteen-year-old standard or a thirteen-year-old standard. The Court simply noted, "[a] child's age is far 'more than a chronological fact.' It is a fact that 'generates common sense conclusions about behavior and perception.' Such conclusions apply broadly to children as a class."[75] Suffice it to say that these points can be made about race as well.[76]

Returning now to Tanya: Taking race into account might mean asking, among other questions, whether the widespread perception of Black Muslims as terrorists could cause someone in Tanya's position to feel compelled to acquiesce to the FBI's request for a "voluntary interview." The Court might well answer that question in the negative (recall my earlier point that, as a substantive matter, the seizure analysis is more normative and policy-driven than empirical factually-driven). But quite apart from how the Court would ultimately resolve the seizure question in any given case, its discussion of race (and, in this case, its intersection with religion) would recognize that social category as a matter of legal concern in ways that might generate public debate about "voluntary interviews" or other surveillance practices the government routinely deploys against Black and other Muslims.

Imagine, for example, that in a case like Tanya's the Court ruled that it considered whether race was relevant to the seizure analysis but concluded that it was not. According to the Court, the claim that people view Muslims as terrorist is "too amorphous" to shape the application of the seizure analysis. The Court reasoned as well that even if people do stereotype Muslims as terrorists, the existence of that stereotype does not mean that a reasonable person in Tanya's position would have felt seized.

A Supreme Court ruling of the foregoing sort would generate significant public debate. Yet, as things now stand, Tanya would not benefit from that kind of debate, because the Court's colorblind approach does not produce nearly as much public controversy. In this respect, the Court's racial avoidance when deciding whether the Tanya's "voluntary interview" was a seizure could affect not only the outcome of her case, but also how much public attention it received.

Another approach the Court could take to address the racial dimensions of policing is not explicitly race-conscious. Here, whenever a police officer approaches a person and asks that person a question, that person is seized and thus the Fourth Amendment protections would kick in. The issue would then become whether the seizure was reasonable. To answer that question, courts would first ask whether the officer dispensed what I will call "free to leave warnings." Those warning would instruct the person of their right to walk away or otherwise terminate the encounter. The absence of those warning would make that seizure unreasonable, and no other inquiry would be necessary.

Informing this approach is the idea that if the seizure analysis is predicated on "whether people are free to leave," why not simply require police officers to offer that instruction? Doing so would increase the likelihood that when people stay put, they are doing so because they want to.

Drawing in part on some of my earlier writings on race and Fourth Amendment law,[77] a recent concurring opinion in *United States v. Knights*,[78] a federal appellate court case in the Eleventh Circuit, advocated for a version of the approach I am advancing here. Referencing some of the very problems I've articulated with respect to current applications of the "free to leave test," the concurrence suggests that "the Supreme Court should consider adopting a bright-line rule requiring officers to clearly advise citizens of their right to end so-called consensual police encounters."[79]

Some readers will undoubtedly think that my "free to leave warnings" tip the scales too heavily in the direction of privacy and liberty without sufficient regard for public safety. Assuming this is your concern, the fix might be to incorporate an exigency exception into my rule: If an officer engages someone but, because of an emergency, did not provide the "free to leave warnings," the absence of those warnings would not without more make that seizure unreasonable. This amendment to my rule could draw on the fact that Fourth Amendment law already embodies an exigency doctrine. For example, although police officers will ordinarily need a warrant to search a home,[80] they may do so without a warrant if they have probable cause and the circumstances are exigent.[81] Some version of that exigency standard could be employed to modify the "free to leave warnings" rule I am advocating. Again, I do not believe that my rule warrants an exigency exception. But I understand why others might disagree.

There's another objection one might level against my warnings: They may not be helpful in the way my arguments assume. This objection would rest on empirical evidence suggesting that even when police officers dish out *Miranda* warnings to suspects, they are still able to elicit confessions from those suspects.

No matter what your knowledge of constitutional criminal procedure, chances are you have heard the *Miranda* warning, a favorite of police procedural television shows and movies:

> You have the right to remain silent. Anything you can and will be sued against you in a court of law. You have the right to an attorney. If you can't afford an attorney, the state will provide one for you.

At least since the 1970s, *Miranda* warnings have been firmly ensconced in police investigation practices. And, researchers have found that when police officers offer those warnings, people still talked.[82] This is worrisome for the "free to leave warnings" not only because a person might not feel "free to leave" after receiving those warnings, but also because if that person didn't leave, they would have a difficult time subsequently arguing that they felt forced to stay. After all, they got the warnings. From that vantage point, the "free to leave warnings" could end up protecting police officers from challenges to the unwanted encounters they stage rather than protecting people from those encounters. That risk is real.

But before you give up on the warnings I'm proposing, you should know that the *Miranda* protections kick in only after a person is in custody, meaning under a formal arrest or its functional equivalent.[83] Under those conditions, warnings may not be enough to remove the coercive nature of the encounter.[84] By contrast, the "free to leave test" would be triggered by *any* encounter with the police, including those that no judge would conclude amounted to an arrest.

The distinction between the *any* encounter trigger for my warnings and the *custodial* encounter trigger for *Miranda* could matter. In the context of *non-custodial* encounters, warnings could be at least somewhat empowering. Armed with warnings, people who might not otherwise terminate or leave a *non-custodial* encounter might decide to do either, even when they would do neither in a *custodial* encounter. Still, the truth is, we just don't know whether warnings would function in the way I am imaging.[85]

What we do know is that none of this debate about warnings is particularly helpful to Tanya. Her misfortune has her stuck in the "here and now" of Fourth Amendment law. As such, the police-dominated environment in which she finds herself—an involuntary interrogation that the Court would masquerade as a voluntary interview—doesn't even trigger the Fourth Amendment.

You might think that some other constitutional provision—such as the very Fifth Amendment's *Miranda* warning about which I've been talking—might be helpful in this context, particularly because the questioning occurred at the FBI's office. They wouldn't be. Quite apart from whether such warning would do any good, you now know that the fact that Tanya is not in custody (indeed, she isn't even seized) means that the Miranda protections wouldn't apply. Remember: We are entitled to *Miranda* warnings only when we are experiencing custodial interrogation. Moreover, even if the officers' conduct amounted to a custodial interaction, Miranda's protections would still be unavailable. Because the state is not yet seeking to admit Tanya's statements against her, there is no self-incrimination issue.[86]

Similarly, the Sixth Amendment right to counsel would not help. That constitutional right applies only when the state has commenced formal proceedings against a person by, for example, issuing an indictment.[87] Finally, because the Supreme Court would perceive "voluntary interviews" as consensual encounters, arguments against the practice that invoke due process—that Tanya was coerced into cooperating with the police—also would fail, and easily so.[88] The reality, then, is that Tanya is stuck with the Fourth Amendment, even as it offers her no protections from the racially motivated "voluntary interview" she experienced.

Decision 8: To Chase

Assume that Tanya has had all the foregoing interactions with the police—and on more than one occasion. She does not want to have another. Now that Tanya is more familiar with the law, she worries that she will be forced to compromise her rights and answer questions or consent to a search to prove that she is innocent. She believes that her failure to cooperate could ultimately lead to her arrest.

Although Tanya has not herself been arrested for refusing to cooperate with the police, many of her friends in the neighborhood have been. Plus, for at least a decade, Black women in the neighborhood have been complaining that police officers use the stop-and-frisk practice as a mechanism to engage in sexual harassment. Tanya thus decides that the next time she sees the police she is going to avoid them altogether—even if it means running away. And, seeing two officers the next day, she does just that.

The police officers chase Tanya down the street, shouting, "Stop, it's the police!" as they do so. Is Tanya now seized? No. The fact that she is not formally under the control of the police, in the sense that she has not submitted to their authority or been apprehended means that she is not seized.[89] Thus, the officers are free to chase Tanya, even if they have no reason to think she has engaged in wrongdoing—and even if their primary reason for doing so is the fact that she is a Black woman.

It gets worse. Initially, the officer has no reason to believe that Tanya has done anything wrong, and she has every right to avoid another police encounter. To use the legal parlance, she is "free to leave." But if Tanya exercises that right by running away, the officer may draw an adverse inference from her decision to flee. And, if Tanya is running in what the officer considers a "high crime area" (which several scholars have suggested is simply code for a predominantly Black or brown neighborhood)[90] the officer may now have a basis to stop her, at least according to Supreme Court law.[91]

A very recent opinion by the highest court in Massachusetts challenges the idea that running from the police necessarily makes a person a suspect. According to the court:

> [T]he finding that black males in Boston are disproportionately and repeatedly targeted for FIO encounters suggests a reason for flight totally unrelated to consciousness of guilt. Such an individual, when approached by the police, might just as easily be motivated by the desire to avoid the recurring indignity of being racially profiled as by the desire to hide criminal activity.[92]

The Supreme Court, however, has not embraced the Massachusetts court's reasoning, and it remains to be seen whether other jurisdictions will.

What this means for Tanya (unless she happens to be in Massachusetts) is quite demoralizing: an officer's decision to chase her will not amount to a seizure, so he is free to do so even if he has no reason to believe that Tanya did anything wrong aside from running. Moreover, if Tanya is subsequently seized—either because the officer apprehends her or because Tanya stops running and submits to his authority[93]—a court may conclude that that seizure is reasonable, particularly if Tanya was running in a "high crime area."

It would be bad enough if Tanya's exposure to police contact ended with this "is there a *seizure*" analysis. But she also must worry about *searches*. Remember that the Fourth Amendment ostensibly protects us from both. Consequently, in addition to deciding lots and lots of cases on what counts as a seizure, the Supreme Court has also had to decide lots and lots of cases about what counts as a search.

As with the *seizure* cases, the Court's *search* cases contain stories that reveal the minimalization of Fourth Amendment's protections against racial harms of policing, on the one hand, and the maximalization of police investigative powers, on the other. Although the Court's caselaw on searches transcends pedestrian checks, they too demonstrate the ease with which police officers can surveil Black Americans and subject them to intrusive practices with zero evidence of criminal wrongdoing. Picking up from the prior hypotheticals, I add four more examples to illustrate.

Decision 9: To Infiltrate

Recall from *Decision 7: To Conduct Voluntary Interviews* that the police suspected Tanya of terrorist activity and asked her to accompany them to the police station, where they conducted a "voluntary interview." Again, there is no evidence that Tanya has engaged in any criminal activity. Indeed, the government's only reason for investigating Tanya for supposed terrorist activity is that she is a Muslim, and that she regularly attends a mosque whose leader routinely and publicly criticizes U.S. foreign policy in the Middle East.

Although that interview did not inculpate Tanya, the officers remain convinced that Tanya is hiding something.[94] They decide, therefore, to infiltrate her mosque and to enlist one of her friends, Mohammed (who goes by "Mo"), to report on her activities. Imagine that Mo surreptitiously records every private conversation he has with Tanya for six months, and gives the recordings to the FBI. Does this violate the Fourth Amendment? No. Indeed, Mo's activity would not even trigger the Fourth Amendment.

Unsurprisingly, if Tanya were to argue that she was seized, she would not get very far. After all, Mo is Tanya's best friend (or so Tanya believes), and Tanya was not aware that Mo was cooperating with the government. Under these circumstances, it stretches credulity to argue that a reasonable person in Tanya's position would *not* feel free to leave or otherwise terminate her many interactions with Mo.

The real question, then, is whether the government's conduct in this case amounts to a search of Tanya or her conversation. The short answer is "no." The Supreme Court would reason that Tanya assumed the risk that the person with whom she had those interactions (Mo) was a government official.[95] The burden is on Tanya to choose her friends more carefully.

Additionally, it does not matter that Mo surreptitiously recorded their conversations.[96] The point remains the same: the Fourth Amendment does not protect us from "misplaced confidence"[97] or "false friends."[98] We supposedly assume the risk that the people with whom we interact will listen to, record, and transmit our conversations, even when they are acting under the direction of law enforcement.[99]

Nor does it matter that the government's decision to focus on Tanya was racially and/or religiously motivated. The fact that Mo's conduct does not trigger the Fourth Amendment means that it is irrelevant, for Fourth Amendment purposes, whether that conduct was racially or religiously motivated.

The freedom with which law enforcement can use informants to investigate terrorism has become a profound problem for Muslim communities. As legal scholar Amna Akbar explains, "There is reason to believe that that there are informants at each and every mosque in the United States."[100] The potential chilling effects of the government's use of informants cannot be overstated. It creates an incentive for Muslims not to attend mosques, and to severely circumscribe their interactions when they do.

Decision 10: To Search Tanya's Trash

Assume that Mo's recording of his conversations with Tanya's yielded no incriminating evidence. Nevertheless, the government continues to believe that Tanya is somehow connected to terrorist activity, and is possibly at what law enforcement sometimes to refer to as "the early stages of radicalization," a concept that many scholars have rightly criticized for relying on perceived "Muslimness" itself as evidence of radicalization.[101]

Because the police lack probable cause with respect to Tanya's connection to terrorism, they are in no position to obtain a search warrant for Tanya's home. Therefore, they determine to examine her trash in hopes of finding some evidence of Tanya's supposed radicalization. If Tanya is like the average person, her trash will reveal some of the most intimate details of her life. For three consecutive weeks, the officers watch Tanya leave her trash on the side of the curb of her two-apartment building, and confiscate the bags once she is out of view.

The Supreme would conclude that the officer's rummaging through Tanya trash is not a search under the Fourth Amendment. In a 1988 case, *California v. Greenwood*, the Court ruled that we do not have a "reasonable expectation of privacy" in trash we put out for the garbage collector to pick up. "It is common knowledge that plastic garbage bags left on or at the side of a public street are readily accessible to animals, children, scavengers, snoops, and other members of the public," the Court maintained. The Court reasoned that requiring police officers to avert their eyes from activity to which the general public is exposed would put them in a worse position than other members of society.

There is much in the Court's analysis to critique. As Justice Brennan observed in his dissent:

> The mere possibility that unwelcome meddlers might open and rummage through the containers does not negate the expectation of privacy in their contents any more than the possibility of a burglary negates an expectation of privacy in the home; or the possibility of a private intrusion negates an expectation of privacy in an unopened package; or the possibility that an operator will listen in on a telephone conversation negates an expectation of privacy in the words spoken on the telephone.

Justice Brennan also challenged the Court's questionable claim that people do not harbor an expectation of privacy in their trash. "Scrutiny of another's trash is contrary to commonly accepted notions of civilized behavior," Brennan insisted. "I suspect, therefore, that members of our society will be shocked to learn that the Court, the ultimate guarantor of liberty, deems unreasonable our expectation that the aspects of our private lives that are concealed safely in a trash bag will not become public."

The problem for Tanya is that Justice Brennan's arguments were for the dissent—not the majority. Thus, the officers may search her trash on the side of curb as many times as they want without running afoul of the Fourth Amendment.

Decision 11: To Investigate to Verify Welfare Eligibility

Assume now that for the past thirteen months, Tanya has been looking for a job, but she has not had much luck. Her friends urge her to apply for welfare benefits, if not for herself, then for her fifteen-year-old son. Tanya is reluctant to do so, however, as she doesn't want to be stigmatized as a "welfare queen."[102]

Another two months pass, and Tanya remains unemployed. She decides that there is no other way. Stigma is better than hunger and homelessness.

Upon applying for benefits, Tanya learns that her county requires that all prospective welfare recipients submit to mandatory home visits by county social workers to verify the recipients' eligibility for welfare benefits. Tanya does not like this arrangement, but she fills out the requisite forms "consenting" to the visits.

The county welfare agency notifies Tanya in advance that the inspection visit will occur at some point during the following week, between the hours of noon and five in the afternoon. When the social workers visit Tanya's home, they find a small bag of marijuana on the floor of Tanya's son's bedroom. The social worker reports this finding to county prosecutors.

Although the district attorney declines to prosecute, the county welfare agency uses the incriminating evidence as the basis to disqualify Tanya from welfare eligibility. Tanya cannot claim Fourth Amendment protection from the social workers' search, because courts, including the Supreme Court, have held either that such investigations do not constitute a Fourth Amendment "search," or else that they represent an exception to the Fourth Amendment that is allowable so long as the primary purpose of the search is for a "special need" (such as health and safety concerns) other than strictly law enforcement purposes.[103]

Decision 12: To Conduct Surveillance of On-the-Street Dwellings

Within months of being found ineligible for welfare benefits, Tanya is evicted from her apartment and finds herself houseless. Making matters worse, her son ends up in the foster care system. Tanya is at her wit's end.

She realizes relatively quickly that in order to survive she needs to join a community with other houseless people. They live together in makeshift structures assembled from tarps and cardboard boxes that serve as their homes in the Skid Row area of town. Like many other cities, Tanya's city has an ordinance against obstructing municipal streets and sidewalks, but her home (and the rest of the "tent city") intrudes a few feet onto a city sidewalk.

One day, police officers appear at the "tent city" to investigate the theft of merchandise from a nearby business. The officers may freely look inside Tanya's dwelling, and may even pull aside a tarp flap or piece of cardboard to do so. Any evidence they may find inside will be—constitutionally speaking—fair game.

Courts generally have held that there is no reasonable expectation of privacy in an unauthorized dwelling illegally erected on public land. Therefore, police surveillance and intrusions into such dwellings do not constitute searches under the Fourth Amendment.[104]

Just because I used hypothetical situations to frame this chapter does not mean that the encounters and surveillance practices I have described are themselves hypothetical problems. Many were drawn straight from the pages of Supreme Court cases. Moreover, almost all of those cases involved interactions between the police and Black Americans.

Take a look at Figure 1 below, which focuses mostly (though not entirely) on pedestrian checks.

Conduct ≠ Search or Seizure	Cases	Race of Defendant
Decision to Follow/ Approach	*United States v. Mendenhall* (1980)	Black
Decision to Question Generally	*United States v. Mendenhall* (1980)	Black
Decision to Question on a Bus	*Florida v. Bostick* (1991) *United States v. Drayton* (2002)	Black Black
Decision to Not Inform of Right to Not Cooperate	*United States v. Drayton* (2002)	Black
Decision to Verify Welfare Eligibility (via Home Inspection)	*Wyman v. James* (1971)	Black
Decision to Chase	*California v. Hodari* (1973)	Black

Figure 1: Supreme Court Cases Involving Black Litigants

The left column lists the police conduct that the Court concluded is neither a search nor a seizure. The middle column reveals the case and year in which the Court ruled. Finally, the column to the right notes the race of the litigant in each of the cases referenced: Black. Black. Black. Black. Black. Black. Black.

Did I cherry-pick the cases in Figure 1? No. Did I leave out important Supreme Court cases that do a better job engaging race? Again, the answer is no. While the cases I have foregrounded do not comprise the entire universe of the Supreme Court's seizure case law, each case establishes or further entrenches significant points of Fourth Amendment law that have helped to make police interactions routine incidents in the life of people.

One might say, borrowing from Toni Morrison, that Figure 1 tells a story about Supreme Court decision-making "on the backs of blacks."[105] The point is that the Court regularly decides cases that include Black Americans as parties and impact Black people as a group in deciding whether a certain police practice triggers the Fourth Amendment, yet does not expressly engage how members of that community perceive and experience the police.[106]

Your question now might be: Does the rest of Fourth Amendment law look any better? Distressingly, the short answer is "no." The next chapter elaborates by describing the state of imperilment Black people can find ourselves in when we drive our cars.

Chapter Two
Traffic Stops

For almost three decades, "Driving While Black," or DWB, has been part of America's racial parlance. The term arose in the 1990s to spotlight the frequency with which police officers were subjecting Black Americans to traffic stops. The idea DWB means to communicate is relatively straightforward, if distressing: It is essentially a crime for Black Americans to drive their cars because when they do so, police officers stop and search the car, and detain and question the driver. The data on this point is striking.

Black men between the ages of twenty-five and twenty-nine are twice as likely to be stopped multiple times in one year by the police than white men within the same age group.[1] A similar point can me made about Black women and white women: Within any given year, the former is more than twice as likely to be stopped multiple times than the latter.[2] While Black vulnerability to being stopped by the police diminishes with age, it is worth noting that "Black men over 50 have the same rate of multiple stops in the past year as white men in their 20s."[3] With respect to Black women over fifty, they have roughly the same rate of multiple stops in the past year as white women in their thirties.[4]

Against the background of statistics of the foregoing sort, it is no wonder that Black people say they experience "Driving While Black" as a crime. This chapter explains the role Fourth Amendment law plays in facilitating that criminalization. The scope of the problem is broader than the traffic stop itself. Traffic stops open the door to more intrusive searches and seizures, including excessive force.

Think back to April 4, 2015. On that day, Michael Slager, a white police officer in North Charleston, South Carolina, shot and killed Walter Scott, a Black American man.[5] Slager's encounter with Scott began as a traffic stop. The officer's alleged reason for stopping Scott was a broken taillight on Scott's car.[6] After requesting Scott's driver's license, Slager returned to his patrol car to check it against police records.[7] Upon discovering that Scott had alighted from the car and was fleeing the scene, Slager shot Scott several times in the back, fatally wounding him.[8]

Commentators rightly struck upon this case as another example of unjustified police violence. But the case also highlights the authority police officers have to conduct traffic stops. Indeed, it is precisely that authority that permitted Slager to legally stop Scott in the first place. But for the broad discretion Fourth Amendment law allocates to police officers over whom to subject to traffic stops and when and how to effectuate them, Walter Scott might still be alive.

Unlike the prior chapter, the story this chapter tells is not about whether police conduct triggers the Fourth Amendment in the sense of counting as a search or seizure. As Chapter 1 discussed, if police conduct is neither a search nor a seizure, the Fourth Amendment analysis ends. There is no need for the government to offer a justification for the conduct.

Not so with traffic stops. Officers are required to justify their decisions to conduct traffic stops because there is no dispute in Fourth Amendment law about whether traffic stops are seizures. They are. The thorny question is: Under what circumstances are traffic stops reasonable? The short answer: under far too many. The Supreme Court has made it very easy for police officers to draw on race as a basis for both stopping people and subjecting them to more intrusive and violent searches and seizures that transcend the traffic stop itself.

To appreciate the low bar for police officers to justify stopping someone for a traffic infraction, and how easily traffic stops can escalate into more intrusive searches and seizures, assume that Tanya is driving her car home from work on a Friday evening.[9] Two officers in a patrol car observe her commit a traffic infraction—failing to use her turn signal prior to changing lanes. Let's say that the officers also observe a white motorist commit the very same traffic infraction. Consider the following decisions the officers might make. Each will reveal the discretion police officers have to practice racial profiling in ways that heighten Black vulnerability to police surveillance and violence.

Police Decision 1: To Enforce the Traffic Violation

Officer A says to Officer B, "We can't stop both cars, so let's stop the car with the Black woman." Assume that the officers stop Tanya's car. Is this stop constitutional?

As a preliminary matter, remember that Fourth Amendment law is clear that traffic stops are considered seizures.[10] The question thus becomes whether this seizure is reasonable. Tanya would argue that it is not, because the officers' decision to stop her was racially motivated. That argument would fail. The Supreme Court has made clear that so long as police officers have probable cause to believe that a suspect has committed a traffic infraction—any traffic infraction—the fact that the decision to stop the car was racially motivated does not make that seizure unreasonable.[11] The Court's decision was unanimous.[12]

But what if the officer is mistaken about whether Tanya has violated a traffic code? Let's say that the officer lacks probable cause. That would not necessarily make the traffic stop unconstitutional. To appreciate how this mistake might play out, assume that the officer stops Tanya's car because she has a broken taillight, but it turns out that the vehicle code indicates that it is permissible to drive with one broken taillight. In the jurisdiction in which Tanya is driving, it's only a problem when both taillights are out. The officer is mistaken as to what the vehicle code proscribes. Does that necessarily make his decision to stop Tanya unconstitutional?[13] No. The question would be whether the officer's mistake of law was reasonable[14] (recall from Chapter 1 that Fourth Amendment law tolerates numerous forms of law enforcement mistakes, including mistakes of law).[15] While an officer would be permitted neither to issue Tanya a ticket nor arrest her based on the foregoing mistake of law, he would, as I discuss more fully below, be permitted to ask Tanya for her identification or seek permission to search her car. Under Fourth Amendment law, Tanya is supposed to know that she has the right to refuse consent and feel empowered to exercise that right.

Police Decision 2: To Use the Traffic Infraction as Pretext

Assume again that the officers see both Tanya and a white man commit identical traffic infractions. Once more, the officers decide to stop Tanya, but this time they do so because they think she may have drugs on her person or in the car. Under this scenario, the officers are employing the traffic infraction for pretextual reasons. They are not interested in enforcing the traffic code but in investigating drug possession or distribution. Let's further assume that the police are members of a special unit that is specifically charged with ferreting out drug crimes, and that departmental regulations provide that officers in this unit should enforce only serious traffic violations, those that present an immediate risk of harm to the officers or the community. Recall that Tanya's infraction is that she failed to use her turn signal. Does this seizure violate the Fourth Amendment?

No. The Court would respond that so long as the officers have probable cause, it does not matter whether their reasons for stopping Tanya were pretextual, that is: facilitated under the guise of completing a traffic stop, with ulterior intentions, such as investigating a drug-related crime for which the officer lacks probable cause.[16]

The Supreme Court case that bears most directly on Decisions 1 and 2 is *Whren v. United States*, a unanimous opinion central to which is the view that if police officers have probable cause to believe that Tanya committed a traffic infraction, then they can stop her on the basis of race and for pretextual reasons.[17] If, however, the officers do not have probable cause to stop Tanya for a traffic infraction, and they stop her on the basis of race or for pretextual reasons, that stop would constitute an unreasonable seizure.

The distinction between these two scenarios is not nearly as significant as you might think. In fact, there's hardly a distinction at all. Consider first Scenario 1:

As Scenario 1 suggests, here the officer has both probable cause to believe that the person has committed a traffic infraction and racial suspicion (but no probable cause) to believe that the person committed a drug crime. Under these circumstances, an officer may legitimately stop the suspect to investigate whether he is in possession of drugs. In other words, that stop is a constitutional seizure.

Consider now Scenario 2:

Here, the officer has only racial suspicion that the suspect is in possession of drugs, but no probable cause to believe that the person committed a traffic infraction. Stopping the car to investigate that crime under these circumstances would constitute an unconstitutional seizure. Again, there is no probable cause.

The difference between Scenarios 1 and 2 is meaningful only if the traffic stop/probable cause "check" is a meaningful one. In truth, however, it is not. Not only is probable cause a relatively easy evidentiary standard for police officers to meet,[18] but traffic infractions are misdemeanors that every driver routinely commits.[19] It is only slightly hyperbolic to say that to drive a car is to violate some provision of a vehicle code. Consider the following vehicle code violations:

- "Dazzling" lights;[20]
- Loud or unnecessary horn;[21]
- Driving too slowly;[22]
- Driving at a speed greater than what is "reasonable and prudent" for the conditions;[23]
- Following too closely;[24]
- Driving left of center on a grade or a curve;[25]
- Making a right turn without being as close to the right-hand curb as possible;[26]
- Failure to approach a left turn nearest to the center line without interfering with the progress of any streetcar;[27]
- Turn signal not given continuously during the last one hundred feet before a turn;[28]
- Entering an intersection or marked crosswalk without sufficient space on the other side;[29]
- Failure to yield entering a traffic circle;[30] and
- Failure to yield when entering the roadway from any place other than another roadway.[31]

In short, if a police officer needs probable cause to stop you, she can always find it. The ease with which police officers can establish probable cause to stop a driver for a traffic infraction means that the traffic stop/probable cause check in Scenario 1 is a very weak restraint. Which is to say, Scenario 1 really looks like this:

The probable cause restraint almost isn't there. This renders Scenario 1 similar to (indeed, almost indistinguishable from) Scenario 2. The weakness of the probable cause/traffic infraction restraint means that police officers are effectively free to stop people on the basis of race whenever they want.[32]

One might reasonably wonder whether police officers are likely to take advantage of the racial loophole *Whren* creates. The fact that *Whren* permits police officers to perform pretextual stops, doesn't necessarily mean that they will. As it turns out, the law enforcement establishment was very much aware of the on-the-ground implications of *Whren*. As one training officer for the California Highway Patrol put it, "After *Whren* the game was over. We won."[33] Moreover, as Charles Epp and his colleagues note in an empirical investigation of traffics stops, "*Police Chief* magazine, the official voice of the International Association of Chiefs of Police (IACP), repeatedly and enthusiastically encouraged police departments" to engage in pretextual stops.[34] One concrete example of this comes from the IACP's director of traffic enforcement:

> Savvy police administrators have rediscovered the value of traffic enforcement. They see it not as simply an end in itself, but also as a valuable tool—as a means to an end and an integral part of both criminal interdiction and community policing. An alert police officer who "looks beyond the traffic ticket" and uses the motor vehicle stop to "sniff out" possible criminal behavior may be our most effective tool for interdicting criminals.[35]

The short of it is that *Whren* is problematic not only because it creates an incentive for police officers to continue to perform pretextual stops, but also because it legalizes those stops, which helps make them an institutional practice. Indeed, only four years after the Supreme Court decided *Whren*, IACP created an award—Looking Beyond the License Plate—to recognize police officers who successfully employed traffic stops to effectuate more serious criminal arrests.[36]

Let's now return to our hypothetical Tanya. We left her at Police Decision 2, the decision the officer makes to stop Tanya for Driving While Black. As it turns out, the policing problem *Whren* creates transcends that decision. As you will now learn, traffic stops open the door to more intrusive and potentially violent searches and seizures. Decisions 3 through 13 explain.

Police Decision 3: To Question Regarding a Drug Crime

Suppose that after the officers stop Tanya, Officer *A* asks her for her driver's license, registration, and insurance. While Officer *A* is checking Tanya's license against police records, Officer *B* asks her a series of questions, first about drugs—"Have you ever used or sold drugs?" "Does anyone in your family use or sell drugs?" "Do you have any drugs in the car?"—then about whereabouts and occupation—"Where are you coming from?" "Where are you going?" "What kind of work do you do?" While none of the questions Officer *B* asks have anything to do with the traffic infraction, Fourth Amendment law permits the officer to ask them.

Police Decision 4: To Do a Records Check

In the context of the traffic stop, the officer conducts a records check, meaning he runs Tanya's license through several databases to see whether she has any outstanding warrants. As Wayne LaFave observes, "This kind of checking of government records incident to a 'routine traffic stop,' which usually takes a matter of minutes, is well established as a part of the 'routine,' and has consistently been approved and upheld by both federal and state courts."[37]

One worrisome dimension of the permissibility of record checks in the context of traffic stops is the point I made in Chapter 1 about outstanding warrants. Police officers have an incentive to use traffic stops as pretext to ascertain whether drivers have outstanding warrants.

Another worrisome dimension relates to my point about mistakes. If the officer is mistaken in his belief about the existence of probable cause because in fact there was no vehicle code violation, but Tanya "voluntarily" hands over her identification and the officer performs a records check that reveals an outstanding warrant, the officer could legally arrest Tanya. This is so even though he had no objective basis to stop Tanya in the first place, as long as the officer's mistake of law as to the vehicle code violation was reasonable. What counts as reasonable? Whatever courts decide is reasonable after the fact.

Police Decision 5: To Contact Immigration and Customs Enforcement

Assume for this decision that the officers perceive Tanya to be an immigrant. Assume as well that in the context of the traffic stop, the officers develop reasonable suspicion (an evidentiary standard that, as you will see from Chapter 3, is greater than a hunch but lower than probable cause)[38] that Tanya is undocumented. Under these circumstances, the officers would be permitted to prolong the encounter to contact Immigration and Customs Enforcement (ICE) to check her citizenship status. The matter is even worse for people the officers perceive to have "apparent Mexican ancestry." As I noted in Chapter 1, an officers' reasonable suspicion could, in part, be expressly based on whether the officer perceives a person to have "apparent Mexican ancestry."[39]

Police Decision 6: To Ask the Driver or the Passenger to Exit the Car

In the context of the traffic stop, the officers are free to ask Tanya to exit the car.[40] They would not need any additional justification to do so. Probable cause to believe that Tanya has committed a traffic infraction is enough.

Incidental to stopping Tanya for a traffic infraction, the officers could also ask any passenger to exit the car. Here, too, the officers would not need any additional justification to do so.[41] That is, without any reason to believe that a particular passenger has done anything wrong, police officers who stop a driver for failing to use a turn signal can ask passengers in that car to exit. Because police need no other justification to ask passengers or the driver to exit the car, police officers can racially select the passengers and the drivers that they subject to this treatment.

Police Decision 7: To Search the Car and Frisk the Driver

If the officers have reasonable suspicion that Tanya is armed and dangerous, they may frisk Tanya and search the car.[42] Because reasonable suspicion is a low evidentiary standard, if the police stop Tanya for a traffic infraction while she is driving in a "high crime area" in the middle of the night, the officers are a long way towards satisfying the reasonable suspicion standard (if not there already). They would thus likely have little difficulty justifying frisking Tanya and searching her car.[43] In the context of that frisk, Tanya would be vulnerable to being sexually violated, a gendered dimension of frisks that figures marginally if at all in our public discussions about race and policing.

As we've seen, then, racial suspicion figures into these hypothetical police encounters in several ways. First, remember that as the officers have probable cause, they may expressly use race to justify pulling Tanya over. Second, reasonable suspicion is a low evidentiary bar for an officer to surmount. Thus, the officers will often be legally empowered to frisk the driver, the passengers, and to search the car itself. Third, the very notion of a "high crime area" already embeds race in the equation in the sense that the term almost always refers to predominantly Black or Latinx neighborhoods, without any articulation of what level of crime justifies characterizing an area as "high crime."[44]

Police Decision 8: To Use a Drug-Detection Dog

After stopping Tanya, the officers contact a colleague, Officer Mathews, and ask him to bring a drug-detection dog to the scene. This colleague arrives within five minutes, while the officers are still checking Tanya's driver's license, insurance, and registration. Upon arriving, Mathews immediately walks the dog around the car, directing the dog to smell the vehicle for narcotics. No drugs are detected. The other officers then return with Tanya's license and ask, "There are no drugs in the car, right?" Tanya responds in the negative. The officers then tell Tanya that she is free to leave. None of this violates the Fourth Amendment. Notwithstanding that the officer's basis for stopping Tanya was a traffic infraction, and that the officers have no reason to believe that Tanya is in possession of drugs, the Supreme Court would conclude that it is constitutionally reasonable for police officers to employ a drug-detection dog in the way I have described.[45]

Police Decision 9: To Seize Money Found in the Car (and the Car Itself)

The dog in the prior example responds positively upon circulating the car. From this, the officer concludes that Tanya has drugs in the vehicle. The officer searches the car yet finds no drugs. He does, however, find $500 in the glove compartment. The officer seizes the money and explains to Tanya that, if she wishes to get it back, she must prove that the money is not related to criminal activity.[46] Fourth Amendment law would not prevent the officer from seizing that money or any other property (such as jewelry or electronics) that the officer finds in the car if the officer alleges that he has reason to believe those items are connected to criminality. As you will learn in Chapter 5 in the context of a discussion about predatory policing, the rules of civil asset forfeiture give police officer broad latitude to seize property under the circumstances I have described, and Fourth Amendment law does not stand in the way.

Police Decision 10: To Seek Permission to Search

Imagine now that the officer asks Tanya for permission to search her. Recall from Chapter 1 that police officers do not seize us when they approach us and ask us for permission to search. Under those circumstances, we are supposedly "free to leave or otherwise terminate the encounter." But my hypothetical assumes that Tanya is not "free to leave or otherwise terminate the encounter"; our assumption is that Tanya has been seized because traffic stops are seizures. Is it permissible for officers to seek permission to search when they have seized someone? Yes. Does it matter that the officer has not informed Tanya that she has a right to refuse consent? No. In theory, Tanya could simply decline the request. Again, the fact that she may not know that she has that right, or may not feel empowered to exercise it, does not matter.

All of this might seem to flow from what I have already stated about consent searches. But it is one thing for police officers to seek permission to search in the context of an encounter that is ostensibly consensual in the sense that we are technically free to leave; it is quite another for police officers to seek permission to search when the person, like Tanya, has already been seized. Here, the possibility that Tanya (or a reasonable person in her position) would feel that she is bargaining in the shadow of a potential (albeit illegal) arrest would be high.[47] Indeed, many people might erroneously think not only that they may not bargain, but also that the right to detain a person carries with it the right to search. The Ohio Supreme Court's approach to consent searches highlights these problems. Here's what that court has to say about the relationship between consent searches and seizures:

> The transition between detention [meaning a seizure] and a consensual exchange can be so seamless that the untrained eye may not notice that it has occurred. The undetectability of that transition may be used by police

officers to coerce citizens into answering questions that they need not answer, or to allow a search of a vehicle that they are not legally obligated to allow.... Most people believe that they are validly in a police officer's custody as long as the officer continues to interrogate them. The police officer retains the upper hand and the accouterments of authority. That the officer lacks legal license to continue to detain them is unknown to most citizens, and a reasonable person would not feel free to walk away as the officer continues to address him ...

Therefore, we are convinced that the right, guaranteed by the federal and Ohio Constitutions, to be secure in one's person and property requires that citizens stopped for traffic offenses be clearly informed by the detaining officer when they are free to go after a valid detention, before an officer attempts to engage in a consensual interrogation. Any attempt at consensual interrogation must be preceded by the phrase "At this time you legally are free to go" or by words of similar import.[48]

In the foregoing case, an officer got almost eight hundred people who he stopped for a traffic violation to consent to search of their cars.[49] That officer's conduct is consistent with data on consent searches in the context of traffic stops. In one study, "none of the 90-95% of [the traffic-stopped] subjects who consented knew of the right to refuse consent, and those few who knew the law were skeptical that the officer would actually take no for an answer."[50] Making matters worse, there is at least some evidence that Black Americans are subject to consent searches at a significantly higher rate than whites.[51]

When the Ohio case reached the Supreme Court, the Court could easily have followed the Ohio Supreme Court approach and required police officers who wish to conduct traffic-stop consent searches to inform people of their right to refuse consent. However, the Court did not do so. The Court made clear that the fact that police officers do not inform people of their right to refuse consent does not automatically make a consent search invalid. In reaching this conclusion the Court evidenced no concern that people seemed to consent to searches during traffic stops because they think they have to, and that police officers seem to employ traffic stops to target Black Americans for consent searches. The end result is that police are free to employ consent search requests both when people are seized and when they are not—whether people are on foot or whether they are in their cars. Across these various scenarios, Fourth Amendment law does not require police officers to inform us of our right to refuse consent.

Police Decision 11: To Arrest and Search

Let's now say that the officers decide to arrest Tanya for the traffic infraction. That would not be unreasonable under the Fourth Amendment.[52] Simply refusing to wear a seatbelt can render one vulnerable to a full custodial arrest.[53] The relevant case here is *Atwater v. City of Lago Vista*,[54] a case in which a woman, Gail Atwater, was arrested and transported to the station house for failing to wear her seat belt, failing to fasten her children in seat belts, and failing to provide her driver's license and proof of insurance.[55] The specific constitutional question the case presents is whether the arrest was unreasonable.[56] Atwater argued that it was.[57] Her claim was that a simple misdemeanor crime could not serve as a predicate for a full custodial arrest.[58] The Supreme Court disagreed,[59] and Justice O'Connor dissented.[60]

It's worth pausing to say a few things about Justice O'Connor's dissent in light of our earlier discussion about the Supreme Court's failure in *Whren* to take concerns about racial profiling seriously. Recall that not a single justice dissented in *Whren*. Nor did any of the justices in that case make the particular racial profiling problem *Whren* presents a matter of Fourth Amendment concern.

But, in *Atwater* Justice O'Connor vociferously quarrels with the majority. More than that, she articulates a profound worry about the implication of the case for racial profiling. Toward the end of her dissent, Justice O'Connor makes the following observation: "[A]s the recent debate over racial profiling demonstrates all too clearly, a relatively minor traffic infraction may often serve as an excuse for stopping and harassing an individual."[61]

The above quote is quite remarkable, though for reasons you might not yet fully appreciate. The quote is a rare moment in constitutional criminal procedure in which Justice O'Connor expresses a concern about racial profiling. But, she does so in a case about a white woman. O'Connor does not express a concern about racial profiling in *Whren*, the traffic stop case involving a Black man I discussed earlier. Nor does she express that concern in *Bostick*, the bus-sweep case involving a Black man I discussed in Chapter 1. To ask the Marvin Gaye question: What's going on?

I suspect that part of what might be going on is that Justice O'Connor sees herself in the person of Atwater (a white woman) and the circumstances under which Atwater was arrested (seatbelt violations). However, she does not see herself in the persons of Whren or Bostick (Black men) and the circumstances under which they were arrested (for being in possession of drugs). I'm not arguing that this is conscious, intentional decision-making. Something more unconscious is plausibly at play, akin to an implicit form of identification with Atwater and an implicit form of dis-identification with Bostick. To put what I am saying slightly differently, Justice O'Connor evidences for Atwater precisely what she lacks for Bostick—empathy.

Recall from Chapter 1 that Bostick was on a bus when two officers approached and questioned him. During the course of the interaction, the officers asked Bostick for permission to search his bag. Bostick supposedly consents and the search reveals incriminating evidence. Bostick moved to suppress the evidence on the theory that it was the product of an unconstitutional seizure.

At least some readers might be thinking: If the police found incriminating evidence on Bostick, surely that ends the story. We should simply applaud the officers for their investigative win, not put them through the ringer. Later chapters will explain why we should neither praise the officers nor mark the evidence they found as a win. For now, consider a scenario in which an officer conducts one thousand warrantless searches of homes. Suppose that one of those searches uncovers evidence of criminal wrongdoing. That the officer got it right in that single case surely shouldn't end the story. In other words, the fact that the officer's warrantless search of the home uncovered evidence of wrongdoing, shouldn't make that particular warrantless search, or warrantless searches of homes generally, constitutional. In the same way, the fact that the officer's search of Bostick produced incriminating evidence, shouldn't, without more, make the search and the overall encounter constitutional. Again, further along in this book, you'll have the opportunity to reflect more deeply on this issue. In the meantime, let's continue to think about the constitutional arguments that were available to Bostick to challenge the police conduct he experienced.

Bostick was in a good position to argue that the government's conduct in the case was an unconstitutional seizure. As you might remember, the officers in the case stipulated that when they approached and questioned Bostick, they had no reason to believe that Bostick had done anything wrong. That stipulation meant a finding that the officers' engagement with Bostick amounted to a seizure was tantamount to a finding that the seizure was unreasonable because the officers had neither probable cause nor reasonable suspicion.

Justice O'Connor makes clear that she does not believe that Bostick was seized. Her reasoning reflects virtually no empathy for Bostick. On the contrary, Justice O'Connor sees the case almost entirely through the eyes of law enforcement. The main theme in her fugue sounds in the register of victim-blaming: To the extent Bostick felt confined while the officer's interacted with him, "this was the natural result of his decision to take the bus; it says nothing about whether or not the police conduct at issue was coercive."[62] Doubling down on this view, O'Connor goes on to argue that "Bostick's freedom of movement was restricted by a factor independent of police conduct—i.e., by his being a passenger on a bus."[63] Under Justice O'Connor's analysis, because Bostick chose to board the Greyhound bus, and because the police had nothing to do with that decision, it was constitutionally permissible for the officers to exploit Bostick's vulnerability as a bus passenger.

Justice O'Connor's lack of empathy for the circumstances under which Bostick found himself is also reflected in her sanitized factual characterization of the case. In O'Connor's account, the officers simply "walked up to Bostick . . . asked him a few questions, and asked if they could search his bags."[64] At no point during the encounter, O'Connor notes, "did the officers threaten Bostick with a gun."[65] While "one officer carried a zipper pouch containing a pistol . . . the gun was [n]ever removed from its pouch, pointed at Bostick, or otherwise used in a threatening manner."[66] Because Justice O'Connor looks for, but does not find, evidence of overt police coercion, she implicitly concludes that the encounter was consensual.

It would have been easy for Justice O'Connor to conclude that Bostick was seized. Justice Marshall's dissent in *Bostick* is exhibit A for what I mean. According to Justice Marshall:

> These facts exhibit all of the elements of coercion associated with a typical bus sweep. Two officers boarded the Greyhound bus on which respondent was a passenger while the bus, en route from Miami to Atlanta, was on a brief stop to pick up passengers in Fort Lauderdale. The officers made a visible display of their badges and wore bright green "raid" jackets bearing the insignia of the Broward County Sheriff's Department; one held a

gun in a recognizable weapons pouch. These facts alone constitute an intimidating "show of authority." Once on board, the officers approached respondent, who was sitting in the back of the bus, identified themselves as narcotics officers and began to question him. One officer stood in front of respondent's seat, partially blocking the narrow aisle through which respondent would have been required to pass to reach the exit of the bus.[67]

Further along in his dissent, Justice Marshall adds:

By consciously deciding to single out persons who have undertaken interstate or intrastate travel, officers who conduct suspicionless, dragnet-style sweeps put passengers to the choice of cooperating or of exiting their buses and possibly being stranded in unfamiliar locations. It is exactly because this "choice" is no "choice" at all that police engage this technique.[68]

I quote Justice Marshall at some length to offer a counter narrative to the one Justice O'Connor provides. My point is to highlight that Justice O'Connor could easily have decided the case differently. There were multiple ways for her to frame Bostick's encounter as a seizure, but she goes out of her way not to do so. Throughout Justice O'Connor's opinion, she blames Bostick, rather than the police officers, for Bostick's sense of confinement.

Moreover, Justice O'Connor is perfectly clear, and in more than a by-the-way sense, that Bostick is no innocent. The issue of innocence surfaces in the opinion because of an argument Bostick advanced to suggest that he was seized. Why would a person in possession of drugs consent to the search of his person? Surely, such a person would not have consented to the search if he was truly "free to leave." Justice O'Connor was not persuaded. She deployed the concept of innocence to explain why. According to Justice O'Connor, courts should conduct the seizure analysis from the perspective of an "innocent" person, not from the perspective of someone like Bostick who was in possession of drugs.[69]

This invocation of innocence here makes very little sense, even putting to one side the oddity of the appearance of the term against the backdrop of our constitutional commitment to the idea that people are innocent until proven guilty—and not by police officers on the street, but in the presence of judges in court. Specifically, with reference to the Fourth Amendment, Justice O'Connor's reliance on innocence ignores the fact that, by and large, courts determine the scope of our Fourth Amendment rights in the context of cases where the defendant is attempting to suppress incriminating evidence. People who are not in possession of incriminating evidence but whose Fourth Amendment rights the police violate typically do not bring Fourth Amendment claims.[70] For the most part, courts determine the constraints the Fourth Amendment imposes on police in the context of cases involving people on whose person the police claim to have found incriminating evidence. Had the police not found drugs on Bostick, the case would not have been litigated. Justice O'Connor's focus on innocence elides all of this. Lacking empathy for Bostick, and certainly not imagining herself in his position, O'Connor turns the Fourth Amendment upside down. She makes Bostick's decision to board a bus in possession of drugs more relevant for Fourth Amendment purposes than the officers' decision to conduct the "dragnet-style sweep" and target Bostick with no evidence that he did anything wrong.

Returning now to the *Atwater* case. What a difference a case (with a white woman) makes. In *Atwater*, Justice O'Connor expresses profound empathy for Gail Atwater. There is no blaming Atwater for the fact that she did not buckle herself or her children in a seatbelt, even though Atwater's failure to do so was an indication of precisely what the officers lacked in *Bostick*—evidence of wrongdoing. Instead, O'Connor focuses attention on the officer's conduct. Moreover, she describes the officer's decision to arrest Atwater from the perspective of how Atwater experienced the arrest:

> Officer Turek handcuffed Ms. Atwater with her hands behind her back, placed her in the police car, and drove her to the police station. Ironically, Turek did not secure Atwater in a seatbelt for the drive. At the station, Atwater was forced to remove her shoes, relinquish her possessions, and wait in a holding cell for about an hour. A judge finally informed Atwater of her rights and the charges against her, and released her when she posted bond. Atwater returned to the scene of the arrest, only to find that her car had been towed. . . .
>
> [T]he decision to arrest Atwater was nothing short of counterproductive. Atwater's children witnessed Officer Turek yell at their mother and threaten to take them all into custody. Ultimately, they were forced to leave her behind with Turek, knowing that she was being taken to jail. Understandably, the 3-year-old-boy was "very, very, very, traumatized." After the incident, he had to see a child psychologist regularly, who reported that the boy "felt very guilty that he couldn't stop this horrible thing . . . he was powerless to help his mother or sister." Both of Atwater's children are now terrified at the sight of any police car. According to Atwater, the arrest "just never leaves us. It's a conversation we have every other day, once a week, and it's—it raises its head constantly in our lives."[71]

The fundamental idea the above passages convey is that Atwater and her children were not supposed to experience that kind of encounter. That is to say, they were not supposed to be traumatized by, or become terrified of, the police. Their family life should not be burdened by an emotionally draining "conversation every other day, once a week" about a police interaction. Officer Turek should not have humiliated Atwater. Nor should he have rendered the family a public spectacle. Implicit in Justice O'Connor's concern for Atwater is the notion that Turek's treatment of Atwater sent a public message about the woman—that she is a criminal. But neither the misdemeanors Atwater committed nor her identity as a white mother invited or justified the dissemination of that message.

Let me be clear: I agree entirely with Justice O'Connor that Atwater should not have endured the treatment she experienced. The problem I am surfacing is that nowhere in Justice O'Connor's criminal procedure cases—and certainly not in *Bostick*—does she evidence anything like the preceding sensibilities about Black Americans' exposure to the police. She never expressly considered whether the frequency with which Black Americans encounter the police makes them less trusting of, and more terrified around, law enforcement. There's no thought in her cases about whether Black Americans' constant exposure to the police ever "leaves us." Nor has Justice O'Connor ever explicitly discussed the fact that Black Americans have "a conversation . . . every other day, once a week," about their encounters with the police. And, in none of Justice O'Connor's cases on the Fourth Amendment involving Black American defendants does she ever articulate what she surely must have known, namely, that Black Americans' worries and frustrations about police contact "raises its head constantly in our lives."

Of course, there are differences between *Atwater* and *Bostick* with respect to the precise Fourth Amendment issues they present. One case is about whether the Fourth Amendment is triggered by way of a seizure (*Bostick*) and the other is about whether a seizure is reasonable (*Atwater*). That distinction should not obscure the point I am stressing here: In *Bostick*, Justice O'Connor blames the defendant and identifies with and speaks in the voice of law enforcement; and in *Atwater* she blames the police officer and identifies with and speaks in the voice of the defendant. The end result is that it is in a case involving a white woman that Justice O'Connor expresses a vigorous critique of over-policing and a concern about racial profiling. One might say, somewhat ungenerously, that in Justice O'Connor's Fourth Amendment world, what happened to Atwater should not have happened to her (in part because she is white?), but what happened to Whren and Bostick was entirely appropriate (in part because they are Black?).

This brings us back to Tanya. Recall that our hypothetical has two police officers arresting her, like Atwater, for a traffic infraction. Had Justice O'Connor's analysis in *Atwater* prevailed, the officers' decision to arrest Tanya for failing to use her turn signal would violate the Fourth Amendment. In this respect, my detour to discuss Justice O'Connor's dissent was not to disagree with her bottom-line conclusion, but to note that that her analysis likely was motivated, at least in part, by Atwater's palatable identity as a white mother.

As for Tanya, the Black woman in our hypothetical, you now know that she is in a difficult spot. Based on *Atwater*, a court would conclude that her arrest is constitutional. Police officers may arrest Tanya for any traffic infraction, no matter how minor. Moreover, even if state law expressly prohibits police officers from arresting people for violating a traffic infraction, an officer's decision to do so would not violate the Fourth Amendment, so long as the arrest is supported by probable cause.[72]

Finally, upon arresting Tanya, the officer may also search her[73] and potentially may search areas in the car.[74] Nothing in Fourth Amendment doctrine prevents police officers from consciously employing traffic infractions to trigger the *search incident to lawful arrest doctrine* along the foregoing lines. Thus, if a police officer believes that a suspect has drugs on her person or in the car, but does not have probable cause to back that up, he can circumvent that drug-suspicion probable cause requirement by trading on another—the probable cause he will always have that the person committed a traffic infraction.[75]

Police Decision 12: To Conduct a DNA Search

Assume that upon arresting Tanya and transporting her to the station, the officers use a cheek swab to take a sample of Tanya's DNA. There is no question that this search would be constitutionally reasonable if Tanya is arrested for a "serious" crime. That much is clear from the Supreme Court case, *Maryland v. King*.[76] What is less clear is whether the serious/nonserious crime distinction on which *King* is based is conceptually sound and one that courts can manage. Dissenting in *King*, Justice Scalia found the distinction to be neither sound nor manageable:

> The Court disguises the vast (and scary) scope of its holding by promising a limitation it cannot deliver. The Court repeatedly says that DNA testing, and entry into a national DNA registry, will not befall thee and me, dear reader, but only those arrested for "serious offense[s]." I cannot imagine what principle could possibly justify this limitation, and the Court does not attempt to suggest any. If one believes that DNA will "identify" someone arrested for assault, he must believe that it will "identify" someone arrested for a traffic offense. This Court does not base its judgments on senseless distinctions. . . . When there comes before us the taking of DNA from an arrestee for a traffic violation, the Court will predictably (and quite rightly) say, "We can find no significant differences between this case and *King*."[77]

At the very least, Justice Scalia's prediction is plausible. If he is right, the ultimate result will be not only that police officers may conduct ordinary searches of the person incidental to arrest but also that they may conduct bodily intrusions in the form of DNA testing as well.[78] Little would prevent police officers from employing race as a basis for determining who, upon arrest, they subject to DNA testing, particularly given the growing interest on the part of law enforcement agencies across the country to create and grow DNA databases.

Police Decision 13: To Strip Search

If subsequent to arresting Tanya, the police decide to place her in the general jailhouse population, they may perform a strip search prior to doing so.[79] This search requires no additional justification, and unlike with the DNA search, there isn't even the formal limitation that the predicate crime be a serious one.[80] Any crime for which Tanya is arrested can be the basis for a strip search if she is placed in the general population.[81] And, remember, the genesis for this strip search could derive from officers' race-based decision to arrest Tanya for failing to use her turn signal!

What are we to make of this chapter's account of traffic stops and their role as gateway seizures? In a nutshell, you should understand that, like the Supreme Court's conclusions about when the Fourth Amendment is triggered, its judgments about when searches and seizures are *reasonable* exposes Black Americans to police contact and thus the possibility of police violence. I focused my discussion on traffic stops because of the broad discretion police officers have to conduct them, because that discretion has made driving while Black effectively a crime, and because traffic stops can open the door to more intrusive and potentially violent searches and seizures.

Things would be bad enough if my race and Fourth Amendment law story ended here. But there is more. I have said nothing thus far about stops and frisks. You have heard about these law enforcement tactics, I am sure. What you may not know is that Fourth Amendment law expressly licenses them, that the constitutionality of stops and frisks came to the Supreme Court in the context of America's civil rights revolution in the 1960s, and that, over the past five decades, the Supreme Court has broadened, rather than narrowed, the circumstances under which police officers may conduct stops and frisks. Chapters 3 and 4 elaborate.

Chapter Three

Stop-and-Frisk

On April 20, 2007, David Floyd—a Black man living in New York City—was walking home down his block on East 172nd Street in the Bronx, when he saw two officers a little more than a block away talking to another person.[1] As he continued walking, the same officers he had observed earlier pulled up next to him in a van and asked whether they could speak to him.[2] David stopped immediately. Three officers got out of the van and asked him for his ID. Though he asked the officers whether he was required to give them his ID, he did not feel like he could refuse their request.[3]

David showed the officers his ID and then reached into his pocket for his cellphone to take down the officers' badge numbers.[4] When he did this, one officer, a white man, jumped toward him, causing David to throw his hands up and say, "It's a cellphone." The officer replied that "it made him nervous when people put their hands in their pockets."[5] He then asked David if he had a weapon, to which David responded that he did not. David was wearing jeans and sneakers, and only carrying his phone, keys, and wallet in his pockets.[6] Although David did not consent to a search,[7] the officer proceeded to pat him down from his groin to his ankles and pulled his cellphone out of his pocket. The episode ended after the officer handed back David's out-of-state ID and told him it was illegal to not have a New York City license.[8] David said the encounter left him feeling "frustrated, humiliated—because it was on my block where I live, and I wasn't doing anything."[9]

Less than a year later, on February 27, 2008, David had another encounter with the police. This time, David was leaving his home to go to school, backpack in hand.[10] David lived in a property owned by his godmother—a three-family dwelling with a guest house—and as he was leaving, a tenant who lived in the basement of the property (also a Black man) asked David for his help because he was locked out.[11] David had several unmarked spare keys on a ring from his godmother's apartment, and began trying each of them to see which would unlock the tenant's door. As David tried to open the door, three plainclothes officers approached him and the tenant and told them to stop what they were doing and put their hands up. David complied.[12] The officers then ordered them against the wall, patted them down, and searched through their pockets, without their consent.[13]

After giving the officers his ID, David asked why he had been stopped. The officer responded that there had been a pattern of burglaries in the area, though that was not the justification the officer would later provide.[14] Instead, when the officer filled out a required form describing the incident, he checked the box for "Furtive Movements," based on witnessing David fiddle with the doorknob and keys, as the basis for searching David and the tenant.[15] Like David's prior encounter with the police, David left feeling demoralized and trapped—engendering the sense that "I shouldn't leave my home."[16] David's experiences with the NYPD led him to become the lead plaintiff in a class-action lawsuit challenging its use of a policing practice often referred to as "stop-and-frisk."

Although both "stop" and "frisk" are likely familiar to most readers, the terms have highly specific legal meanings. A "stop" is an investigatory practice wherein an officer detains and questions a person. A "frisk" is a precautionary measure wherein an officer stops a person and "pats down" their outer clothing to determine whether they might be armed or dangerous.[17] To better capture the full dimensions of these practices, I often refer to "stops" as "stop-and-question," and "frisks" as "stop-and-frisk."

Among other things, the lawsuit against the NYPD alleged that the department deployed both stop-and-frisk and stop-and-question disproportionately against Black and Latinx people.[18] Judge Shira Scheindlin, a federal district court Judge, agreed.[19]

In concluding that the NYPD's stop-and-frisk and stop-and-question policing practices violated the Constitution, Judge Scheindlin relied heavily (though not entirely) on an empirical study of the NYPD's UF-250 forms, conducted by Dr. Jeffrey Fagan. NYPD officers were required to complete the forms—also known as the "Stop, Question and Frisk Report Worksheet"—after each such stop.[20] Fagan's analysis revealed that:

- The number of stops per year significantly increased "from 314,000 in 2004, to a high of 686,000 in 2011."
- "Between January 2004 and June 2012, the NYPD conducted over 4.4 million" stops.
- Only 12% of the 4.4 million stops culminated in an arrest or a summons. 88% of stops ended without an additional law enforcement sanction or prosecution.
- New York City was roughly 52% Black and Latinx, and 33% white—yet Blacks and Latinx were the subjects of 83% of the 4.4 million stops; whites were the subjects of 10%.
- The NYPD frisked 52% of the people they stopped.
- Police found weapons on 1.0% of the Blacks they frisked, on 1.1% of Latinx, and on 1.4% of whites. Put another way, the NYPD *did not* find weapons on 98.5% of the roughly 2.3 million people they frisked.
- The NYPD conducted a full search (meaning, they reached into the clothing) of 8% of the people they stopped. Their justification for doing so was that while

conducting the frisk, they felt a weapon. Yet, only 9% of those searches uncovered a weapon—91% of the time the person fully searched was unarmed.

- The rate of stops could be predicted by the racial demographics of an area, even when controlling for crime rates.
- Further, less than 10% of the stops resulted in an arrest or in finding weapons or other contraband.[21]

These findings are striking. They tell a story about constitutional violations in which "stops" and "frisks" function as racialized rites of passage. One might conclude from Fagan's study, however, that if only police officers complied with the constitutional rules governing "stops" and "frisks," Black people would be safe from both intrusions.

This chapter tells a different story. It contends that the way that the Supreme Court has interpreted the Fourth Amendment's protections against "stops" and "frisks" all but ensures that many Black people will experience both stop-and-frisk and stop-and-question as a routine part of their American life.[22]

From Street Injustice to Constitutional Law

By the mid-1960s, in the context of the "Second Reconstruction"—when the United States was muddling through how to bring about meaningful civil rights—a number of factors converged to make it relatively clear that "stops" and "frisks" would soon move from the streets of America's cities to the halls of the Supreme Court.

To begin, Black leaders complained that police officers were using these practices to harass the Black community and to quell Black aspirations for civil rights.[23] Moreover, President Lyndon Johnson's Commission on Law Enforcement and Administration of Justice urged states to articulate the precise scope of police authority to use "stops" and "frisks."[24] Many states did just that, with New York at the forefront, passing a law that expressly allowed officers to use both.[25] Police departments thus increasingly began to rely upon stop-and-frisk and stop-and-question as important law enforcement tools.[26]

Meanwhile, hundreds of "race riots" were occurring across Black urban landscapes—in Philadelphia, Harlem, Watts, Cleveland, Omaha, Chicago, Detroit, Baltimore, and Washington, D.C., among other places.[27] According to the National Advisory Commission on Civil Disorders (the task force that President Johnson appointed in 1967 to investigate the causes of these rebellions), the tense relationship between the police and Black communities—caused in part by the rampant use of stops and frisks—played a role in each uprising.[28]

The convergence of these factors made it relatively clear that the Supreme Court would soon need to decide whether stops and frisks were constitutional. It did so in 1968, in the case of *Terry v. Ohio*.[29]

On the afternoon of October 31, 1963, Cleveland Police Detective Martin McFadden saw two Black men, John Terry and Richard Chilton, standing on a downtown Cleveland street corner.[30] Though he had never seen the two men before, Detective McFadden testified that, based on his thirty-nine years as a policeman, Terry and Chilton "didn't look right" to him.[31] After watching both men, Detective McFadden became convinced that they were about to rob a store. McFadden feared that they might have a gun because, from his perspective, the men were "casing a job, a stick-up."[32] He thus approached the men, identified himself as a police officer, and asked them for their names.[33] When they "mumbled" a response, McFadden grabbed Terry, spun him around, and patted him down. Upon doing so, he felt a gun in Terry's overcoat and removed a .38 caliber revolver from the inside pocket.[34] Terry was arrested, convicted of carrying a concealed weapon, and sentenced to three years in prison.[35] Nearly five years later his appeal reached the U.S. Supreme Court in the landmark decision, *Terry v. Ohio*.

The author of the Supreme Court's *Terry* opinion was none other than Chief Justice Warren, who penned one of the most important decisions in American constitutional history—*Brown v. Board of Education.* One can debate whether *Brown v. Board of Education* went far enough to protect Black Americans from state-sanctioned racial segregation. *Terry v. Ohio,* however, undoubtedly went *too far* in protecting police officers from constitutional scrutiny.

I promised in the Introduction that there would be moments in this book in which I would bring the law school classroom to you. A standard law school exercise involves professors posing hypothetical situations to their students. Though I employed hypotheticals in Chapters 1 and 2 to argue various points, I did not "call on you"—as I would were you in my class—to give answers to those hypotheticals. That is what I will do now.

Remember from Chapter 1 that Fourth Amendment law is structured around two questions: First, *"Was there a search or seizure?"* If the answer is yes, the protections of the Fourth Amendment are triggered. Next, *"Assuming that there was a search or seizure, was it reasonable?"* meaning, was the government justified in conducting that search or seizure? Only *unreasonable* searches or seizures are considered constitutional violations.

The first question illustrates why the Supreme Court's determinations about whether certain policing practices *are* or *are not* a search or seizure is monumentally important. When the answer is "no," officers receive a free pass to employ that practice free from Fourth Amendment restraint. For example, as we discussed in Chapter 1, police officers may conduct "pedestrian checks"—following, questioning, and asking us for identification or to search us or our belongings—without *any* reason to believe we've done anything wrong. Because the Court has ruled that pedestrian checks are neither searches nor seizures, the Fourth Amendment does not apply.

On the flipside, when a policing practice *is* considered a search or seizure, it triggers the Fourth Amendment and some form of justification for the behavior becomes necessary—zero evidence of wrong-doing won't do. Sometimes, however, the justification ends up being rather thin. For example, as we learned in Chapter 2, an officer who wishes to stop someone for a traffic infraction must have *probable cause* to believe that the driver violated a traffic code. But, because all of us regularly commit traffic infractions when we drive, probable cause does little to constrain a racially motivated police officer from stopping people for "Driving While Black."

Armed with this recap of Chapters 1 and 2, the first hypothetical I want you to consider is this: Assume that you represent the government in the *Terry* case—your role is to defend the exercise of police power. More specifically, you want to make it as easy as possible for officers to conduct both stop-and-question and stop-and-frisk.

Arguing before the Supreme Court, Justice Warren asks you a pointed question: "Is stop-and-question a seizure?" How would you respond: "Yes" or "No"?

Take a moment to think about it. Remember—you want the Court to make it dead easy for police officers to stop-and-question people. Presumably then, your answer would be "No, stop-and-question is *not* a seizure." Likely, you understand that if stop-and-question is not a seizure, police officers receive a free pass to stop-and-question any-one they choose without any evidence of wrongdoing. The Fourth Amendment does not apply.

Stay in your role as the government's lawyer. Warren asks his next question: "Is a frisk a search?" Again, pause and think about it. Here, too, you would answer "No." Such a ruling also would give officers another free pass, this time to stop-and-frisk anyone without any evidence that a person is armed or otherwise dangerous. No justifica-tion required. In other words, your argument would be that because there is no "search," there cannot be an *unreasonable* search—which is all that the Fourth Amendment guards against.

Let's return to the *Terry* case itself.

You will not be surprised to learn that, to some extent, the government's argument in *Terry* tracks the one you just articulated in your role as a government lawyer, with one curious exception. Although the lawyers argued that "stop-and-question" is not a seizure, and "stop-and-frisk" is not a search, they did not reach the conclusion that neither practice required any justification.[36] Instead, they posed a slightly less aggressive standard: While officers need *some* evidence of suspicious activity to stop someone (but lower than probable cause), they do not need an additional reason to conduct a frisk. Put another way, if an officer believes that a person is suspicious in some way (How suspicious? You tell me), not only does that suspicion give the officer the power to stop-and-question that person, but to frisk them as well—even if there is no reason to believe the person poses a danger to the officer or to the community.

Back to your law school desk. This time, imagine you represent the defendant, John Terry. Justice Warren poses the same questions: "Is stop-and-question a seizure?" "Are frisks a search?" Your answers should maximize your client's freedom and constrain police power by requiring officers to separately justify both stop-and-question and stop-and-frisk. What's your answer now? Likely, you would respond "yes" to both: Stop-and-question *is* a seizure and frisks *are* searches. In doing so, your goal is to limit the possibility that police officers could be free to conduct stops and frisks without evidence of wrongdoing.

Assume the chief justice agrees with you that stop-and-question is a seizure and that stop-and-frisk is a search. His next question is: "*How much* evidence of wrongdoing does an officer need to conduct either practice?" If you're a relatively aggressive defense attorney, you might insist that officers obtain a judicially approved warrant, based upon probable cause (you have no reason to know this, but there's a line in Fourth Amendment law that states that *warrantless* searches and seizures are presumptively unconstitutional).[37]

Let's say you lose that argument—and you would. It turns out that lots of searches and seizures don't require a warrant (including traffics stops, as you learned from Chapter 2). What's your move now? What kind of justification should the Fourth Amendment impose on police officers to conduct "stops" and "frisks"? Chances are, you're thinking, "Okay, no warrant, but officers at least need probable cause, right?" That was the argument John Terry's attorney advanced, and for good reason. Prior to *Terry*, probable cause was the gold standard and dominant framework used to justify searches and seizures.[38] Terry thus had every reason to believe that if he convinced the court that stops are seizures and frisks are a search, they also would conclude that police officers needed to have probable cause to justify both practices—after all, the probable cause standard is written in the Fourth Amendment.[39]

But Warren had a different standard in mind.

Lawyers often find clues about how the Court will rule in a given case based upon the way the justices frame the issue they are deciding, and the chief justice's introduction in *Terry* provides such a clue: "Whether it is *always* unreasonable for a policeman to seize a person and subject him to a limited search for weapons unless there is probable cause for arrest."[40] Here, Warren signals that he did not believe the absence of probable cause would not necessarily make "stops" and "frisks" unconstitutional. In reality, few forms of police conduct have been ruled to be "always unreasonable." As a result, by framing the legal question as whether X or Y is "always unreasonable," the inevitable answer will be "no."

It was relatively easy for the Court to land on that "no" because the search in question is framed as "limited" in scope, and its purpose is to discern whether the suspect has "weapons." Be honest: Do you think that a "limited search" for "weapons" should "always [be] unreasonable" just because an officer lacks "probable cause"? Some of you, like Justice Warren, presumably answered that question in the negative: No, it is not *always* unreasonable to stop-and-frisk someone without probable cause. That answer was a win for the government. It meant that, going forward, police officers could stop-and-frisk people without probable cause. Instead, Warren named a new burden of proof, below probable cause, which officers need: *reasonable suspicion* (though he didn't use that precise term).

Although few judges would articulate the reasonable suspicion and probable cause standards as percentages, a crude way to think about the difference between the two would be to say that probable cause kicks in when an officer is 30–35 percent suspicious, whereas reasonable suspicion kicks in somewhere between 15–29 percent. I will say more on the weak limits of reasonable suspicion later on, but for now you should understand that the lower the Court sets the standard for a particular police practice, the less persuasive an officer need to be about their decision to use that practice.

The Migration of Reasonable Suspicion from Stop-and-Frisk to Stop-and-Question

It is one thing to say that an officer may stop-and-frisk someone for weapons when she has a reasonable concern about her safety or the safety of others. As Justice Harlan argued in his concurring opinion in *Terry*, we don't want police officers to approach people, ask them questions, "and take the risk that the answer might be a bullet."[41] Allowing an officer to stop-and-frisk a person when that officer fears that the person is dangerous reduces that risk.

It is quite another to say that officer should be able to stop-and-question someone who poses no threat to her safety or the safety of others—there is no "risk of a bullet." Under those circumstances, one might assume the ordinary standard of probable cause, not the exceptional standard of reasonable suspicion, should apply. Yet, although the chief justice made clear that reasonable suspicion could justify stopping-and-frisking Terry if an officer believed he was armed, he punted on deciding whether the officer would require probable cause to stop-and-question him if he posed no such threat.

Warren's silence on the question subsequently gave courts the room they needed to rule that reasonable suspicion could justify stop-and-question, and not just stop-and-frisk. This migration of reasonable suspicion from a justification for "frisks" to a justification for "stops" was not just a possibility—it was almost a foregone conclusion. Even Warren hinted at this, writing:

> One general interest is of course that of effective crime prevention and detection; it is this interest which underlies the recognition that a police officer may in appropriate circumstances and in an appropriate manner approach a person for purposes of investigating possibly criminal behavior even though there is no probable cause to make an arrest.[42]

Nothing in the quote requires an officer be concerned for their safety. Instead, his words appear to support the idea that an officer may stop-and-question a person simply based upon a reasonable suspicion that the person has committed or will commit a crime.

Moreover, across the country, state legislatures had passed laws expressly authorizing stop-and-question and stop-and-frisk as critical law enforcement practices.[43] A particularly important example was right before the chief justice's eyes. On the same day that Warren issued his ruling in *Terry*, he decided *Sibron v. New York*,[44] a case in which the defendant challenged the constitutionality of New York's stop-and-question/stop-and-frisk statute.

Under New York's statute, an officer could stop any person in a public "whom he reasonably suspects is committing, has committed or is about to commit a felony or any of the offenses specified in section five hundred fifty-two of this chapter, and may demand of him his name, address and an explanation of his actions."[45] This appeared to authorize stop-and-question even when an officer is not concerned about her or anyone else's safety—which is exactly the argument the defendant made. Justice Harlan agreed.[46] According to Harlan's concurring opinion: "The core of the New York statute is the permission to stop any person reasonably suspected of crime."[47]

The chief justice, however, avoided a decision about whether the law was constitutional. Instead, he ruled that because the officer in *Sibron* reasonably believed that the defendant was armed and dangerous before he was stopped and frisked, *that* stop-and-frisk was constitutional. And because *that* stop-and-frisk was constitutional, Warren did not need to decide whether New York's law authorized unconstitutional conduct to rule against the defendant.

Whether Warren decided *Sibron* correctly is not my concern. I reference it here because the case, and certainly Justice Harlan's concurrence, should have alerted Warren to a view about stop-and-question that many states believed: Officers did not need probable cause, nor a concern about officer safety, to conduct stop-and-question.

One final reason Warren should have understood that the reasonable suspicion standard might soon extend from stop-and-frisk to stop-and-question was that several groups argued this position to the Court. The U.S. Government, State of New York, Americans for Effective Law Enforcement, and National District Attorneys' Association all made it clear that they believed that reasonable suspicion should not be limited to cases in which officers were concerned about their safety or the safety of others.[48] These groups' briefs argued that the door of reasonable suspicion, which the chief justice left cracked behind stop-and-frisks, should be flung wide open to include stop-and-question.

In short, in 1968, the writing was on the wall that police officers would push for a constitutional rule that would allow them to invoke reasonable suspicion to justify stop-and-question. Less than a decade later, the Court would grant officers their wish.[49] Without much fuss or fanfare, the Court ruled that officers could justify their decisions to stop-and-question people through reasonable suspicion alone.[50]

What began as an exceptional application—indeed, *invention*—of the reasonable suspicion standard to protect officers from danger has migrated to everyday circumstances in which concerns for officer safety do not exist. Chapter 4 will describe some of the circumstances. It's a long list that many of you may find surprising, if not shocking.

You would be right to wonder whether it is at all unusual for the Supreme Court to invent constitutional doctrine. Not really. Notwithstanding conservative arguments about "strictly" reading the Constitution, the Constitution doesn't fully speak for itself. It never has. For example, terms like "due process" and "equal protection" and "liberty" require Courts to give them meaning. What's different about the Fourth Amendment is that the text of that provision provides a pretty strong signal as to what, at a minimum, reasonableness should mean—probable cause. That standard is explicitly written into the Fourth Amendment.

I am not saying that the Fourth Amendment explicitly states that all searches and seizures require probable cause to be reasonable. It doesn't. It states that warrants must be supported by probable cause to be reasonable. The point is that probable cause is the only evidentiary standard the amendment names. Nowhere does the Fourth Amendment mention reasonable suspicion or any other standard of proof.

That reasonable suspicion applies to both stop-and-frisk and stop-and-question might lead you think that the standard applies to both practices in the precisely the same way. It doesn't. The fact that an officer has reasonable suspicion to "stop" a person doesn't mean that he will necessarily have authority to conduct a "frisk."[51] That is because an officer may suspect that a person has engaged in criminal activity without believing that they are armed and dangerous. Under those circumstances, the officer would be permitted to conduct a "stop" but not a "frisk." Whether this formal distinction in the *law* matters in *practice* is discussed further below (spoiler alert: it does not). The larger point is that, as the law stands, probable cause no longer applies to either practice.

The Weakness of Reasonable Suspicion

Replacing "probable cause" with "reasonable suspicion" is particularly troubling in the context of stops and frisks, considering how weak it is as a standard. I have made this point a few times now, but I've yet to provide any examples. To appreciate *how weak* reasonable suspicion is, recall our hypothetical from Chapter 2 in which Tanya was running from the police.

To remind you, the police have no reason to believe that Tanya has done anything wrong, and that her decision to run is based on her prior bad experiences with police. She does not want to have another encounter where the police will effectively force her to prove that she is innocent by compromising her rights (e.g., "consenting" to questioning or a search). Tanya thus decides to avoid an encounter altogether by graduating her fast-paced walk away to a run. Upon observing Tanya run, the police chase after her. Tanya is now in trouble.

More than two decades ago, David Harris observed that "[a] substantial body of law now allows police officers to stop an individual based on just two factors: presence in an area of high crime activity, and evasive behavior."[52] The Supreme Court came close to adopting this "high crime + evasion" rationale in the case *Illinois v. Wardlow*.[53] Sam Wardlow, the defendant, suddenly ran away after noticing an officer in an area the officers claimed was known for narcotics trafficking. Officers chased after, caught, and frisked him, revealing that he had a handgun. Wardlow argued his decision to run from officers was not enough to provide them with reasonable suspicion that he had committed or was about to commit a crime.

According to the Court in its *Wardlow* decision, nervous or evasive behaviors are relevant factors in determining reasonable suspicion. "Headlong flight—wherever it occurs—is," the Court reasoned, "the consummate act of evasion."[54] To paraphrase Justice Scalia in an earlier case, innocent people do not run.[55] The Court went on to note that it was additionally relevant that Wardlow's flight took place in a "high crime area."[56]

Although the Court never expressly states that unprovoked flight in a "high crime area" gives rise to reasonable suspicion, that is a sensible way to read the *Wardlow* opinion, given that the Court stresses that "it was not merely [Wardlow's] presence in an area of heavy narcotics trafficking that aroused the officer's suspicion, but his unprovoked flight,"[57] and ultimately concludes that the officers were "justified in suspecting that Wardlow was involved in criminal activity."[58] As Andrew Ferguson notes, this was a case in which reasonable suspicion was "based on the 'totality of circumstances' of only two factors—a high crime area plus unprovoked flight."[59]

Wardlow's ruling invites us to ask whether Black people fleeing the police is an "unprovoked" act. A good argument can be made that it is not. The historical and contemporary over-policing of Black communities is an existential provocation to Black people: Avoid the police. In other words, one could argue that it is both reasonable and rational for Black people to try and avoid the police as a prophylactic measure to avoid police harassment and violence. Recall from the prior chapter that the Massachusetts Supreme Court reached precisely this conclusion. But that is not a view the Supreme Court shares. Under the Court's Fourth Amendment law, fleeing the police counts as suspicious activity, particularly when it occurs in a "high crime area."

But what's the relevance of this "high crime area" factor to Tanya? After all, the hypothetical does not have her in a "high crime area"—I only said that Tanya was in a predominantly Black neighborhood, a factor which courts do not expressly state gives rise to reasonable suspicion. But, remember the following two observations I made earlier. One was that there is no clear definition of what constitutes a "high crime area."[60] The other was that "high crime neighborhood" can function as "code for poor Black ghetto."[61] At the very least, one may wonder whether different courts' use of the phrase "high crime area" is a way of not expressly referring to, but still implying, predominantly Black neighborhoods. Some scholars certainly think so.[62]

Accordingly, it will not surprise you to learn that data from the NYPD revealed that officers used "high crime area" as a basis for stop-and-question in 55 percent of their stops.[63] And an empirical study by Ben Grunwald and Jeffrey Fagan found that the NYPD was 8–9 percent more likely to call any particular block a "high crime area" when it was entirely Black compared to a block with no Black residents, regardless of actual crime rates.[64] More surprising, however, was that the same study found that the NYPD labeled 98 percent of New York City blocks as "high crime areas" at one time or another.[65] One could argue that aside from approving a racially inflected factor, another practical effect of the Court's reasoning was that officers understood that the simplest way to achieve a constitutionally acceptable level of suspicion was to simply label *every* area as "high crime."

Separate from whether running in a "high crime area" gave officers reasonable suspicion to stop-and-question Tanya is if it also would permit them to frisk her. At least as a formal matter, the answer is no. The officers would still need to show that they had a reasonable suspicion that she was armed or dangerous. An officer who went to court and asserted that Tanya's flight from the police in a "high crime area" gave the officer reasonable suspicion to believe that Tanya was armed or dangerous would lose that argument.

Just because courts draw a clear line between stop-and-question and stop-and-frisk "on the books" does not mean that officers draw that same line "on the ground." While it would not be accurate to say that police routinely frisk the people they stop, it is fair to say that they often frisk people whom they have no reason to believe are armed or dangerous. Take, for example, the New York Police Department. As

I mentioned at the outset of the chapter, David Floyd was part of a class action lawsuit against the NYPD alleging that the department employed stop-and-frisk and stop-and-question to target Black and Latino people, primarily men. The evidence in that case makes clear that NYPD officers did not take seriously the rule that frisks required independent justification.[66] The NYPD frisked more than half of all the people they stopped.[67] In 99 percent of those cases, officers found no weapons.[68]

If merely running in a high crime area effectively gives officers reasonable suspicion to stop-and-question someone, it could also render Tanya vulnerable to arrest. As discussed in Chapter 1, in many states with "stop-and-identify" laws, if the officers have reasonable suspicion to believe that Tanya engaged in criminal wrongdoing, they may insist that she provide her name.[69] Failing to do so would give the officers probable cause to arrest her for failing to comply.

To summarize Tanya's predicament: At the outset, Tanya was technically "free to leave" or "terminate the encounter," because the police officers had no reason to believe that she did anything wrong.[70] If Tanya chose to exercise her right to leave by running, and does so in a place the officers identify as a "high crime area," that alone could potentially give officers the reasonable suspicion they need to *lawfully* stop her.[71] If she is seized in a jurisdiction with a stop-and-identify law, and does not provide her name, the officers may arrest her.

You might be thinking that things are not as dire as my hypothetical suggests. After all, Tanya's options are not limited to running away or staying put: She could simply walk away. Assuming Tanya did this, the officers would be perfectly free to follow her, and ask her questions as they follow her (remember from Chapter 1 that officers are free to do both without any reason to believe we've done anything wrong and their actions will not trigger the Fourth Amendment). During the walk-and-question, Tanya is *technically* "free to leave." But how? Moreover, how likely is it that even if Tanya knows that she is free to leave, that she would exercise that right when faced with armed officers? Far more likely, she will simply "consent" to an encounter with the officers, and a court—if the case ever got to a court—would subsequently rule that she did so of her own free will.

In light of what you learned in Chapter 1 about what does or does not count as a stop, the *Terry* regime makes it virtually impossible for Black people in predominantly Black neighborhoods to avoid contact with the police. The relatively high threshold before Fourth Amendment protections against seizures are triggered (in other words, the fact that lots of police interactions don't count as seizures), combined with the relatively low threshold of reasonable suspicion needed to justify stop-and-question (in other words, the fact that it's easy for police officers to prove that they have reasonable suspicion), makes contact between the police and Black people almost entirely a matter of police discretion.

More worrisome still, because reasonable suspicion allows police officers wide discretion for the stops-and-question and stop-and-frisks they conduct, and courts largely defer to their explanations, it is easy for officers to substitute *racial suspicion* as an investigatory tool without admitting that they are doing so.[72] Although officers cannot say that they engaged in either type of stop just because someone is Black, or that they systematically targeted Black people for stops, reasonable suspicion's low hurdle enables them to do both.

Not only does reasonable suspicion allow police officers to conceal conscious racial biases, it also enables them to act on racial biases they may not know they have. If officers implicitly view Black people as dangerous or criminally suspect, those biases may lead them to target Black people for investigation, including through the use of "stops-and-frisks."[73] Research suggests that police officers, like the rest of us, harbor precisely such stereotypes.[74]

In a compelling collection of studies, Jennifer Eberhardt and colleagues revealed that people have a robust association between race and crime.[75] In one, subjects were initially exposed to a series of Black or white male faces for 30 milliseconds each, such that subjects consciously perceived each face only as a flash—they were not aware that they had seen a face.[76] They were then asked to identify an object image as quickly as possible.[77] The image moved through forty-one progressive frames, becoming clearer in each frame. The figure below captures three of these frames at different stages of degradation.[78]

Frame 1   **Frame 20**   **Frame 41**

The researchers found that participants primed with Black faces were able to identify the gun more quickly (meaning, in a more degraded state) than those who saw white faces or no faces at all.[79] Surprisingly, those primed with white faces recognized crime-related objects even more slowly than those shown no primes at all. These findings were interpreted to mean that viewing Black faces made the category of "crime" more present in participants' minds, while white faces made it *less* present.[80]

Perhaps more remarkably, the same study showed that priming a subject with the *concept* of crime led them to focus more on Black faces, rather than white faces.[81] What this means is that race and crime are associated in both directions: Not only does seeing a Black person unconsciously arouse suspicions of criminality, but thinking about criminality brings to mind an image of a Black person.[82]

This suggests that the theoretically race-neutral project of crime prevention and detection is already racially inflected, even if only unconsciously. To put it plainly, when police officers think about or observe Black people, crime is at least implicitly on their minds. And when officers think about crime and criminality, Black people are at least implicitly.[83] The takeaway is that even when officers do not intentionally act on racial stereotypes, they might end up doing so unwittingly because of their implicit biases.[84]

Against this background, legal scholar L. Song Richardson observes that, Chief Justice Warren's suggestion that "reasonable suspicion" would not allow an officer to stop-and-frisk someone on the basis of a "hunch" might have been unrealistic. The strength of unconscious biases, combined with the weak "reasonable suspicion" standard, perpetually puts Black people in the United States under greater scrutiny and increased jeopardy, with officers likely acting on "racial hunches" about Black people as criminally suspect and dangerous.[85] And, as discussed above, these racial hunches can also color entire Black neighborhoods as "high crime areas" in officers' minds, moving them one step closer to a *legal* justification for a stop.

To Blame or Not to Blame Chief Justice Warren

You may be asking whether I mean to lay the blame for Black peoples' vulnerability to stop-and-frisk and stop-and-question entirely at the feet of Chief Justice Warren? Not quite—but he certainly deserves some. He did not need a crystal ball to know that the reasonable suspicion door he created, and then refused to close, would be a problem for Black people in particular.[86]

Justice Brennan had urged the chief justice to be mindful of the racial implications of the decision, worrying, in problematic language to be sure, that *Terry* would "aggravate the already white heat resentment of ghetto Negroes against the police."[87]

Apart from Justice Brennan's cautioning, Warren also received ample warning from briefs to the Court, against a backdrop of a country experiencing open racial unrest. First, the NAACP's Legal Defense Fund (LDF) emphasized the racial risks of stop-and-frisk and stop-and-question in its brief to the Court. They argued explicitly for the eradication of stop-and-frisk, as it was one of the "practices in our society that bear with discriminatory harshness upon

Negroes and upon the poor, deprived, and friendless, who too often are Negroes."[88] They argued that all available evidence showed that police used stop-and-frisk "most frequently against the inhabitants of our inner cities, racial minorities and the underprivileged."[89] "Speaking bluntly, we believe that what the ghetto does *not* need is more stop-and-frisk."[90]

Additionally, the broader racial backdrop should have primed the chief justice to think critically and carefully about race and policing. By the time *Terry* was decided, the term "Black Power" was in full circulation,[91] and the Black Panther Party for Self-Defense had been founded, in part, with the goal of policing the police.[92] Moreover, "Bloody Sunday," during which Alabama state troopers brutally attacked unarmed civil rights demonstrators marching from Selma to Montgomery, was still fresh in Black peoples' collective consciousness.[93] Coded appeals to whites about the criminality of Blacks, or what Ian Haney López calls dog-whistle politics, were everywhere, particularly in candidate Richard Nixon's run for the White House.[94] Meanwhile, protests against the Vietnam War had intensified,[95] and Medgar Evers, President John F. Kennedy, Malcolm X, the Reverend Martin Luther King, Jr., and Attorney General Robert F. Kennedy had all been assassinated, further heightening a collective experience of racial despair.[96] In sum, race amounted to more than an elephant in the room.

The chief justice presumably knew that he had to say something about race in *Terry*—and he did. But he largely left the voice of racial justice he used to craft *Brown v. Board of Education* at home. Warren drew no connections between the on-the-books separate-and-unequal educational regime he struck down in *Brown* and the on-the-ground separate-and-unequal policing regime he upheld in *Terry*. Nor did he consider whether the frequency with which police officers stopped and frisked Black people stigmatized them as racially inferior, communicated a message to them that they were criminally suspect, or relegated them to a second-class citizenship.[97]

Instead, Warren acknowledged that the aggressive use of

stop-and-frisk in African American communities exacerbated tensions between Black people and the police,[98] but stated that there
was little a case like *Terry v. Ohio* could do to solve the problem. To
understand his argument, we must discuss the Fourth Amendment's
"exclusionary rule."

Fourth Amendment cases are, to a large extent, about the exclusion of evidence from a criminal trial.[99] Generally, a case begins
with a search of a defendant's person or property which turns up
incriminating evidence—say, an unregistered gun. Prior to trial, in
what is called a "suppression hearing," the defendant argues that the
government cannot use the incriminating evidence at trial because
the search that led to the gun was unconstitutional. Specifically, the
defendant will invoke the "exclusionary rule," which permits defendants to "suppress" evidence (meaning, prosecutors cannot use it at
trial) that the police have obtained by violating the Fourth Amendment, or any other constitutional provision. The government, meanwhile, will argue that the search was constitutionally valid, and that
the evidence should be admitted.[100]

For several decades now, courts have reasoned that we have the
exclusionary rule because it deters unconstitutional police behavior.[101]
The theory is that if officers know that any evidence they acquire by
violating a person's constitutional rights will be inadmissible at trial,
the less likely they are to engage in unconstitutional behavior, including unreasonable searches and seizures.[102] Officers who disregard the
Constitution risk losing their case if a judge excludes relevant and
potentially compelling evidence of criminal wrongdoing.[103]

For example, if a defendant is charged with carrying an unregistered firearm, but officers obtained the gun through an unreasonable
search which was then ruled inadmissible, it would be incredibly difficult for prosecutors to prove their case if they could not show or
even mention the unregistered gun at trial. As the Supreme Court
has explained, "the only effectively available way" to ensure that
police officers respect the Constitution is to eliminate "the incentive

to disregard it."[104] Excluding illegally obtained evidence potentially eliminates that incentive.

Not all forms of policing involve an interest in collecting evidence, however, or even in seeing a case through to prosecution. The chief justice made this point in *Terry*, arguing that the exclusionary rule would not deter officers whose motivation was to harass Black people—not a desire to secure evidence. In his words, the exclusionary rule is "powerless to deter invasions of constitutionally guaranteed rights where the police either have no interest in prosecuting or are willing to forgo successful prosecution in the interest of serving some other goal."[105] According to Warren, "some other goal" is precisely what police officers have in mind when they racially target Black people. That is why he concluded that racially motivated stops and frisks "will not be stopped by the exclusion of any evidence from any criminal trial."[106]

I have read *Terry v. Ohio* many times, and I continue to find Warren's reasoning disappointing and unpersuasive. Why did he think that police officers could not simultaneously be motivated by "legitimate" law enforcement goals *and still* racially harass Black people? Longstanding associations between Blacks and crime, openly expressed during this period, would make it "rational" for police officers to repeatedly stop-and-frisk and stop-and-question Black people—in other words, racially harass them—as an evidence-gathering technique.[107] As mentioned above, there are mountains of evidence demonstrating that many people implicitly and explicitly associate Black people with crime.[108] Indeed, to borrow from Khalil Muhammad, part of the reason Black Americans have long experienced a kind of social "condemnation" comes directly from the multiple ways in which racism projects crime onto Blackness.[109]

Wholesale racial harassment *as* a law enforcement strategy can take many shapes. Consider a city that wants to deter Black Americans in particular from carrying weapons in public. The police department may instruct its officers to aggressively deploy stop-and-question and stop-and-frisk against Blacks as a *deterrent* strategy. The theory? If people know that officers are likely to either stop or frisk Black people any time they are in public—regardless of their behavior—then Black people will be deterred from carrying weapons when they go out. The officers who carried out this effort would not necessarily *reasonably suspect* that the individuals whom they stop will have a weapon. General deterrence is not about the efficient retrieval of weapons—it is about instilling a general fear of frisks among the Black population.

Michael Bloomberg defended just this view of preventive stops and frisks when he was mayor of New York.[110] According to Bloomberg, "by making [a gun] 'too hot to carry,' the NYPD is preventing guns from being carried on our streets."[111] He went on to add that "our real goal [is] preventing violence before it occurs, not responding to the victims after the fact."[112] Other New York City officials expressed similar views. In testimony for the *Floyd* suit against the NYPD, New York senator Eric Adams testified that in a meeting he had with police commissioner Raymond Kelly, Kelly allegedly endorsed the use of stops and frisks to target Blacks and Latinos on the grounds that he "wanted to instill fear in them, every time they leave their home, they could be stopped by the police."[113]

Bloomberg's endorsement of stop-and-frisk as a racially targeted crime-prevention strategy is a very prominent example that Justice Warren was wrong to believe that police officers would not use the "wholesale harassment" of Black people as an ordinary law enforcement technique. Bloomberg, for his part, apologized for the position he held on stop-and-frisk while he was seeking the Democratic nomination for the United States presidency.[114] Some might well doubt Bloomberg's sincerity, and I am tempted to digress and offer my own views on the matter. But I won't. Suffice it to say that whatever Bloomberg's views now, the harm of possibly millions of stops and frisks in New York City is part of not only his legacy, but of Justice Warren's as well.

One final challenge to the chief justice's treatment of race in *Terry* is to note the relationship between "rights" and "remedies" in Fourth

Amendment law. A general principle in law is that if your right is violated, you are entitled to a remedy. As you now know, one remedy that flows from the violation of a Fourth Amendment right is the suppression of evidence. But what you might not appreciate is that each time a judge decides whether or not to apply a remedy—such as the exclusionary rule—*shapes* the scope of our Fourth Amendment rights.[115] For example, Warren's decision to admit the gun Detective McFadden found upon frisking Terry shaped our right to be free from stop-and-frisk, making it turn on whether police officers can plausibly claim *reasonable suspicion*. If Warren had suppressed the gun, our right to be free from stop-and-risk would be protected by *probable cause* instead.

In this regard, the decision to apply the exclusionary rule is not just about the suppression of evidence—it shapes the contours of our Fourth Amendment rights. This can have serious implications for our daily lives: how free we feel in public; how safe we feel from governmental intrusions; how much autonomy we feel to resist the police; or how safe we feel from racialized policing. The question for Warren should not have been if the exclusionary rule can *deter*—in some abstract sense—the "wholesale harassment" of Black people. Instead, he should have asked whether reasonable suspicion could *enable* and *legitimize* such harassment.

Conclusion: Splitting the Baby

Many scholars of constitutional criminal procedure give the chief justice a break for his *Terry* opinion. Some even describe the case as the perfect compromise because, in their view, Warren split the proverbial baby. The defendant won the argument that "stops" are seizures and "frisks" are searches, subject to Fourth Amendment scrutiny. The government won the argument that, with respect to that scrutiny, probable cause should not be the standard.

I am not going to say that there's nothing to the Solomonic representation of the chief justice. But the "split-the-baby" account of

Terry v. Ohio obscures that what Warren took away from police officers with one hand, he gave back to them with the other.

As this chapter has argued, the chief justice undermined his ruling that stop-and-frisk triggers the protections of the Fourth Amendment in two important ways. First, he weakened the form that Fourth Amendment scrutiny would take from probable cause to reasonable suspicion; and, second, he refused to state that reasonable suspicion only applied to stop-and-frisk when officers were concerned for their safety or the safety of others—not to stop-and-question people when they have no such concern. Paradoxically, my critique might suggest that the Solomonic "baby-splitting" metaphor is even more instructive than scholars have thus far recognized. Like Solomon, Warren only *feigned* compromise, but in reality, he handed the entire baby to the government, wrapped in the blanket of *reasonable suspicion*.[116]

Many have made the point that reasonable suspicion is a weak restraint on police, and effectively expands the scope of their power.[117] Frank Rudy Cooper, for example, has argued that the doctrine of reasonable suspicion should be abolished,[118] and Bennett Capers has observed that "if the Fourth Amendment itself has a poisonous tree, its name is *Terry v. Ohio*."[119] The problem with stop-and-frisk and stop-and-question is not simply that officers frequently deploy both *without* reasonable suspicion—it is also that officers have very little difficulty finding reasonable suspicion to justify their decision to stop-and-frisk and stop-and-question, because the standard is so low.

Distressingly, reasonable suspicion is not limited to the stop-and-frisk and stop-and-question street encounters that gave rise to *Terry v. Ohio*. As Chapter 4 will explain, *Terry's* reasonable suspicion standard extends all the way to the border. There, reasonable suspicion is enough not only to justify stop-and-question and stop-and-frisk, but also a more coercive and invasive law enforcement practice that I refer to as stop-and-strip.

Chapter Four
Stop-and-Strip

At the border, officers armed with reasonable suspicion alone may subject individuals to a lengthy and incredibly invasive form of detention, which I refer to as "stop-and-strip."[1] Stop-and-strip is one of many examples in which we see reasonable suspicion transcending its stop-and-frisk origins. In this chapter, I focus on the United States border. There, courts have allowed officers to use reasonable suspicion to terrifying effect. At the border, reasonable suspicion authorizes types of severe—and often shocking—intrusions that one might think would require a warrant.

To illustrate how easy it is for border agents to target a person for stop-and-strip, imagine that Tanya is returning to the United States from a weekend trip to Jamaica.[2] Arriving at the airport, Officer Jackson, a U.S. Customs Officer, asks her a series of questions: "Where are you coming from?"; "For how long were you there?"; "What kind of work do you do?"

When Tanya responds that she was returning from a three-day trip to Jamaica, and that she works as a teacher, Officer Jackson sternly replies, "And you can afford to take a weekend trip to Jamaica?"

Taken aback, Tanya responds, "Excuse me—have I done anything wrong?"

Officer Jackson asks to see her ticket, and tells her, "This is a random stop. Do you know what random means?" Before Tanya has the opportunity to respond, the officer asks her again, this time a little more firmly, to show him her ticket. Tanya complies.

"You purchased this ticket in cash, and only have one piece of luggage?"

"Yes. My travel agent prefers cash to avoid fees. And, as I told you, I was in Jamaica for only three days."

Officer Jackson motions for Tanya to hand him her passport, and while examining it, asks if she's ever been to Jamaica before. She replies, "Yes, for a wedding several years back."

Abruptly handing back the passport, he asks her, "Are you bringing back any drugs?"

Stunned, Tanya stammers, "Drugs? Me? Carrying drugs?"

"Will you please just answer my question: Do you have any drugs?"

Tanya remains baffled and upset. What about *her* prompted Officer Jackson to ask about drugs?

Tanya manages, however, to contain her anger. Like other Black people, Tanya's parents had "The Talk" with her—the discussion Black families have with each other about how to approach interactions with the police.

To remind you, though the words of "The Talk" vary, the underlying message is always the same: Do whatever you can to quickly and safely end the encounter—your overarching goal is to survive the incident and to return to your family physically unharmed. Efforts to preserve your dignity, or simply invoking rights, can prove deadly.

Although Tanya does not feel that her life is in danger, she knows that nothing good will come from pushing back.

"No . . . I don't have any drugs."

Officer Jackson then instructs Tanya to follow him to a room in which he will ask her some additional questions.

"I've done nothing wrong," Tanya responds, walking the fine line between obedience and resistance. "Is this really necessary?"

"Ma'am. The quicker you follow me to this room over here, the sooner this will all be over."

Once in the room, Officer Jackson searches her luggage, finding nothing incriminating. Tanya asks if she may leave.

"That depends," Jackson responds. "Are you carrying any drugs on your body?"

"What?"

"Did you swallow any balloons?"

At this point Tanya is livid. Breaking the warnings her parents gave her long ago, she decides to speak her mind. "This is outrageous. Is this how you treat everybody? Do I look like I'm carrying drugs on my body?"

"I don't know," Officer Jackson responds. "That's what I'm trying to figure out. I can't let you go unless I know for certain that you don't have any drugs." Frustrated that, from his vantage point, Tanya is not doing her part to ease his suspicions, the officer tells Tanya, "It might be more appropriate if Officer Johnson takes over."

Tanya wonders why another officer may be "more appropriate." In what way? She decides not to keep quiet and simply asks Officer Jackson if she may use the restroom.

"You may use the wastebasket in the corner after I leave," Officer Jackson responds in a matter-of-fact tone that suggests Tanya is not the first person whom he has directed to use the basket. He leaves the room, locking the door behind him.

Forty minutes later a woman walks in. Before I say more, I should warn you that Tanya is about to be subjected to a strip search.

"Hi, I am Officer Johnson. I understand that you are coming back from Jamaica. I'm here to make sure that you're not carrying drugs on your body. Can you please remove your clothing?"

"You want me to undress?! Why?!"

"That's the only way we will know whether you're carrying drugs on your body," Officer Johnson replies.

"You could just believe me," Tanya responds. "I've told you I'm not carrying drugs and the other agent searched my bags. What makes you think I still have drugs?"

Officer Johnson is visibly annoyed. Officer Jackson warned her that Tanya would be a "difficult nut to crack," and Johnson was beginning to get a sense of what he meant. "Look, you can argue if you want, but that's only going to drag this whole thing out."

Grudgingly, Tanya begins to undress. As she does so, Officer Johnson carefully searches through her luggage. Standing as boldly and defiantly as she can in her underwear, Tanya asks, "Satisfied?"

"I need to see what's in your underwear. By the way, are you on your period?"

"You know I am," Tanya responds. "You pulled the tampons out of my luggage."

"Can you please remove your tampon as well?"

"You want me to show you my bloodied tampon?!"

"Please just do as I ask," Officer Johnson replies.

Visibly distraught, Tanya removes her tampon and places it on the table.

"Are you satisfied now?"

Officer Johnson does not respond.

"I was married for twenty-five years, and my partner never saw what you saw in this room today," Tanya manages to say.

"I am sorry you find this upsetting . . ."

"It's not upsetting," Tanya interrupts, "It's humiliating and infuriating! Would I be in this room—experiencing this violation—if I were white?"

"Are you calling me a racist?" Officer Johnson pushes back, feeling wounded at Tanya's mention of race. A classic example of racial table-turning, Johnson's performance of the "are-you-calling-me-a-racist?" script transforms her from the perpetrator of racism to the survivor.

Framing Officer Johnson's behavior as racist is not the same thing as saying she's a member of the Ku Klux Klan. It's a way of saying that the ease with which the officer bureaucratized Tanya's degradation was intersectionally enabled by Tanya's race and gender.[3] More precisely, the ordinariness of the violence Officer Johnson enacted was made possible not simply by stereotypes or attitudes Johnson may (consciously or unconsciously) have held about Black women, but also by longstanding racial and gender presumptions about Black women that make it natural and even necessary for the state to violate their bodily integrity and circumscribe the control they have over their bodies.

Tanya doesn't respond to the officer. She has said what she wants to say for now. She thus stands by her words in silence.

Officer Johnson, meanwhile, has more to say: "I am not a racist! I have never been a racist. This has nothing to do with race."

Tanya frees her tongue: "What did I do to deserve this treatment? What about me makes this okay? What *am* I supposed to think?"

"I'm just doing my job," Officer Johnson replies after zipping up Tanya's luggage and placing it next to the wastebasket in which Tanya was expected to relieve herself. She informs Tanya that she may leave. "We're done here. After you're dressed, you are free to go. The door is unlocked. Please close it behind you when you exit."[4]

The law is now relatively clear that if U.S. Customs officials have reasonable suspicion to believe a person is carrying drugs on their body, those officials may seize that person, subject them to questioning, and even conduct a strip search.[5] Of course, if Tanya wanted to challenge her stop in court, she could argue that the officers' conduct nevertheless violated her rights because they had no reasonable suspicion to subject her to a stop-and-strip. But Tanya would not get very far.

As discussed in Chapter 3, reasonable suspicion is a decidedly easy standard for the government to meet.[6] It is likely that the government could easily convince a court that the officers had reasonable suspicion to believe that Tanya was carrying drugs on her body, because:

- Tanya had purchased her ticket in cash;
- Tanya was travelling from a "source country" (a country from which people allegedly travel with drugs);

- Tanya had only one item of luggage; and
- Tanya was in Jamaica for only three days.

You may be nodding your head—these things might *seem* suspicious to you too. And, thinking back to Chapter 3, you might say, "Well, it is reasonable to ask Tanya questions." Maybe you believe it is reasonable to stop her, or even reasonable to pat her down.

But how can reasonable suspicion alone satisfy the protections of the Fourth Amendment when the search and seizure in question is a demand to strip naked and be subjected to an invasive personal search? The government could find all the support it needed to justify such a practice in a Supreme Court case from 1985, *United States v. Montoya de Hernandez.*

In that case, customs officials argued they had reasonable suspicion to believe that a woman arriving at an airport, Rose Elvira Montoya de Hernandez, was using her body to smuggle drugs into the United States.[7] First, inspectors patted her down, and noted her stomach had a "firm fullness" as if she was "wearing a girdle."[8] A further strip search revealed no contraband, but inspectors found that she wore two pairs of elastic underpants lined with paper towels.

Inspectors told Montoya de Hernandez that they suspected she was smuggling drugs inside of her alimentary canal—essentially, that she had swallowed balloons of drugs and would later pass them in her stool. She denied this, and agreed to be X-rayed, but added that she was pregnant. She agreed to a pregnancy test before the X-ray, but then refused to go to the hospital when she was told she would need to be handcuffed on the way there.

The inspector then gave her three choices: (a) return to Colombia on the first flight the following morning; (b) agree to an X-ray; or (c) wait in the customs office until she had a bowel movement, which would be examined to either confirm or dispel the inspector's suspicions. She chose the first option, and was placed under observation for the rest of the night. Furthermore, she was told she could only relieve herself in the wastebasket, and was not allowed to make any phone calls.

That night, officials attempted to place Montoya de Hernandez on a flight to Mexico City which connected to Bogotá the following morning. The airline refused, however, noting that she lacked the proper Mexican visa. Despite not being able to return to Colombia, she was told she was not allowed to leave the office unless she agreed to an X-ray or had a bowel movement. She waited, refusing to eat, drink, or defecate, with the lower court noting that she underwent "heroic efforts to resist the usual calls of nature."[9]

On the following afternoon, nearly sixteen hours after her original flight, Montoya de Hernandez had still not eaten or had anything to drink, nor had she relieved herself. At that point, inspectors obtained a court order "authorizing a pregnancy test, an x ray, and a rectal examination."[10] The order was issued just before midnight, and she was taken to a hospital, where she was issued a pregnancy test and underwent a rectal exam. During the examination, the physician removed a balloon containing an unknown substance. Montoya de Hernandez was formally placed under arrest. Over the next four days she would pass a total of 88 balloons containing 528 grams of cocaine.[11]

Having given that background, Justice Rehnquist concluded that the entire episode was constitutional. Writing for the Court, he reasoned that although the inspectors did indeed seize Montoya de Hernandez, and that seizure included a strip search, reasonable suspicion sufficed to justify the encounter.[12] Probable cause was not required.[13]

Recall from the preceding chapters that the Fourth Amendment protects us from unreasonable searches and seizures.[14] Chapter 1 emphasized that the Fourth Amendment protections kick in only if the conduct at issue is either a *search* or a *seizure*. If the conduct is neither, such as asking someone for their identification, it is considered a "consensual encounter" requiring no justification. Chapters 2 and 3 then made clear that the Fourth Amendment does not protect us from all searches and seizures—only *unreasonable* ones. You learned that probable cause is generally enough to make a traffic stop "reasonable" (Chapter 2) and that reasonable suspicion is generally enough to make "stop" and "frisks" "reasonable" (Chapter 3).

In *Montoya de Hernandez*, there was no dispute as to whether the agents searched and seized Montoya de Hernandez. They did both. The question was whether the search and seizure were reasonable. The answer implicates an additional nuance of Fourth Amendment law that, if you are anything like my law students, you may find it maddening.

Under the Fourth Amendment, both *stops* and *arrests* are considered *seizures*. As such, both require some level of justification. Because arrests are more intrusive and coercive than stops, however, police officers must meet a higher burden to justify an arrest than a simple stop.[15] It bears repeating: Both stops and arrests are seizures. I emphasize this point because it is one that law students often miss. Put simply, because an arrest is a "bigger" seizure than a stop, an arrest requires a "bigger" justification (probable cause) than a stop (reasonable suspicion). Here's a visual that illustrates these points.

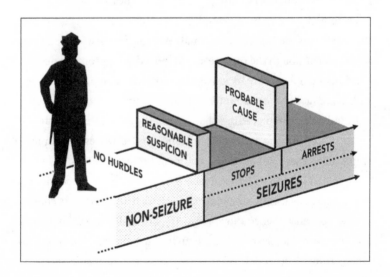

Let's start with the border that separates non-seizures from seizures. Because non-seizures—such as requesting someone's permission to search their bag or asking that person a question—are considered consensual, there is no justification hurdle for the officer. But at some point, a consensual encounter can become a seizure—such as when an officer demands, not simply requests, that a person produce their identification. In that case, the officer would need to "hop" the reasonable suspicion hurdle.

Now, note that there is an internal border within the seizure portion of the diagram separating stops from arrests. As you can see, the hurdle for stops (reasonable suspicion) is lower than the hurdle for arrests (probable cause) because stops are less intrusive seizures than arrests. View the visual one more time before reading on.

The distinction between the lower level of justification necessary for stops and the higher justification for arrests is important, given that a legitimate stop (supported by reasonable suspicion) can quickly morph into an illegitimate arrest (unsupported by probable cause).[16] Courts have used several factors to guide their analysis as to when a stop becomes an arrest. These factors include: the location of the detention (e.g., whether it occurs on the street or in a police station), the nature of the officer's conduct (e.g., whether the officer drew his gun or handcuffed the person), and the length of the detention (e.g., whether the encounter lasted hours rather than minutes).[17] One could imagine that as a judge decides which factors they deem relevant to their analysis, they shift the distance between the boundary between stops and arrests, either by bringing them closer together or further apart. The further apart the boundary between stops and arrests, the more actions Fourth Amendment law allow officers to take based upon reasonable suspicion alone.

Montoya de Hernandez raised each of the preceding factors in her argument, including that officers moved her from one place to another, that her detention occurred in a government facility, and that she was handcuffed at a certain point. She also emphasized the length of her detention,[18] arguing that the government could not rely on reasonable suspicion to justify seizing her for sixteen hours.[19] In effect, she was saying that, after sixteen hours, her detention morphed from a stop to an arrest—for which the government never claims to have probable cause.[20] As such, her detention was an unreasonable seizure.

The Court disagreed.[21] First, Justice Rehnquist emphasized that all of this occurred at the border.[22] He noted that courts have repeatedly stated that the government's interests in regulating the border are strong, and an individual's right to privacy at the border is relatively weak.[23] Stated differently, the scales are tipped in the government's favor at the border.

Next, Rehnquist focused on the nature of the suspected crime.[24] Cases "involving alimentary canal smuggling at the border," he maintained, "give[] no external signs and inspectors will rarely possess probable cause to arrest or search, yet governmental interests in stopping smuggling at the border are high indeed."[25] On this view, a person suspected of smuggling drugs on their bodies may be detained on *less evidence* than probable cause and their detention may be *more prolonged* than would be reasonable for other crimes.

Commenting further on the length of detention in the case, Justice Rehnquist argued that both the length of the detention and the defendant's "discomfort resulted solely from the method by which she chose to smuggle illicit drugs into this country."[26] He contended, moreover, that "[b]ut [for] her visible efforts to resist the call of nature" (in other words, her refusal to defecate in the wastebasket), the encounter would have ended far sooner.[27] According to Rehnquist, "[the Court's] prior cases have refused to charge police with delays in investigatory detention attributable to the suspect's evasive actions."[28]

Nor, Justice Rehnquist reasoned, has the Court ever ruled that the duration of a seizure alone is enough to elevate the evidentiary showing the government needs to justify that seizure. From Rehnquist's perspective, just because the seizure of Montoya de Hernandez lasted sixteen hours, doesn't mean that the government needed probable cause, rather than reasonable suspicion, to make that seizure reasonable.

Let's put to one side the question of whether reasonable suspicion should be enough to justify a sixteen-hour detention. A separate issue whether reasonable suspicion should be enough to justify seizure in which a strip search occurs. The question arises because strip-searching a person, like handcuffing them, can transform a stop into an arrest by ratcheting up the coercive and intrusive dimensions of the seizure. If an officer handcuffs a person and places them in the back of a patrol car, most courts would conclude that that person is not merely "stopped" but is under arrest. Therefore, probable cause, and not reasonable suspicion, would be required. In the same way, if a border patrol agent strip-searches a person, a court should conclude that that person is not merely "stopped" but under arrest, and not an ordinary arrest (whatever that might be), but a sexually violent one for which reasonable suspicion should not be enough.

The point here is that Montoya de Hernandez's encounter may have started as a stop that was supported by reasonable suspicion, but the strip search to which she was subjected—and not just the overall length of encounter—transformed that stop into an arrest that was unsupported by probable cause.

Another way to challenge the Court's reasoning in the case is to modify an image I showed you earlier to focus on "frisks" and "full searches," rather than "stops" and "arrests." Fourth Amendment law is clear that while reasonable suspicion permits police officers to "frisk" a person (by patting down the outer part of that person's clothing), it permits officers to conduct neither a fuller search of the person (by reaching into the person's clothing) nor a general search of the person's car. Because these latter searches are "bigger" searches than frisks, they require a "bigger" justification than reasonable suspicion—probable cause. Once again, a visual may help.

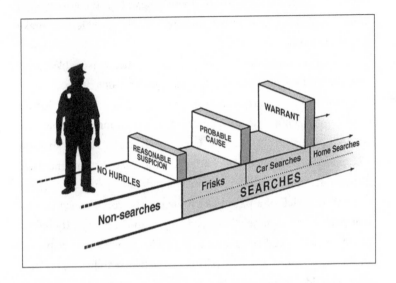

Let's start with the border that separates non-searches from searches. Because non-searches don't trigger the Fourth Amendment, there is no justification hurdle for the officer to jump. But if an officer's conduct moves beyond the non-search territory by, for example, becoming a frisk, that officer would need to jump the reasonable suspicion hurdle to justify the search.

Now, note that there are internal borders within the search portion of the diagram separating frisks, car searches, and home searches. As you can see, although frisks are searches, the hurdle to conduct them— reasonable suspicion—is lower than the hurdle to conduct a general search of a car (which typically requires probable cause). Moreover, the probable cause hurdle for car searches is lower than the hurdle the government must jump to conduct a general search of the home (typically a warrant). View the image one more time before reading on.

That's a lot of Fourth Amendment law, I know, but I'm hoping you got the takeaway: The more intrusive the search, and the greater our expectation of privacy in the area searched, the higher the hurdle the government must jump. It is precisely because we have a heightened expectation of privacy in our homes that the government generally needs a warrant (not reasonable suspicion and not just probable cause) to search them. Were you in my class, I would ask whether you had any questions before I pushed on. Needless to say, I can't do that here. So, carry on I must.

The preceding technical legal points can have large social consequences. To understand how, let's bring strip searches back into focus. The question is: Should strip searches require reasonable suspicion (and be treated like frisks)? Probable cause (and be treated like car searches)? Or a warrant (and be treated like searches of the home)? While Justice Rehnquist doesn't tee up the issue in exactly this way, his opinion invites an answer: "Stopping and stripping" people at the United States border is equivalent to "stopping and frisking" them within the nation.[29] Reasonable suspicion is enough to justify both. From that point of view, when we are at the border, courts should accord our bodies less constitutional protection than they accord our cars and our homes.

A final way to think about why Justice Rehnquist's ruling is troubling relates to the doctrine of excessive force. The constitutionality of an officer's use of deadly force is litigated under the Fourth Amendment. The precise question is whether an officer's use of deadly force was "excessive" and therefore constituted an "unreasonable" seizure.[30] Though police officers don't always follow the rule of excessive force, particularly with respect to Black people, those rules include the principle that just because an officer has probable cause to believe that someone has committed a crime, even a violent crime, does not mean that the officer is empowered to shoot that person dead. Doing so would be considered "excessive."

Just as the Supreme Court has evidenced some (not nearly enough) concern about the use of physical violence in the context of seizing people, it should be concerned about officers' use of sexual violence in the context of seizing people—even when those seizures occur at the border. Reasonable suspicion should not be enough to justify stop-and-strip. When strip searches are supported by only reasonable suspicion, the Court should conclude that they are "excessive" seizures, unreasonable under the Fourth Amendment.

As Justice Brennan wrote in a scathing dissent, the government's conduct in the case represents "a 'disgusting and saddening episode' at our Nation's border."[31] Brennan maintained that "the nature and duration of the detention here may well have been tolerable for spoiled meat or diseased animals, but not for human beings."[32] From Brennan's perspective, the case represented "the most extraordinary example to date" of the Court's push to extend the reasonable suspicion standard well beyond the context of its initial articulation.[33] He reasoned that "It is simply staggering that the Court suggests that *Terry* would even begin to sanction a *27-hour criminal-investigative detention*, even one occurring at the border."[34] And, let's not forget that this "criminal-investigative detention" included a strip search!

Staggering. Saddening. Disgusting. All of that might well be true. None of it changes the extraordinary ways in which reasonable suspicion empowers the government at the border.[35] And none of it helps Tanya.

The story of race, gender, stop-and-strip, and the courts did not end with *Montoya de Hernandez*. In the late 1990s, a group of Black women filed a class action lawsuit against the U.S. Customs and Border Protection, alleging that customs officials systemically targeted Black women for strip searches, among other things.[36] The evidence revealed that Black women were nearly twice as likely to be searched as white men and white women, almost three times as likely to be searched as Black men, more than six times as likely as Latinos, and twice as likely as Latinas.[37] Despite the disproportionate strip searches of Black women, customs agents "virtually never found drugs."[38] The government settled the suit for $1.9 million in 2006.[39]

Six cases filed since that settlement, between 2013 and 2018, allege the continued use of strip searches, sexual assault, and other violations by border agents, primarily of Black and Latina women. The cases provide accounts of stop-and-strip practices that, if true, justify Justice Brennan's phrase "'disgusting and saddening episode[s]' at our Nation's border."[40] The experiences I am about to detail include both invasive and violent intrusions into the body, the details of which some readers, particularly survivors of sexual violence, may not wish to confront—in which case I would recommend readers skip past the bulleted list:

- Searched while menstruating[41] and subjected to the forcible removal of their menstrual products;[42]
- Interrogated, sometimes for hours,[43] with no explanation as to why they were being searched and seized;[44]
- Handcuffed[45] and shackled;[46]
- Forced to remove clothing[47] and to let down hair for inspection;[48]
- Forced to squat and cough;[49]
- Subjected to the probing of their breasts and/or underwear;[50]
- Subjected to the visual inspection of their vaginal and anal areas, including with flashlights;[51]
- Subjected to other bodily intrusions, including the pressing of fingers into the vaginal[52] and rectal area,[53] the "insert[ing of] speculum into . . . vagina"[54] in the presence of others, and using the same examination gloves for multiple detained people;[55]
- Subjected to canine sniffs;[56]
- Forcibly transported to a hospital or other medical center,[57] directed to ingest laxatives,[58] to undergo X-ray procedures,[59] to provide DNA and urine samples,[60] to undergo gynecological exams,[61] and to be sedated;[62]
- Detained for hours in a confined space[63] without access to restrooms,[64] food and water,[65] and denied the right to contact family.[66]

Words can hardly describe the in-the-moment, and after-the-fact, harms described in these cases. Even the terms "trauma" and "sexual assault" may prove inadequate. We could, of course, have a debate about exactly when, during the above incidents, the government crossed the line drawn by the Court between reasonable and unreasonable searches. But such an exercise would miss this important point: It is exactly because *Montoya de Hernandez* opens up constitutional space for debate—beyond the kinds of evidence on which the government may rely to establish reasonable suspicion—that Black and Latinx women will continue to find themselves navigating the boundaries between the varieties of stop-and-strip violence that are constitutional and those that are not.

Yet, the practice of stop-and-strip has not had much of a presence in public discourses about race, policing, and state violence. With all of the discussion we have had on those topics over the past several decades—from the height of debates about racial profiling in the 1990s to the more recent and ongoing organizing around Black Lives Matter—scholars, policymakers, and community organizers rarely invoke border searches and seizures, including the often gendered and racialized violence of stop-and-strip (even as there is some recognition that policing the interior of the country is very much a border patrol activity designed to keep people in their proper places).

Sexual violence at the border is not without precedent. As Sarah Haley demonstrates in her compelling book, *No Mercy Here: Gender, Punishment, and the Making of Jim Crow Modernity*, sexual violence against Black women was a pervasive feature of, and used to construct, the Jim Crow system.[67]

Similarly, a long list of writers, including Khiara Bridges, Kimberlé Crenshaw, Angela Y. Davis, Ruth Wilson Gilmore, Cheryl Harris, Priscilla Ocen, Dorothy Roberts, and Hortense Spillers, among others, argue that the regulation of Black women's sexual autonomy and violence against their bodies (including in the form of sterilization) have been core—and not peripheral—features of racism.[68] This compelling body of work suggests the routine manner in which border officials lawfully violate Black women's bodies through stop-and-strip has historical roots in the routine and lawful ways in which private and state actors violated Black women's bodies from slavery to Jim Crow to the present. Put plainly, the subjugation of Black women as racial inferiors on whose bodies sexual violence can be lawfully enacted "back then" remains a disturbing feature of our constitutional landscape "right now."

That Black women's experiences are a useful barometer for the experiences of Black people as a group is a critical insight of Kimberlé Crenshaw's theory of intersectionality. I won't define the full contours of that theory here, except to say that people who invoke intersectionality typically fail to connect two important (but not the only) branches of the theory.[69] I will call one of these branches the "uniqueness prong" and the other the "representative prong." These terms sound academic but they are easy enough to understand.

The "uniqueness prong" suggests that Black women have experiences as Black women that diverge or differ from the racial experiences of Black men and the gender experiences of other women. Thus, with respect to Black men and other women, some of Black women's experiences are unique.

The "representative prong" suggests that Black women have experiences as Black women that converge with or are roughly the same as the racial experiences of Black men and the gender experiences of other women. Thus, with respect to Black men and other women, some of Black women's experiences are representative.[70]

Stop-and-strip bears out the lessons of both prongs. Drawing attention to the role reasonable suspicion plays constitutionalizing stop-and-strip has the potential both to reveal Black women's unique vulnerability to this form of violence and illustrate a broader problem in Fourth Amendment law—the various incursions into Black life reasonable suspicion authorizes. I will provide concrete and shocking examples of these incursions towards the close of this chapter. The point here is that the relative silence about how Fourth Amendment law exposes Black women to stop-and-strip has not only made their suffering less visible, but limits our ability to see the true scope of how the Fourth Amendment impacts all Black people.[71]

Even those familiar with intersectional critiques of laws, social policies, and social movements, including the critiques that have fueled the powerful #SayHerName Campaign that has successfully broadened public consciousness about police violence against Black women,[72] may be surprised by how little attention has been paid to *Montoya de Hernandez* in scholarly, legal, and policy debates about race, racial profiling, and state violence. Although it is arguably the most important constitutional decision on stop-and-strip, the case has received virtually no scholarly, media, or judicial engagement. Some limited illustrations are presented in the tables below.

TABLE 1

	Terry v. Ohio: # of Results	*U.S. v. Montoya de Hernandez*: # of Results
Race or Racial Profiling	Cases: 359	Cases: 5
	Trial Court Orders: 11	Trial Court Orders: 0
	Statutes & Court Rules: 6	Statutes & Court Rules: 0
	Secondary Sources: 679	Secondary Sources: 12
	Total: 1,055	**Total: 17**

Table 1 compares the results for searches run on a leading legal database, Westlaw. The searches cross-reference search terms with citations to two cases we've discussed at length: *Terry v. Ohio* and *United States v. Montoya de Hernandez*. Essentially, the search results demonstrate the extent to which those cases are associated with the terms "race" or "racial profiling" in subsequent case decisions, trial documents, statutes, or secondary sources—such as scholarly articles, legal treatises, or practical guides. As Table 1 demonstrates, this search produces just over 1,000 results for "*Terry* + race or racial profiling,"[73] yet only seventeen for "*Montoya de Hernandez* + race or racial profiling."[74] That's a massive disparity.

Now consider Table 2 which compares the frequency with which

Black men are associated with *Terry* to the frequency with which Black women are associated with *Montoya de Hernandez*. "*Terry* + Black man" produces 533 results,[75] while the "*Montoya de Hernandez* + Black woman" search returns three.[76] Again, a huge difference.

TABLE 2

	Terry v. Ohio: **Black Men: # of Results**	*U.S. v. Montoya de Hernandez*: **Black Women: # of Results**
Race or Racial Profiling	Cases: 244	Cases: 0
	Trial Court Orders: 4	Trial Court Orders: 0
	Statutes & Court Rules: 6	Statutes & Court Rules: 0
	Secondary Sources: 279	Secondary Sources: 3
	Total: 533	**Total: 3**

Table 3 suggests that Black women's experiences are largely absent from racial discussions of the reasonable suspicion standard more generally. Whereas Black men are mentioned 1,044 times in relation to reasonable suspicion,[77] the number for Black women—seventy-three—is decidedly smaller.[78]

TABLE 3

	Black Men: # of Results	**Black Women: # of Results**
Reasonable Suspicion	Cases: 635	Cases: 38
	Trial Court Orders: 23	Trial Court Orders: 0
	Statutes & Court Rules: 26	Statutes & Court Rules: 2
	Secondary Sources: 360	Secondary Sources: 33
	Total: 1,044	**Total: 73**

Moreover, when one counts the number of times Black men and Black women are discussed in the context of *Terry*—as demonstrated in Table 4—the results are consistent with the prior tables. A search of "*Terry* + Black man" yields 533 results,[79] while "*Terry* + Black woman" yields thirty-two.[80]

TABLE 4

	Black Men: # of Results	Black Women: # of Results
	Cases: 244	Cases: 14
	Trial Court Orders: 4	Trial Court Orders: 0
Terry v. Ohio	Statutes & Court Rules: 6	Statutes & Court Rules: 1
	Secondary Sources: 279	Secondary Sources: 17
	Total: 533	**Total: 32**

Two points deserve emphasis. First, these numbers do not fully speak for themselves. Undoubtedly, more nuanced stories are embedded within these searches that careful qualitative analyses would reveal. Still, the numbers are striking.

Second, I do not intend to suggest that we are learning too much about Black men or their experiences of criminal injustice. We are not. The formal and informal ways through which Black men are socially surveilled, supervised, disciplined, and put down—sometimes quite literally—largely continue to occupy a marginal space in our national consciousness. Though the uprisings sparked by the police-killing of George Floyd are changing that,[81] we need to know more, not less, about how Black men are policed,[82] including the ways in which they might experience stop-and-frisk as form of sexual violence.[83]

I am saying, then, that we should continue talking about Black men and police violence. I presented the above tables not to disrupt those conversations but to suggest that, although *Terry* was decided more than forty years ago, we have learned virtually nothing about the impact of that case or its offspring on the lives of Black women.

One pushback against that tables I have presented might be that the disparities they reflect make sense. After all, neither *Terry* nor *Montoya de Hernandez* were about Black women. Therefore scholars, policymakers, and the media have no reason to invoke those cases when discussing Black women. That explanation is not particularly compelling because the rulings in both cases clearly affect Black women.

Moreover, were one to put *Terry* or *Montoya de Hernandez* to the side and focus more narrowly on "Black women + strip searches" at the border, the search yields a total of only seven results.[84] That result further suggests that Black women's vulnerability to strip searches at the border is not part of our collective consciousness.

There is a case, however, that directly involves law enforcement personnel strip-searching a Black woman defendant: *United States v. Mendenhall*.[85] While the facts of *Mendenhall* are not nearly as disturbing as those in *Montoya de Hernandez*, they, too, reveal the sexual violence to which Black women are vulnerable when they travel. As you will soon learn, even this case is largely absent in discussions about race and policing.

In *Mendenhall*, two Drug Enforcement Administration agents approached Sylvia Mendenhall in the airport terminal as she arrived in Detroit from Los Angeles. The agents claimed that Mendenhall fit a "drug courier" profile, which the Court described as "an informally compiled abstract of characteristics thought typical of persons carrying illicit drugs."[86]

At the time of the litigation, law enforcement officers routinely relied on the drug courier profiles, notwithstanding that those profiles were based almost entirely on innocuous behavior and were replete with contradictory factors on which law enforcement officers could rely. For example, if you were the first to leave the plane, you fit the drug courier profile. You also fit the profile if you were the last to deplane, or if you deplaned in the middle. If you purchased a one-way ticket, you fit the drug courier profile. You also fit the profile if your ticket included a return trip. If your flight was non-stop, you fit the drug courier profile. And if your itinerary included a layover, you fit the profile as well. Acting too calmly corresponded to the drug courier profile, as did acting nervously. Finally, if you travelled alone, you fit the drug courier profile. And, yes, if you travelled with a companion, you fit the profile as well.

While courts have ruled that officers may no longer invoke the "drug courier profile" as such to justify their decision to detain a person, police officers may still rely on any of the factors that went into constructing those profiles (such as whether a person appeared to be acting nervously) to argue that they had reasonable suspicion to stop and question a person.

Upon approaching Mendenhall, the agents asked her for her identification and travel documents. Seeing that the names on the documents did not match, the agents asked her to accompany them to a DEA office. At the office Mendenhall was asked for permission to search her bag, to which she responded, "Go ahead."[87] That search revealed no incriminating evidence.

Soon thereafter, a woman agent arrived in the room and requested to search Mendenhall's person. According to the agent, Mendenhall agreed. She was then escorted to a private room, and again asked permission to search her body. This time Mendenhall expressed concerns that she might miss her flight. The agent responded that if Mendenhall was not carrying any drugs, she had nothing to worry about. Mendenhall proceeded to undress and removed a package of heroin from her underwear. The officer subsequently arrested Mendenhall. The question for the court was whether the arrest was constitutional.

This presents another good opportunity for you to review what you've learned about Fourth Amendment law thus far. Assuming you're the government lawyer in this case, how would you defend the officer's conduct?

Drawing from Chapter 1, you would argue that following Mendenhall, approaching her, requesting that she show her identification and travel documents, asking her to accompany the officers to the DEA office, and seeking permission to search her person and belongings were all consensual actions. In other words, drawing on the language the Court employs to determine whether a person is seized, at all times Mendenhall was "free to leave or otherwise terminate the encounter." That she chose not to leave is on her, not the officers. You'd insist, therefore, that the officers needed no justification to proceed as they did—the Fourth Amendment simply doesn't apply. You would add, moreover, that she freely consented to the search of her bag and her body. No seizure. A consensual search. No justification necessary.

Let's say you lose that argument, with a court ruling that by the time Mendenhall found herself in the DEA's office she was seized. What's your move now?

Hint: Earlier in this chapter you learned that there are two types of seizures—a stop and an arrest. Which type of seizure would you argue occurred here? Presumably, you would describe the seizure as a stop, not an arrest, and claim that the officers only needed reasonable suspicion—not probable cause. You would then point to the facts that you think gave rise to reasonable suspicion, including the discrepancy between the name on Mendenhall's identification and the name on her travel documents.

Unable to point to other concrete incriminating facts, you would echo the actions Mendenhall took which matched the supposed actions of a drug-courier, as the agents claimed in this case. These included that (a) Mendenhall arrived from Los Angeles, a city believed by the agents to be the place of origin for much of the heroin brought to Detroit; (b) she was the last person to leave the plane, "appeared to be very nervous," and "completely scanned the whole area where [the agents] were standing"; (c) after deplaning, she "proceeded past the baggage area without claiming any luggage;" and (d) she "changed airlines for her flight out of Detroit."[88]

Hearing such arguments, a majority of the Court concluded that either Mendenhall was not seized, and therefore the officers needed no justification for asking Mendenhall to accompany them to the DEA office and to the private room, or that she was seized, but that the seizure was reasonable because it amounted to a stop (not an arrest) and the officers had reasonable suspicion.[89] Under either theory, the events leading to the strip search became irrelevant—the only issue was whether Mendenhall voluntarily consented to that search. The Court believed she did.[90]

Mendenhall has been cited more than twenty-thousand times,[91] over a thousand of which include secondary sources, like academic journals, newspapers, and magazines.[92] Because the case concerns a Black woman who was subjected to a strip search, one might believe that the case has been cited numerous times to discuss Black women's vulnerability to sexual violence. The data suggests otherwise.

To begin, of those 4,000-plus citations, the case has been discussed only twenty-six times with specific reference to Black women.[93] Narrowing the search to focus on "Black women + sexual violence"[94] returns no results; even "police violence"[95] more generally, returns only two results. It is fair to say that while *Mendenhall* has received some amount of attention, discussions of the case have largely sidelined the gendered dimensions of Black women's exposure to searches and seizures.

Mendenhall is important not just because the case provides us with a concrete example of how the Supreme Court's creation of the reasonable suspicion standard increases Black women's vulnerability to intimate scrutiny by law enforcement. It also reveals two problematic features of Fourth Amendment law that potentially impact all Black people.

First, the case exposes a law-and-order practice that police officers routinely mobilize against Black people—drug courier profiles. As I mentioned earlier, although courts have since prohibited officers from justifying their decision to detain a person based on a "drug courier profile," officers may still rely on the same factors that produced those profiles—such as leaving a plane last, or not carrying luggage—to generate reasonable suspicion.

Second, the Court's intersectional analysis in the *Mendenhall* decision is cause for both optimism and pessimism. Recall that in determining whether a person has been seized, courts ask "whether a reasonable person would feel free to leave or otherwise terminate the encounter." When a certain population—here, Black women—often experiences policing more frequently and perhaps forcefully than the justices deciding their case—here, eight white men and one Black man—it can be difficult to generalize about whether someone feels "reasonably free to leave" without taking race and gender into account. In *Mendenhall*, the Court gestured in this direction, noting that Sylvia Mendenhall's race and gender "were not irrelevant" to understanding whether or not she believed she could terminate the encounter.[96] Scholars and lawyers would do well to lift up and redeploy this part of the analysis.

My pessimism derives, however, from the Court's conclusion that although race and gender "were not irrelevant" to deciding whether Mendenhall was seized, they were also "not decisive."[97] So, while the Court indicated that these factors may have some bearing on whether a person is seized, it is unclear what types of arguments they might find persuasive, or how much weight they give to them. For now, *Mendenhall* can still serve as a useful case for talking about the racial harms produced by the reasonable suspicion standard, both for particular harms faced by Black women and more general harms affecting Black people as a whole.

I mentioned at the outset of this chapter that stop-and-strip violence exists as part of a broader expansion of reasonable suspicion, which covers far more circumstances than the stop-and-frisk context out of which the standard arose. I will conclude this chapter by providing a specific indication of what I mean.

In Chapter 3, I faulted Justice Warren for not realizing how the move away from probable cause would make Black people easy targets for police officers. I do not fault him, however, for failing to anticipate the multiple contexts in which reasonable suspicion would come to be applied. Its migration from *Terry v. Ohio* to just about every dimension of policing is quite remarkable and should surprise even the most ardent proponent of "law and order." Consider the following:

1. Although Chief Justice Warren contemplated that an officer would stop someone only if the officer had reasonable suspicion that they were armed and dangerous, officers now use reasonable suspicion to stop-and-question people even where there is no such safety concern.[98]

2. Officers may now stop and investigate luggage, not just people, based upon the reasonable suspicion that it contains drugs.[99]

3. Officers may stop vehicles based upon reasonable suspicion.[100]

4. Officers may also use reasonable suspicion to frisk any passengers in a vehicle, not just the driver.[101]

5. Individuals may be required to disclose their names during a stop if there is reasonable suspicion of their involvement in criminal activity. Failure to comply could subject them to arrest.[102]

6. Officers may ask whatever questions they want of the individual or anyone else incidentally detained (such as the passenger of a vehicle) during the course of a stop supported by reasonable suspicion, as long as the questions do not unduly prolong the detention.[103]

7. Officers may choose not to knock or announce their presence when executing a warrant if they have reasonable suspicion (not probable cause) of some kind of urgency.[104]

8. When executing an arrest or search warrant in the home,

officers are permitted to use reasonable suspicion to justify an expanded search for suspects who might be armed and dangerous.[105]

9. Officers may search the home of a person on probation based on reasonable suspicion alone.[106] And they may search the home of a parolee for any reason whatsoever, or no reason at all.[107]

10. Law enforcement officials may take "apparent Mexican ancestry" into account in determining whether they have reasonable suspicions to believe that a person is undocumented.[108]

11. Reasonable suspicion can be used to add someone to the "No Fly List."[109]

12. Reasonable suspicion applies to past and future crimes, and not just crimes currently underway.[110]

13. Reasonable suspicion may be based on an informant's tip, not just an officer's direct observation and expertise.[111]

14. An anonymous tip to a 911 operator that a person is driving erratically essentially gives police officers reasonable suspicion to justify stopping the vehicle the tip describes.[112]

15. "Evasive behavior," such as the "furtive movement" of someone in a "high crime area" is almost enough to constitute reasonable suspicion.[113]

16. Officers may rely on generalized factors that are consistent with so-called "drug courier profiles" to establish reasonable suspicion.[114]

17. Reasonable suspicion may be used to justify subjecting a suspect to a "show up," which is effectively a line-up conducted on the street.[115]

18. An officer may demand and take a person's fingerprints during a stop justified only by reasonable suspicion.[116]

19. There is no time limit required by the reasonable suspicion standard.[117] Courts have upheld reasonable suspicion-based stops that have lasted more than thirty minutes.[118]

20. Not only can reasonable suspicion be used to justify stopping

and frisking children in schools, but strip-searching them as well.[119]

21. Government employers may rely on reasonable suspicion to conduct workplace searches.[120]

22. Officers may rely on reasonable suspicion to perform full searches at "extended borders"—areas miles away from actual border crossings—if they possess a reasonable certainty that the subject recently crossed the border.[121]

23. Reasonable suspicion allows border agents to forensically search the personal property of both citizens and non-citizens—such as laptops and other electronic storage devices.[122]

24. The government may rely on reasonable suspicion to justify searching international mail at the border.[123]

25. Reasonable suspicion permits border agents to stop-and-strip people at the border.[124]

These examples are not equally problematic, of course. As one adds them all up, however, they create a world in which government agents may search and seize people on the streets, in their homes, in their cars, in schools, at work, and at the border—all on the thinnest of justifications.

The next chapter also centers the constitutionality of searches and seizures on the thinnest of justification. Here again sexual violence is implicated—and so is economic extraction. In this chapter, too, you will see the ease with which law enforcement can—under cover of law—effectuate incursions into Black life. This time, the target of my critique is a phenomenon I will call "predatory policing." The story begins in Ferguson, Missouri.

Chapter Five
Predatory Policing

Roughly six months after officer Darren Wilson shot and killed unarmed Michael Brown in Ferguson, Missouri, the Department of Justice released a report summarizing the results of its investigation into the Ferguson Police Department.[1] To those of you who have not read the Ferguson Report, you should. It is a sobering look at a criminal justice system in which racism and classism were turned into central and ordinary features of the city's governance. It revealed how ordinary policing mechanisms were deliberately used to extract revenue from Black and impoverished communities in Ferguson, in a manner that touched the heart of those peoples' economic lives. The report includes a compelling example of the debt-upon-debt scenarios produced by Ferguson's revenue-generating policing:

> We spoke, for example, with an African-American woman who has a still-pending case stemming from 2007, when, on a single occasion, she parked her car illegally. She received two citations and a $151 fine, plus fees. The woman, who experienced financial difficulties and periods of homelessness over several years, was charged with seven Failure to Appear offenses for missing court dates or fine payments on her parking tickets between 2007 and 2010. For each Failure to Appear, the court issued an arrest warrant and imposed new fines and fees. From 2007 to 2014, the woman was arrested twice, spent six days in jail, and paid $550 to the court for the events stemming

from this single instance of illegal parking. Court records show that she twice attempted to make partial payments of $25 and $50, but the court returned those payments, refusing to accept anything less than payment in full. One of those payments was later accepted, but only after the court's letter rejecting payment by money order was returned as undeliverable. This woman is now making regular payments on the fine. As of December 2014, over seven years later, despite initially owing a $151 fine and having already paid $550, she still owed $541.[2]

This chapter places the story of revenue generation in Ferguson into a broader context of predatory policing and explains how Fourth Amendment law is an important driver of such practices.

"Predatory policing" describes the use of ordinary policing mechanisms such as warrants, arrests, and citations not only to exploit the economic and social vulnerabilities of a group, but also to generate revenue for cities and police departments, and to secure pay increases and promotions for police officers as well.[3] Examples of predatory policing include using the threat of arrest and incarceration to commit acts of sexual violence against poor Black women, seizing people's property (jewelry, cash, and cars) by alleging that it is connected to a crime, or using traffic and pedestrian stops to issue multiple misdemeanor citations, each of which carries its own fine and sometimes a mandatory court appearance. The result of predatory policing is that, across the United States, Black people often find themselves paying for and going into debt through forms of police contact that leave them violated, economically exploited, and incarcerated.

Before I illustrate the precise contours of predatory policing and the toll it exacts in the lives of Black people, you should know about a widespread *legal* phenomenon on which predatory policing relies—mass criminalization. The term may sound familiar to you. Thanks in no small part to Michelle Alexander's groundbreaking text, *The New*

Jim Crow: Mass Incarceration in the Age of Colorblindness, "mass incarceration" comfortably rolls off the tongues of people of all ideological stripes. Before Alexander's book was published, and its thesis widely accepted, uttering the words "mass incarceration" would have marked the speaker disparagingly as a radical. But today, the problem of mass incarceration is part of our collective consciousness about criminal justice, even if we don't all agree about what to do about the problem.

By contrast, public discussions of *mass criminalization*—or the criminalization of relatively non-serious behavior or activities, most often as misdemeanor offenses,[4] and the diffusion of criminal justice actors, logics, and practices into other parts of the welfare state, including immigration enforcement, public schools, and hospitals— are virtually non-existent. Here's a list of the kinds of conduct cities and municipalities routinely criminalize:

a. Spitting in public places;[5]

b. Possession of spoons, bowls, and blenders (as indicative of drug paraphernalia);[6]

c. Loitering for illicit purposes;[7]

d. Loitering;[8]

e. Sleeping in a public place;[9]

f. Sitting or lying down in particular public places;[10]

g. Camping or lodging in a public place;[11]

h. Panhandling anywhere in the city;[12]

i. Storing personal property in a public place without a permit;[13]

j. Drinking in public;[14]

k. Jaywalking;[15]

l. Riding bicycles on the sidewalk;[16] and

m. Removing trash from a bin.[17]

Though the criminalization of these acts may seem trivial, the social effect of that criminalization is sweeping: Misdemeanors such as these account for approximately 80 percent of all state criminal cases,[18] with "most Americans encounter[ing] the criminal system through the petty offense process."[19] According to legal scholar Alexandra Natapoff, "[i]t turns out that the lowly misdemeanor—not homicide or rape—is the paradigmatic American crime and the paradigmatic product of the American criminal system."[20]

A few points bear emphasis. First, several of the crimes, like "sleeping in public," are far more likely to be committed by those living in poverty than anyone else. Indeed, it's fair to say that mass criminalization results in the criminalization of poverty.[21] The challenges of poverty become compounded when your inability to afford access to basic necessities like food, shelter, or bathrooms can additionally mark you as criminal.

Second, in addition to being non-serious, some of the listed crimes, such as "loitering," are decidedly vague. This combination of non-serious and vague crimes means police officers can easily establish the necessary probable cause to arrest nearly anyone. For example, if the law criminalizes jaywalking, and most pedestrians regularly jaywalk, the question is not whether the police will have probable cause to arrest—they will. Instead, the question becomes whether the police will use that probable cause selectively to arrest members of particulars groups (for example, Black teenagers). In that sense, the more cities criminalize activities in which many people engage, the wider the pool from which police officers may arrest gets.

Finally, criminalizing relatively non-serious activities is compounded by an issue I explored in Chapter 2—the broad discretion which police officers have when deciding whom they arrest. Assuming that an officer has probable cause to arrest a person, and that the person is in public, the officer's choice whether or not to carry out the arrest is nearly unbridled.

Mass criminalization is thus not simply a source of criminal sanction; it is also an important source of police power. That power provides officers with a kind of perpetual probable cause that they may use both to arrest Black people for a wide range of non-serious activities[22] and to predatorily target them, including as a source of revenue generation.

Predatory Policing as Revenue Generation

Civil asset forfeiture and citations and fines are two mechanisms police officers can use, with virtually no Fourth Amendment constraint, to generate revenue. Here's how.

Civil Asset Forfeiture

Civil asset forfeiture allows law enforcement officers to seize *any property* they believe was used in the commission of, or purchased with proceeds from, a crime.[23] As you see, here too police officers' power to arrest is implicated.

To understand the civil asset forfeiture form of predatory policing, assume that a police officer stops Tanya for failing to use her turn signal (a traffic infraction) in order to investigate a crime the officer has no probable cause to believe she has committed: drug distribution. Recall from Chapter 2 that the stop would not be unconstitutional—the Supreme Court has expressly stated that such pretextual stops are consistent with Fourth Amendment law.[24]

While questioning Tanya, the officer informs her that he smells marijuana, and asks to search her car. She consents, both because she does not know she has the right to refuse the officer's request and because the officer did not—and is not required to—inform her of that right.[25] The officer searches the car but finds no drugs. He does, however, find $500 in cash in the glove compartment, which Tanya explains that she earned by babysitting. The officer responds that, "Even though I did not find any drugs, I believe that this money is linked to drugs." The officer seizes the money and explains to Tanya that if she wants it back, she must prove it is not related to criminal activity.[26]

As a technical legal matter, and this will likely strike you as odd, the government's seizure of Tanya's cash is considered an action against the property, not Tanya herself. In other words, the government is suing the property! This legal fiction—that the alleged crime is committed by the property, not the person—is reflected in the name of cases litigating asset forfeiture: *State of Texas v. One Gold Crucifix*, *United States v. Approximately 64,695 Pounds of Shark Fins*, and *United States v. One Pearl Necklace*.[27] Importantly, under the rules of civil asset forfeiture, even if the government does not charge the person, their property remains in police custody until they can prove that it is not related to criminal activity.

Property seized under civil asset forfeiture often is used to fund the very police departments who conducted the seizures, providing a perverse incentive for law enforcement to seize as much property as possible. Since 2001, there have been at least 61,998 cash seizures made without warrants or indictments under the Federal Equitable Sharing Program, which rewards local police for cooperating with the Federal Government in its efforts against drug trafficking, terrorism, and other crimes. In exchange, local police departments retain a large share of the proceeds. How large? According to one study, the Federal Equitable Sharing Program has resulted in the seizure of over $2.5 billion from people who were not charged with crimes, of which approximately $1.7 billion was returned to local law enforcement departments for their use.[28]

Hoping to pad their budgets, police officers may use their arrest power to seize property in the form of "cash for freedom" arrests. For example, police officers pull over motorists for minor traffic infractions, such as in Tanya's case. They then obtain consent to search the car, and seize any money, jewelry, or other valuables found during the search by asserting a link to some sort of criminal activity. Once seized, the officer presents the driver with two options: either face criminal charges, arrest, and possible jail-time, or sign over a release waiver for the seized property, and be free to go.[29] Under these coercive circumstances, many motorists will choose to forfeit their property, even if they believe the charges won't ultimately stick, to avoid the harms that flow from arrest and even a few hours in jail.

Alternatively, an officer might give Tanya a receipt for her money, and tell her that it will remain in police custody or be absorbed into the forfeiture fund if she does not claim it in a timely manner. In many states, the burden would be on Tanya to prove that her babysitting money was not connected to a crime—a difficult standard to meet for a job without a paper trail.[30] She could not rely on a public defender for help; there is no right to counsel in a civil case and the government isn't charging Tanya with a crime. And she would likely find that the cost of hiring a lawyer to fight the case on her behalf would greatly exceed the $500 the government seized.

This type of petty cash forfeiture, or police petty robbery on the highways, is commonplace.[31] One report from the ACLU found that nearly half of all the cash forfeitures in Philadelphia from 2011–2013 were for less than $192.[32] Although there are many high-profile cases where the government seized large sums of cash from innocent victims, officers often prefer small seizures over large seizures as a form of revenue generation.[33] For one thing, small seizures are harder to track and therefore lead to less transparency and accountability. For another, the difficulties and costs of retrieving smaller cash seizures are a disincentive for those interested in recovery. These factors make it unlikely that Tanya will ever see her babysitting money again.

Similar to other policing practices, Blacks are burdened by civil asset forfeiture to a greater extent than whites.[34] Our hypothetical Tanya would be as well. No matter where Tanya is going, every time she drives she is vulnerable not only to being pulled over, but also to a form of predatory policing that could extract her salary.

And, to make matters worse, she could even lose her car. An officer's made-up probable cause that the car is connected to crime is all an officer would need to seize it.[35] In this instance as well, the burden would be on Tanya to prove that her car is "innocent."

Citations and Fines

Civil asset forfeiture is not the only economically extractive dimension of predatory policing—police officers also use citations, fines, and fees to generate revenue for their departments and cities as well. Two documents—the *Arch City Defenders: Municipal Courts White Paper* and the Department of Justice's report on the Ferguson Police Department—provide a window into how this works.[36] Both describe an organized and racially biased economic exploitation system that mobilized police officers as frontline revenue generators. Broadly framed, the documents describe the system as follows.

Predatory policing was an institutional feature of everyday policing in Ferguson. According to the Justice Department, the city's focus on generating revenue had "a profound effect on [the Ferguson Police Department's] approach to law enforcement. Patrol assignments and schedules are geared toward aggressive enforcement of Ferguson's municipal code, with insufficient thought given to whether enforcement strategies promote public safety. . . ."[37]

Ferguson's city leadership incentivized its police force to target Black residents to generate revenue for the city of Ferguson.[38] This included "carrots" and "sticks," such as signaling to police officers that their pay, promotions, and job assignments could be positively or negatively impacted by the rate at which they issued citations.[39] Police responded by stopping Ferguson's Black residents for minor infractions (recall the problem of mass criminalization) and issuing citations (that carried fines).[40]

Officers often issued multiple citations to each person they stopped, and many of these citations included a mandatory court appearance to pay a fine.[41] People who showed up to court but did not have the means to pay their fines were subject to arrest, faced additional fines, or had their driver's licenses revoked.[42] Those who drove on a revoked license (including those who did so to go to work or to transport children to and from school or daycare) were vulnerable to being arrested, after which they would find themselves back in court and subject to the possibility of additional fines.[43]

Those who failed to show up to the mandatory court appearances for their citations had warrants issued for their arrest.[44] Over 9,000 warrants, covering more than 30,000 offenses, were issued in one year alone. As recently as 2014, at least 16,000 people were vulnerable to arrest on an outstanding warrant.[45]

There is also no indication that the municipal court made any determination as to someone's financial ability to pay before assessing these fines.[46] People who found themselves caught up in any part of Ferguson's revenue generating system rarely had the advice of counsel, and the city did not provide indigent defense representation when people could not otherwise afford retaining a lawyer.[47]

This predatory revenue scheme permeated almost every aspect of government in Ferguson. In fact, the city's budget was dependent on revenue generation from municipal fines.[48] For example, chief of police Thomas Jackson regularly reported the police department's level of revenue generation to the city manager, among others.[49] In an email to Chief Jackson, the city finance director commented that "unless ticket writing ramps up significantly before the end of the year, it will be hard to significantly raise collections next year."[50] He also recommended that the police department develop specific traffic enforcement strategies "to fill the revenue pipeline."[51] Chief Jackson committed to "looking at different shift schedules which will place more officers on the street, which in turn will increase traffic enforcement per shift."[52]

Other institutions and officials actively participated in this scheme, including:

- The municipal court system, which tracked "the number of tickets issued by each officer and each squad,"[53] and issued "severe penalties when a defendant fail[ed] to meet court requirements, including added fines and fees and arrest warrants that [were] unnecessary and r[a]n counter to public safety";[54]

- The prosecutor, who, among other things, instructed police to ensure that "all necessary summonses [were] written for each incident, i.e. when DWI charges [were] issued, [were] the correct companion charges being issued, such as speeding, failure to maintain a single lane, no insurance, and no seatbelt, etc.";[55]

- Police supervisors, who incentivized and pressured rank-and-file officers to issue as many citations as possible;[56] and

- Patrol officers, who competed among themselves with respect to the number of citations they issued.[57]

The strategy was effective. In one email correspondence, Chief Jackson indicated that "May is the 6th straight month in which court revenue (gross) has exceeded the previous year."[58]

My colleague, Beth Colgan, describes an administrative structure in Ferguson that highlights the extent to which revenue generation was thoroughly embedded as an ordinary feature of governance: The chief executive officer for the city—the city manager—oversaw the city's finances, selected judicial candidates for the municipal court, approved prosecutorial appointments, and managed and supervised the chief of police. In turn, the chief of police oversaw the municipal court (housed within the police department), with court staff—including the clerks responsible for accepting guilty pleas or discharging cases—reporting directly to him. "In other words, although the city manager did not himself have the ability to convict, acquit, or sentence, he selected and supervised those who did."[59]

Colgan describes how various actors worked together to prioritize revenue generation:

Take, for example, the court clerk, who, as noted above, had the power to dispose of charges. Ferguson city officials consulted the court clerk with respect to how to improve revenue generation and to set goals regarding how much funding the court might generate in a given year. In turn, the court clerk put pressure on other actors to work toward revenue generation. Emails located by the Department of Justice, for example, revealed that the court clerk prodding a prosecutor to seek higher economic sanctions with the warning, "We need to keep up our revenue."

Ferguson's prosecutors also had adjudicative power in Ferguson's system, as they were given authority to deny requests for extensions of time to pay debts stemming from economic sanctions. This occurred with apparent regularity so that prosecutors could "aid in the court's efficient collection of its fines." That prosecutors in St. Louis County's municipalities felt intertwined with the court as a revenue-generating partner is also obvious from a comment made by a prosecutor who agreed to reduce a fine after a plea negotiation with a pro bono attorney from the ArchCity Defenders: "You're taking money right out of my pocket, here."[60]

Colgan's account puts into sharp relief predatory policing's role as one part of a systemic and normalized practice of revenue generation, in which the more economically and racially marginalized a community, the more vulnerable members of that community are to predatory policing.[61] The focus on predatory policing in Ferguson and across the state of Missouri has raised questions about whether the practice is prevalent in other parts of the United States.[62] The answer, quite likely, is yes.[63]

The story I have told about the revenue-generating features of predatory policing is also, distressingly, a story about warrants. This may
not be obvious. To see the connection between warrants and revenue generation it may help to remember that in one year alone,
Ferguson—a city of approximately 21,000 residents—issued 9,007
warrants and that in 2014, at least 16,000 people were vulnerable to
arrest on an outstanding warrant (approximately 3/4 of all residents).
The sheer number of warrants allowed police officers to indiscrimi-
nately stop people on the assumption that they may have had an outstanding warrant and then arrest them or pile on other fines.

This kind of policing might sound far-fetched. Yet, a relatively
recent Supreme Court case effectively encourages police officers to
do just that—stop people on the assumption that they will have an
outstanding warrant.[64]

Here's how that could happen.

Assume that a police officer observes Tanya walking home one
evening. He has no reason to believe that Tanya has done anything
wrong. Nevertheless, he stops her. In the context of doing so, he
demands that Tanya produce her identification. At this point, the
officer's conduct is clearly unconstitutional. The officer isn't simply
asking for Tanya's identification, he is insisting that she produce it.
Tanya has thus been seized.

The officer then runs Tanya's name through a warrant database
and discovers that she has an outstanding warrant arising from a
parking violation that she neglected (or could not afford) to pay. The
officer uses the warrant as justification to handcuff, arrest, and transport Tanya to the stationhouse.

How would you resolve this case if you were the judge? From one
view, the arrest is constitutional. It was based on the fact that Tanya
had an outstanding warrant. Had Tanya taken care of her warrant,
like the law required her to do, she would not have been arrested.

But how did the officer come to learn of that warrant? By illegally
seizing Tanya and demanding that she produce her identification.

But for that illegal act, the officer would not have learned about Tanya's outstanding warrant. The discovery of the warrant was thus the "fruit of the poisonous tree."

A critical part of the Fourth Amendment's exclusionary rule, the rule I discussed in Chapter 3, the "fruit of the poisonous tree" doctrine prohibits the police from using evidence obtained through a constitutional violation. The rationale, as you might remember, is that police officers may not benefit from violating our constitutional rights and that suppressing the evidence creates a disincentive for them to do so.[65]

Back to your representation of Tanya. As her lawyer, you would draw on the "fruit of the poisonous tree" doctrine to claim that without the officer's initial decision to illegally stop and demand that Tanya produce her identification (the "poisonous tree"), he would not have known about the warrant for her parking ticket (the "fruit").[66]

Assuming you make the "fruit of the poisonous tree" argument, there is no guarantee that you would win. First, and as you might remember from prior chapters, under Fourth Amendment law, police officers not only have tremendous discretion, they also have broad latitude to make mistakes.[67] If a court believed that the unconstitutional stop was the result of a *reasonable* mistake, it would also likely find that the officer's discovery of Tanya's outstanding warrant effectively "cured" the unconstitutional seizure, in that it was a separate "intervening act."

If you are confused by that argument, you should be. How does Tanya's warrant, which was discovered by an unconstitutional stop, become an "intervening act"—something that happened *between* the unconstitutional seizure and the discovery of the warrant? The warrant was not an intervening act. It was the product of an illegal one! To state this point using another metaphor from Fourth Amendment law, there was no break in the chain of causation between the illegal act (the baseless seizure of Tanya) and the discovery of the warrant. The following image makes all of this clear:

Follow the chain of events. There are no breaks in the chain. The illegal arrest of Tanya is part of an unbroken link to Tanya's arrest. The fact that the warrant itself might otherwise be legitimate should not matter. The point is that an illegal seizure led to the discovery of the warrant and the discovery of the warrant was the basis for Tanya's arrest.

There is a more sensible way of thinking about intervening acts provided in a foundational case, *Wong Sun v. United States.*[68] Simplifying the case, the government wanted to submit two of the defendant's confessions into evidence. The first confession, the Court concluded, was obtained after an unconstitutional seizure, and was therefore the "fruit of the poisonous tree."

The second confession, however, could be admitted. This was because, following the unconstitutional seizure and first confession, the defendant was released on his own recognizance (meaning, the defendant didn't have to pay bail) and then voluntarily returned to the police station two days later—not against his will, not summoned by the police—and gave a second confession. This, the Court believed, represented an "intervening act" which broke the chain of causation between the first unconstitutional seizure to the evidence. In the Court's view, it made little sense to hold the police responsible for the second confession when they did not ask, let alone compel, the defendant to show up at the stationhouse. The defendant's showing up at the stationhouse was an "intervening act," and so the second confession was not the "fruit of the poisonous tree." Again, a diagram might help.

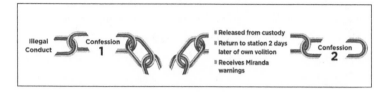

Note the break in the chain after the first confession. Tanya's unrest (which flows from an unbroken link that begins with an illegal seizure) is not like Confession 2 (which flows from a broken link that disconnects the confession from the initial illegal conduct). Look at the diagram one more time. Tanya did nothing like the defendant in *Wong Sun* who voluntarily showed up at the station two days after the initial illegal conduct. Instead, there is a clear and uninterrupted chain from an unconstitutional seizure (the officer's decision to stop Tanya without reasonable suspicion) to the discovery of the outstanding warrant to the Tanya's arrest.

Nevertheless, because of the Supreme Court's recent expansion of what qualifies as an "intervening act," the argument that Tanya's arrest is the "fruit of the poisonous tree" of an illegal stop could fall on deaf ears.[69] Even though the officer had no reason to believe that Tanya did anything wrong when he approached her, he could end up with a legitimate basis on which to arrest her.

We can now trace how a system of predatory policing intended to generate revenue, which in turn generates a stream of warrants, increases a Black person's vulnerability to a *legal* arrest that began as an *illegal* stop. A police officer can easily exploit the existence of such warrants by asking people for identification (which many people will present "voluntarily" on the assumption that they must comply) or by demanding it (when people refuse to comply or assert their rights). If the identification check reveals that the person has an outstanding warrant, the officer may proceed to *legally* arrest them even if the demand for the identification occurred in the context of an *illegal* seizure.

And what if it turns out that the person the officer stops does not have a warrant? The officer will simply send that person on her way. While the pressure to make stops, generate revenue, and make arrests in policing-for-revenue schemes often is enormous, the disincentives that might keep an officer from making such illegal stops are trivial. Worst case, the person subject to an illegal stop may file a formal complaint against the officer, though it is highly unlikely. Certainly, they won't file a lawsuit—would you?

Predatory Policing As Sexual Violence

In addition to being economically extractive and revenue-generating, predatory policing can also be sexually violent. The 2015 conviction of a former Oklahoma City police officer Daniel Holtzclaw on eighteen counts of sexual assault while on duty, including rape, forcible oral sodomy, and sexual battery is a case in point.[70] Though the case warranted more media attention than it received, the prosecution of Daniel Holtzclaw, and the fact that he was subsequently sentenced to 263 years in prison, raised public consciousness about the predatory nature of sexual violence committed by the police.[71]

Sexual assault is the second-most reported form of police misconduct in the United States—perhaps marking it as a prototypical form of predatory policing.[72] That statistic is all the more alarming when one keeps in mind the systemic underreporting of sexual violence,[73] an underreporting that likely is particularly acute in the context of police sexual violence.

As Kimberlé Crenshaw has observed, Black women and girls are especially vulnerable to sexual violence because of the multiple ways in which they are disadvantaged in society and because Black women and girls have labored under the stereotypes that they are sexually deviant and promiscuous.[74] Andrea Ritchie similarly contends that the intersection of race and gender can structure sexual violence vulnerability. According to Ritchie, women of color, including trans women and cis women who do not fit within the normative boundaries of male and female heterosexuality, are salient targets for police violence, including sexual assault.[75] Crenshaw's and Ritchie's work suggests that Holtzclaw likely preyed upon the Black women he sexually violated exactly because he perceived them to be vulnerable and marginalized.[76]

The thirteen women who accused him were between the ages of seventeen and fifty-seven, and they were all Black.[77] Most of the women were poor and lived in the most economically depressed neighborhoods of Oklahoma, where Holtzclaw was assigned to patrol.[78] Some had pending warrants for unpaid tickets or had prior criminal records, including for sex work and substance use, making them more vulnerable to being arrested.[79]

Holtzclaw likely understood that he could target these women because he held immense power over their personhood and bodily autonomy as a police officer.[80] From the outset, these women were in a weak position to say "no"—any initial resistance to Holtzclaw would eventually give way to coerced compliance upon threat of arrest. Arrests are costly not just because of the stigma they impose and the material conditions of jails, but also because of the economic extraction they effectuate.

Many people may not know that some states enforce police investigation fees for arrests as well as booking fees.[81] If the arrest involves a vehicle, the arrestee may be required to pay impound fees.[82] More generally, people who are arrested also face fees for "law enforcement costs and pretrial detention."[83] For instance, Texas has a $50 fee for the execution of an arrest warrant, as well as a fee of 15 cents per mile traveled by a police officer.[84] Making matters worse, people who are jailed sometimes have to pay for their incarceration.[85] In Florida, there is a "subsistence fee" of several dollars a day.[86] North Carolina, meanwhile, charges $10 a day for its pre-conviction jail fee.[87]

People who manage to post bond may also find themselves paying fees to secure their freedom. The revenue that can be generated from these fees is significant. For example, New Orleans collected $1.7 million in bond fees in 2015,[88] and New York courts can keep up to 3 percent of any bail payment.[89]

People for whom the courts appoint attorneys may be charged a "contribution" at the time of appointment, including application fees, user fees, administrative fees, and others.[90] Application fees range "from $10 in New Mexico to $480 in Wisconsin."[91] Jurisdictions may also attempt "recoupment" for the costs of appointed counsel even in situations where defendants are acquitted or otherwise not convicted.[92] Florida has recoupment fees of $50 "minimum for misdemeanors and $100 for felonies."[93] Florida even has a $50 fee in order to file for a determination of indigency![94]

All of the foregoing would be bad enough. But as you've already learned back when we were focused on Ferguson, jurisdictions also add on fees just for the process of making payments or for failing to do so. North Carolina imposes a "$25 late fee for failure to pay a fine or other court cost on time and a $20 surcharge to set up an installment payment plan."[95] In New Mexico, failing to pay fines and fees results in a bench warrant and a corresponding $100 bench warrant fee as well as a $30 fee to reinstate the person's license.[96] Finally, Florida also suspends drivers' licenses for a lack of payment, and reinstatement costs there can add up to hundreds of dollars.[97] All of this is Ferguson redux. And, the unfortunate reality is that every state, including Oklahoma, has at least some of these fee structures on their books.[98]

While the women whom Holtzclaw targeted need not have had knowledge of the precise details of the foregoing fees, they likely understood that being arrested could end up costing them an arm and a leg. The women's economic precarity in that regard made Holtzclaw's "bargaining power"—his ability to get the women to do whatever he wanted them to do—particularly strong.

Holtzclaw's bargaining power may also have strengthened by his sense that any thoughts the women had about reporting his sexual violence would give way to reticence and then silence, given their perceived lack of respectability and credibility, particularly against a police officer.[99] Although some of the women told their family members, boyfriends, and friends that Holtzclaw had sexually assaulted them, only one of them reported the incident to the police.[100] By and large, the women were "so terrified of police—or resigned to the fact that the system is designed to protect officers and white America, not Black victims—that he knew he could threaten them with jail if they dared to refuse or report him."[101]

Particularly relevant to this point is that the only woman who reported Holtzclaw's assault was Jannie Ligons, a fifty-seven-year-old Black grandmother who did not live in the poor neighborhood that Holtzclaw patrolled.[102] Unlike the rest of the survivors, Ligons was not poor and she reported the assault immediately after it happened.[103] After Holtzclaw was convicted, Ligons stated, "I wasn't a criminal. I have no record. I didn't do anything wrong . . . I was innocent, and he just picked the wrong lady to stop that night."[104] It was not until Ligons, the least economically marginalized of the women, and who did not live in the community Holtzclaw patrolled, reported her account of sexual violence that the other women came forward.

Significantly, it is not clear whether *any* of the women Holtzclaw assaulted were involved in criminal activity when he stopped them.[105] This is important, not because Holtzclaw's conduct would have been any less disturbing had the women been committing a crime when he stopped them, but because Holtzclaw had no real reason to interact with these women to begin with.

But that doesn't matter. Remember from Chapter 1: Police officers are empowered to approach and question people even when they have no reason to believe that such people have done anything wrong. Pedestrian checks of that sort don't trigger the Fourth Amendment. Moreover, as you've learned from this chapter, if an officer is really motivated to arrest someone, mass criminalization makes it easy for officers to establish the requisite probable cause to do so.

Moreover, every jurisdiction in the United States likely has some form of a "failure to comply with an officer" offense on the books, which officers might charge even if their commands are unlawful and a person's resistance to those commands are lawful. For example, residents in Ferguson complained about the extent to which Ferguson police officers weaponized non-compliance; when people refused to comply, they were arrested.[106] Tellingly, Black residents comprised almost all of the "failure to comply," "resisting arrest," "disturbing the peace," and "failure to obey" charges.[107] That these charges did not often stick—meaning they are not followed by prosecution or conviction—doesn't negate the incentive to comply with an officer's commands to avoid the burden, stigma, and economic costs of being arrested.

It was precisely this coercive incentive to cooperate that Holtzclaw exploited when he approached women and asked them to produce some form of identification. Upon receiving their identification, he ran their names through law enforcement databases for existing warrants and to check their arrest records (think back to our discussion about *mass criminalization* and warrant checks—the former encourages the latter).[108] After determining that some of the women had outstanding warrants for unpaid tickets, Holtzclaw leveraged that information to enact a kind of "quid pro quo" police sexual violence.[109]

In the workplace sexual harassment context, quid pro quo cases involve supervisors who demand sexual acts from employees with less power. In Holtzclaw's case, he threatened to use his power as a police officer to arrest women who refused his sexual advances.[110] More generally, Holtzclaw used his police authority and constant presence in the community to harass and psychologically intimidate the women.[111] He stalked at least three of them, with one moving her family to another part of town after he came looking for her at her home three times.[112]

These women were bargaining under the twin shadows of

Holtzclaw's power and their vulnerability. Holtzclaw's power and the women's vulnerability were shaped by the presumptive legitimacy of police conduct, the invisibility of sexual assault as a form of police violence, the historical myth that Black women cannot be sexually violated, and the unfortunate reality that these particular women were unlikely to become icons of victimization around whom the public at large or even the Black community specifically would organize.[113]

Below is a visual representation of some of the different types of predatory policing: civil asset forfeiture, citations and fines, and sexual violence. It is significant that each of these manifestations of predatory policing occurs against a backdrop of the possibility of arrest. In this sense a police officer's power to arrest serves as a gateway to predatory policing.

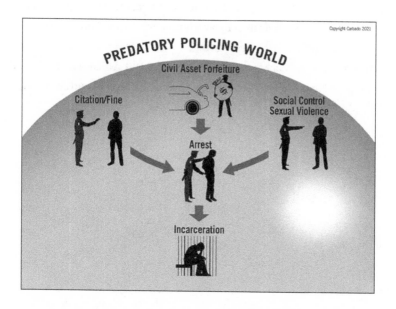

The image reveals not only that all pathways in the system of predatory policing can lead to arrest and incarceration, but also that the moments up to and including incarceration are moments of indebt-edness, economic extraction, and capital accumulation for the state. And because predatory policing is likely to affect the same person multiple times, each new police contact is likely to place them further into debt. Furthermore, they will be less able to pay new fines and fees, which can lead to more serious enforcement actions.

In Ferguson, for example, it was not uncommon for Black residents to find themselves incarcerated for up to three days if they did not have the means to post bail, though this is hardly unique to that city.[114] As legal scholar Jocelyn Simonson has noted, at any given time in the U.S., there are nearly half a million people in pre-trial detention simply because they cannot afford to pay bail. This includes people who are arrested for precisely the kind of minor infractions upon which mass criminalization rests.[115] When we add money bail to the problem of predatory policing, we end up with a criminal legal system in which racially and economically marginalized people are forced to pay for their own incarceration, for the exploitative, racial-ized policing that put them there, and for their freedom. And all of this against the background of a constitutional Amendment that is supposed to protect them from "unreasonable searches and seizures."

Chapter Six
Unreasonable

One of the clearest examples of how Fourth Amendment law under-protects Black people is *Whren v. United States*. My surmise is that it's a case about which you know nothing. Indeed, you may not even have heard the case name. Have you? Because I spent the prior chapters describing how the Supreme Court has interpreted the Fourth Amendment, I wanted to create space for the Supreme Court to speak in its own voice, in this instance through *Whren v. United States*. Armed with what you've learned in this book, your job is to read the case for yourself and make sense of it.

As you engage the opinion, keep the following in mind. First, remember from Chapter 2 that *Whren* was a unanimous opinion. Not a single justice dissented. Second, the case is not about whether there is a seizure, but about whether the seizure (in this instance, the traffic stop) the officers effectuated is reasonable. Third, stop reading after you've gotten through the first paragraph. Then, ask yourself this: Does that paragraph contain any clue that what's at stake in the case is whether the Supreme Court would name, condemn, and mitigate the degree to which "Driving While Black" had, by the 1990s, become a core feature of African American life? Finally, when you return to the case, keep track of the number of times the Court references race (not many) and what the Court says about race and policing more generally (essentially nothing, except to insist that its Fourth Amendment hands are tied). The opinion is a prelude to Chapter 7, which presents a rewritten version of the case, one that makes the precarity of Black life a matter of constitutional concern.

517 U.S. 806 (1996)

WHREN et al.
v.
UNITED STATES

UNITED STATES SUPREME COURT.

Scalia, J., delivered the opinion for a unanimous Court.

In this case we decide whether the temporary detention of a motorist who the police have probable cause to believe has committed a civil traffic violation is inconsistent with the Fourth Amendment's prohibition against unreasonable seizures unless a reasonable officer would have been motivated to stop the car by a desire to enforce the traffic laws.

I

On the evening of June 10, 1993, plainclothes vice-squad officers of the District of Columbia Metropolitan Police Department were patrolling a "high drug area" of the city in an unmarked car. Their suspicions were aroused when they passed a dark Pathfinder truck with temporary license plates and youthful occupants waiting at a stop sign, the driver looking down into the lap of the passenger at his right. The truck remained stopped at the intersection for what seemed an unusually long time—more than 20 seconds. When the police car executed a U-turn in order to head back toward the truck, the Pathfinder turned suddenly to its right, without signaling, and sped off at an "unreasonable" speed. The policemen followed, and in a short while overtook the Pathfinder when it stopped behind other traffic at a red light. They pulled up alongside, and Officer Ephraim Soto stepped out and approached the driver's door, identifying himself as a police officer and directing the driver, petitioner Brown, to put the vehicle in park. When Soto drew up to the driver's window, he immediately observed two large plastic bags of what appeared to be crack cocaine in petitioner Whren's hands. Petitioners were arrested, and quantities of several types of illegal drugs were retrieved from the vehicle.

Petitioners were charged in a four-count indictment with violating various federal drug laws, including 21 U.S.C. §§ 844(a) and 860(a). At a pretrial suppression hearing, they challenged the legality of the stop and the resulting seizure of the drugs. They argued that the stop had not been justified by probable cause to believe, or even reasonable suspicion, that petitioners were engaged in illegal drug-dealing activity; and that Officer Soto's asserted ground for approaching the vehicle—to give the driver a warning concerning traffic violations—was pretextual. The District Court denied the suppression motion, concluding that "the facts of the stop were not controverted," and "[t]here was nothing to really demonstrate that the actions of the officers were contrary to a normal traffic stop." App. 5.

Petitioners were convicted of the counts at issue here. The Court of Appeals affirmed the convictions, holding with respect to the suppression issue that, "regardless of whether a police officer subjectively believes that the occupants of an automobile may be engaging in some other illegal behavior, a traffic stop is permissible as long as a reasonable officer in the same circumstances *could have* stopped the car for the suspected traffic violation." 53 F. 3d 371, 374–375 (CADC 1995). We granted certiorari. 516 U.S. 1036 (1996).

II

The Fourth Amendment guarantees "[t]he right of the people to be secure in their persons, houses, papers, and effects, against unreasonable searches and seizures." Temporary detention of individuals during the stop of an automobile by the police, even if only for a brief period and for a limited purpose, constitutes a "seizure" of "persons" within the meaning of this provision. See *Delaware v. Prouse*, 440 U.S. 648, 653 (1979); *United States v. Martinez-Fuerte*, 428 U.S. 543, 556 (1976); *United States v. Brignoni-Ponce*, 422 U.S. 873, 878 (1975). An automobile stop is thus subject to the constitutional imperative that it not be "unreasonable" under the circumstances. As a general matter, the decision to stop an automobile is reasonable where the police have probable cause to believe that a traffic violation has occurred. See *Prouse*, *supra*, at 659; *Pennsylvania v. Mimms*, 434 U.S. 106, 109 (1977) (*per curiam*).

Petitioners accept that Officer Soto had probable cause to believe that various provisions of the District of Columbia traffic code had been violated. See 18 D.C. Mun. Regs. §§ 2213.4 (1995) ("An operator shall . . . give full time and attention to the operation of the vehicle"); 2204.3 ("No person shall turn any vehicle . . . without giving an appropriate signal"); 2200.3 ("No person shall drive a vehicle . . . at a speed greater than is reasonable and prudent under the conditions"). They argue, however, that "in the unique context of civil traffic regulations" probable cause is not enough. Since, they contend, the use of automobiles is so heavily and minutely regulated that total compliance with traffic and safety rules is nearly impossible, a police officer will almost invariably be able to catch any given motorist in a technical violation. This creates the temptation to use traffic stops as a means of investigating other law violations, as to which no probable cause or even articulable suspicion exists. Petitioners, who are both black, further contend that police officers might decide which motorists to stop based on decidedly impermissible factors, such as the race of the car's occupants. To avoid this danger, they say, the Fourth Amendment test for traffic stops should be, not the normal one (applied by the Court of Appeals) of whether probable cause existed to justify the stop; but rather, whether a police officer, acting reasonably, would have made the stop for the reason given.

A

Petitioners contend that the standard they propose is consistent with our past cases' disapproval of police attempts to use valid bases of action against citizens as pretexts for pursuing other investigatory agendas. We are reminded that in *Florida v. Wells*, 495 U.S. 1, 4 (1990), we stated that an "inventory search[1] must not be a ruse for a general rummaging in order

---

1.   An inventory search is the search of property lawfully seized and detained, in order to ensure that it is harmless, to secure valuable items (such as might be kept in a towed car), and to protect against false claims of loss or damage. See *South Dakota v. Opperman*, 428 U.S. 364, 369, 49 L. Ed. 2d 1000, 96 S. Ct. 3092 (1976).

to discover incriminating evidence"; that in *Colorado v. Bertine*, 479 U.S. 367, 372 (1987), in approving an inventory search, we apparently thought it significant that there had been "no showing that the police, who were following standardized procedures, acted in bad faith or for the sole purpose of investigation"; and that in *New York v. Burger*, 482 U.S. 691, 716–717, n. 27 (1987), we observed, in upholding the constitutionality of a warrantless administrative inspection,[2] that the search did not appear to be "a 'pretext' for obtaining evidence of . . . violation of . . . penal laws." But only an undiscerning reader would regard these cases as endorsing the principle that ulterior motives can invalidate police conduct that is justifiable on the basis of probable cause to believe that a violation of law has occurred. In each case we were addressing the validity of a search conducted in the *absence* of probable cause. Our quoted statements simply explain that the exemption from the need for probable cause (and warrant), which is accorded to searches made for the purpose of inventory or administrative regulation, is not accorded to searches that are *not* made for those purposes. See *Bertine*, *supra*, at 371–372; *Burger*, *supra*, at 702–703.

Petitioners also rely upon *Colorado v. Bannister*, 449 U.S. 1 (1980) (*per curiam*), a case which, like this one, involved a traffic stop as the prelude to a plainview sighting and arrest on charges wholly unrelated to the basis for the stop. Petitioners point to our state-

---

2. An administrative inspection is the inspection of business premises conducted by authorities responsible for enforcing a pervasive regulatory scheme—for example, unannounced inspection of a mine for compliance with health and safety standards. See *Donovan v. Dewey*, 452 U.S. 594, 599–605, 69 L. Ed. 2d 262, 101 S. Ct. 2534 (1981).

ment that "[t]here was no evidence whatsoever that the officer's presence to issue a traffic citation was a pretext to confirm any other previous suspicion about the occupants" of the car. *Id.*, at 4, n. 4. That dictum *at most* demonstrates that the Court in *Bannister* found no need to inquire into the question now under discussion; not that it was certain of the answer. And it may demonstrate even less than that: If by "pretext" the Court meant that the officer really had not seen the car speeding, the statement would mean only that there was no reason to doubt probable cause for the traffic stop.

It would, moreover, be anomalous, to say the least, to treat a statement in a footnote in the *per curiam Bannister* opinion as indicating a reversal of our prior law. Petitioners' difficulty is not simply a lack of affirmative support for their position. Not only have we never held, outside the context of inventory search or administrative inspection (discussed above), that an officer's motive invalidates objectively justifiable behavior under the Fourth Amendment; but we have repeatedly held and asserted the contrary. In *United States v. Villamonte-Marquez*, 462 U.S. 579, 584, n. 3 (1983), we held that an otherwise valid warrantless boarding of a vessel by customs officials was not rendered invalid "because the customs officers were accompanied by a Louisiana state policeman, and were following an informant's tip that a vessel in the ship channel was thought to be carrying marihuana." We flatly dismissed the idea that an ulterior motive might serve to strip the agents of their legal justification. In *United States v. Robinson*, 414 U.S. 218 (1973), we held that a traffic-violation arrest (of the sort here) would not be rendered invalid by the fact that it was "a mere pretext for a narcotics search," *id.*, at 221, n. 1; and that a lawful postarrest search of the person would not be rendered invalid by the fact that it was not motivated by the officer-safety concern that justifies such searches, see *id.*, at 236. See also *Gustafson v. Florida*, 414 U.S. 260, 266 (1973). And in *Scott v. United States*, 436 U.S. 128, 138 (1978), in rejecting the contention that wiretap evidence was subject to exclusion because the agents conducting the tap had failed to make any effort to comply with the statutory requirement that unauthorized acquisitions be minimized, we said that "[s]ubjective intent alone . . . does not make otherwise lawful conduct illegal or unconstitutional." We described *Robinson* as having established that "the fact that the officer does not have the state of mind which is hypothecated by the reasons which provide the legal justification for the officer's action does not invalidate the action taken as long as the circumstances, viewed objectively, justify that action." 436 U.S., at 136, 138.

We think these cases foreclose any argument that the constitutional reasonableness of traffic stops depends on the actual motivations of the individual officers involved. We of course agree with petitioners that the Constitution prohibits selective enforcement of the law based on considerations such as race. But the constitutional basis for objecting to intentionally discriminatory application of laws is the Equal Protection Clause, not the Fourth Amendment. Subjective intentions play no role in ordinary, probable-cause Fourth Amendment analysis.

B

Recognizing that we have been unwilling to entertain Fourth Amendment challenges based on the actual motivations of individual officers, petitioners disavow any intention to make the individual officer's subjective good faith the touchstone of "reasonableness." They insist that the standard they have put forward—whether the officer's conduct deviated materially from usual police practices, so that a reasonable officer in the same circumstances would not have made the stop for the reasons given—is an "objective" one.

But although framed in empirical terms, this approach is plainly and indisputably driven by subjective considerations. Its whole purpose is to prevent the police from doing under the guise of enforcing the traffic code what they would like to do for different reasons. Petitioners' proposed standard may not use the word "pretext," but it is designed to combat nothing other than the perceived "danger" of the pretextual stop, albeit only indirectly and over the run of cases. Instead of asking whether the individual officer had the proper state of mind, the petitioners would have us ask, in effect, whether (based on general police practices) it is plausible to believe that the officer had the proper state of mind.

Why one would frame a test designed to combat pretext in such fashion that the court cannot take into account *actual and admitted pretext* is a curiosity that can only be explained by the fact that our cases have foreclosed the more sensible option. If those cases were based only upon the evidentiary difficulty of establishing subjective intent, petitioners' attempt to root out subjective vices through objective means might make sense. But they were not based only upon that, or indeed even principally upon that. Their principal basis—which applies equally to attempts to reach subjective intent through ostensibly objective means—is simply that the Fourth Amendment's concern with "reasonableness" allows certain actions to be taken in certain circumstances, *whatever* the subjective intent. See, *e.g., Robinson, supra,* at 236 ("Since it is the fact of custodial arrest which gives rise to the authority to search, it is of no moment that [the officer] did not indicate any subjective fear of the [arrestee] or that he did not himself suspect that [the arrestee] was armed") (footnotes omitted); *Gustafson, supra,* at 266 (same). But even if our concern had been only an evidentiary one, petitioners' proposal would by no means assuage it. Indeed, it seems to us somewhat easier to figure out the intent of an individual officer than to plumb the collective consciousness of law enforcement in order to determine whether a "reasonable officer" would have been moved to act upon the traffic violation. While police manuals and standard procedures may sometimes provide objective assistance, ordinarily one would be reduced to speculating about the hypothetical reaction of a hypothetical constable—an exercise that might be called virtual subjectivity.

Moreover, police enforcement practices, even if they could be practicably assessed by a judge, vary from place to place and from time to time. We cannot accept that the search and seizure protections of the Fourth Amendment are so variable, cf. *Gustafson, supra,* at 265; *United States v. Caceres,* 440 U.S. 741, 755–756 (1979), and can be made to turn upon such trivialities. The difficulty is illustrated by petitioners' arguments in this case. Their claim that a reasonable officer would not have made this stop is based largely on District of Columbia police regulations which permit plainclothes officers in unmarked vehicles to enforce traffic laws "only in the case of a violation that is so grave as to pose an *immediate threat* to the safety of others." Metropolitan Police Department, Washington, D. C., General Order 303.1, pt. 1, Objectives and Policies (A)(2)(4) (Apr. 30, 1992), reprinted as Addendum to Brief for Petitioners. This basis of invalidation would not apply in jurisdictions that had a different practice. And it would not have applied even in the District of Columbia, if Officer Soto had been wearing a uniform or patrolling in a marked police cruiser.

Petitioners argue that our cases support insistence upon police adherence to standard practices as an objective means of rooting out pretext. They cite no holding to that effect, and dicta in only two cases. In *Abel v. United States*, 362 U.S. 217 (1960), the petitioner had been arrested by the Immigration and Naturalization Service (INS), on the basis of an administrative warrant that, he claimed, had been issued on pretextual grounds in order to enable the Federal Bureau of Investigation (FBI) to search his room after his arrest. We regarded this as an allegation of "serious misconduct," but rejected Abel's claims on the ground that "[a] finding of bad faith is . . . not open to us on th[e] record" in light of the findings below, including the finding that "'the proceedings taken by the [INS] differed in no respect from what would have been done in the case of an individual concerning whom [there was no pending FBI investigation],'" *id.*,

at 226–227. But it is a long leap from the proposition
that following regular procedures is some evidence of
lack of pretext to the proposition that failure to follow regular procedures *proves* (or is an operational
substitute for) pretext. *Abel*, moreover, did not involve
the assertion that pretext could invalidate a search or
seizure for which there was probable cause—and even
what it said about pretext in other contexts is plainly
inconsistent with the views we later stated in *Robinson, Gustafson, Scott*, and *Villamonte-Marquez*. In the
other case claimed to contain supportive dicta, *United
States v. Robinson*, 414 U.S. 218 (1973), in approving
a search incident to an arrest for driving without a
license, we noted that the arrest was "not a departure
from established police department practice." *Id.*, at
221, n. 1. That was followed, however, by the statement that "[w]e leave for another day questions which
would arise on facts different from these." *Ibid.* This is
not even a dictum that purports to provide an answer,
but merely one that leaves the question open.

III

In what would appear to be an elaboration on the "reasonable officer" test, petitioners argue that the balancing inherent in any Fourth Amendment inquiry
requires us to weigh the governmental and individual interests implicated in a traffic stop such as we
have here. That balancing, petitioners claim, does not
support investigation of minor traffic infractions by
plainclothes police in unmarked vehicles; such investigation only minimally advances the government's
interest in traffic safety, and may indeed retard it by

producing motorist confusion and alarm—a view said to be supported by the Metropolitan Police Department's own regulations generally prohibiting this practice. And as for the Fourth Amendment interests of the individuals concerned, petitioners point out that our cases acknowledge that even ordinary traffic stops entail "a possibly unsettling show of authority"; that they at best "interfere with freedom of movement, are inconvenient, and consume time" and at worst "may create substantial anxiety," *Prouse*, 440 U.S., at 657. That anxiety is likely to be even more pronounced when the stop is conducted by plainclothes officers in unmarked cars.

It is of course true that in principle every Fourth Amendment case, since it turns upon a "reasonableness" determination, involves a balancing of all relevant factors. With rare exceptions not applicable here, however, the result of that balancing is not in doubt where the search or seizure is based upon probable cause. That is why petitioners must rely upon cases like *Prouse* to provide examples of actual "balancing" analysis. There, the police action in question was a random traffic stop for the purpose of checking a motorist's license and vehicle registration, a practice that—like the practices at issue in the inventory search and administrative inspection cases upon which petitioners rely in making their "pretext" claim—involves police intrusion *without the probable cause that is its traditional justification.* Our opinion in *Prouse* expressly distinguished the case from a stop based on precisely what is at issue here: "probable cause to believe that a driver is violating any one of the multitude of applicable traffic and equipment regulations." *Id.*, at 661. It noted approvingly that "[t]he foremost method of enforcing traffic and vehicle safety regulations . . . is acting upon observed violations," *id.*, at 659, which afford the "'quantum of individualized suspicion'" necessary to ensure that police discretion is sufficiently constrained, *id.*, at 654–655 (quoting *United States v. Martinez-Fuerte*, 428 U.S., at 560). What is true of *Prouse* is also true of other cases that engaged in detailed "balancing" to decide the constitutionality of automobile stops, such as *Martinez-Fuerte*, which upheld checkpoint stops, see 428 U.S., at 556–562, and *Brignoni-Ponce*, which disallowed so-called "roving patrol" stops, see 422 U.S., at 882–884: The detailed "balancing" analysis was necessary because they involved seizures without probable cause.

Where probable cause has existed, the only cases in which we have found it necessary actually to perform the "balancing" analysis involved searches or seizures conducted in an extraordinary manner, unusually harmful to an individual's privacy or even physical interests—such as, for example, seizure by means of deadly force, see *Tennessee v. Garner*, 471 U.S. 1 (1985), unannounced entry into a home, see *Wilson v. Arkansas*, 514 U.S. 927 (1995), entry into a home without a warrant, see *Welsh v. Wisconsin*, 466 U.S. 740 (1984), or physical penetration of the body, see *Winston v. Lee*, 470 U.S. 753 (1985). The making of a traffic stop out of uniform does not remotely qualify as such an extreme practice, and so is governed by the usual rule that probable cause to believe the law has been broken "outbalances" private interest in avoiding police contact.

Petitioners urge as an extraordinary factor in this case that the "multitude of applicable traffic and equipment regulations" is so large and so difficult to obey perfectly that virtually everyone is guilty of violation, permitting the police to single out almost whomever they wish for a stop. But we are aware of no principle that would allow us to decide at what point a code of law becomes so expansive and so commonly violated that infraction itself can no longer be the ordinary measure of the lawfulness of enforcement. And even if we could identify such exorbitant codes, we do not know by what standard (or what right) we would decide, as petitioners would have us do, which particular provisions are sufficiently important to merit enforcement.

For the run-of-the-mine case, which this surely is, we think there is no realistic alternative to the traditional common law rule that probable cause justifies a search and seizure.

———

Here the District Court found that the officers had probable cause to believe that petitioners had violated the traffic code. That rendered the stop reasonable under the Fourth Amendment, the evidence thereby discovered admissible, and the upholding of the convictions by the Court of Appeals for the District of Columbia Circuit correct. The judgment is

Affirmed.

Chapter Seven
Reasonable

For this final chapter I have drawn on a prior essay I wrote with law professor Jonathan Feingold to rewrite *Whren v. United States,* the Supreme Court case you read in the preceding chapter, to demonstrate the ease with which the Court could have incorporated race into its analysis. My approach not only disrupts the colorblind fiction that policing is race-neutral, it also opens the door to treating the precarity of Black life as a matter of serious constitutional concern when interpreting the Fourth Amendment.

Think back to the original *Whren* opinion. In no part of its analysis did the Court acknowledge the longstanding ways in which Black people (both individually and as a community) have suffered under various forms of policing in the United States. That omission is particularly disturbing if you consider how policing has—as a matter of law—helped to effectuate and maintain racial inequality throughout this country's history. The table below offers a simplified visual of what I mean:

Form of Policing	Form of Racial Subordination
Slave patrol policing	Slavery
Jim Crow policing	*De jure* segregation
Anti-protest/civil disobedience policing	*De jure* racial segregation Contemporary racial inequality
Order maintenance/proactive policing	Racial profiling, excessive force, stop-and-frisk Circumscribed freedom of movement
"War on Drugs" policing	Mass incarceration

Slave patrol policing propped up the institution of slavery by enforcing the criminalization of Black freedom (the act of "running away") as a form of theft. Jim Crow policing vigorously and violently enforced the pervasive borders of the colorline and in so doing entrenched formal racial segregation. Anti-protest/anti-civil rights policing target not only organizers and activists under the guise of maintaining "law and order," but also people perceived to be aligned with such causes. By restricting the acceptable expressions of dissent, anti-protest/anti-civil rights policing also limit the terms of Black political expression and erects barriers to dismantling historical and contemporary forms of racial inequality.

Order maintenance policing employs various law enforcement techniques, including those discussed in prior chapters (such as "pedestrian checks," "traffic stops," and "stops" and "frisks"), to violate Black people's privacy, sense of security, personal integrity, and dignity. More broadly, order maintenance policing imposes time, place, and manner restrictions on "when" Black people can be "where" doing "what"—effectively disciplining and exerting social control over their freedom and mobility. Finally, war-on-drugs policing—which rose in prominence as a law enforcement technique during the same period that colorblindness rose in prominence as a constitutional technique—helped to advance and legitimize mass incarceration. The relationship among colorblindness, war-on-drugs policing, and mass incarceration in that regard is precisely why Michele Alexander includes both "colorblindness" and "mass incarceration" in the title of her book, *The New Jim Crow: Mass Incarceration in the Age of Colorblindness*.

Needless to say, there is quite a lot more to say about the ways in which policing has long been an instrument of racial inequality. And yet in *Whren*, the Supreme Court is silent—nothing in the decision even hints at how policing has functioned as a racialized state practice, not to "protect and serve" Black people, but to discipline and social control them in ways that "protect and serve" the interests of white supremacy.

The opinion is also troubling in that the Court refused to make the argument that state-sanctioned racism is constitutionally unreasonable. Just because an officer has probable cause to believe that a person has committed a traffic infraction, should not mean that it is "reasonable" for that officer to use the driver's race to determine whether or not to take enforcement action. Nothing prevented the Court from ruling that such racial profiling was "unreasonable" under the Fourth Amendment—no constitutional text, no constitutional history, and no constitutional precedent.

As I mentioned in the introduction, by presenting a reimagined version of the *Whren* opinion, I do not intend to suggest that Black people can find our way out of being over-policed through legal reforms alone—we certainly cannot. But we cannot afford to cede the terrain of law completely; it plays too important a role in shaping how Black people are racially subordinated through police powers. In prior chapters, you learned about the racially pernicious ways that *legally sanctioned* police powers played out in Tanya's life. Wouldn't diminishing or abolishing those powers make her life at least somewhat less precarious?

For example, imagine if we abolished certain pedestrian checks, including the power officers have to approach, question, and to seek permission to search a person or belongings, when they have no reason to believe that the person has done anything wrong. Or suppose we abolished the power to conduct "stops" or "frisks," unless officers had probable cause. More radically, let's say we abolished the doctrine of reasonable suspicion altogether, raising the standard to probable cause across the board. Would Tanya be better off? Probably.

Minimizing police power could include interpreting the Fourth Amendment to require that police officers to show cause—other than the simple fact that a driver has committed a traffic infraction—to justify asking the driver or the passenger to exit the car. The law could also minimize an officer's power to use deadly force by making the question of whether an officer's use of force was reasonable turn on whether that use of force was necessary.

Each of these examples of abolishing or minimizing police powers targets the legal source of those powers, rather than "good" or "bad" officers—though none solves the problem of race and policing entirely. Because both strategies are fundamentally about limiting police power, they provide another entrance into the debate on defunding the police.

This brings us to my rewrite of *Whren v. United States*, which is itself an effort to diminish the scope of police power. The opinion demonstrates how the Supreme Court could have acknowledged and mitigated the criminalized experience of "Driving While Black" through a straightforward—almost literal—interpretation of the Fourth Amendment: namely, that racially motivated traffics stops are "unreasonable seizures."

I have attributed the opinion to the late Thurgood Marshall, the extraordinary civil rights lawyer who argued *Brown v. Board of Education*, and the first African American to serve on the Supreme Court. His constitutional jurisprudence routinely centered the experiences of the marginalized, the minoritized, and the forgotten.[1]

WHREN *v.* UNITED STATES
Opinion of the Court

JUSTICE MARSHALL delivered the opinion of the Court.

In this case, we decide whether it is consistent with the Fourth Amendment for a police officer who observed a traffic violation to use that violation as the justification to perform a racially-selective traffic stop, or as the pretext to investigate a crime for which the officer does not have probable cause. We answer that question in the negative.

I

On the evening of June 10, 1993, a team of District of Columbia (D.C.) plainclothes vice officers, were patrolling for drug activity in an unmarked car. Investigator Tony Howard drove the vehicle, in which officers Ephraim Soto, Jr. and Homer Littlejohn were also present.[1] While driving in Southeast D.C., the officers noticed two Black men sitting in a dark Nissan Pathfinder paused at a stop sign. The Pathfinder had temporary tags. Officer Soto testified that he had observed James Lester Brown, the driver, looking into the lap of Michael Whren, the passenger. As the officers proceeded slowly down the street, Soto continued to watch the Pathfinder. He testified that the

---

1. *United States v. Whren*, 53 F.3d 371, 372 (D.C. Cir. 1995).

Pathfinder remained stopped at the intersection for more than 20 seconds obstructing traffic behind it.[2]

Investigator Howard had already begun to make a U-turn to tail the Pathfinder when Soto instructed him to follow it. As the officers turned around, the Pathfinder turned without signaling. Officer Soto added that the Pathfinder "sped off quickly" and proceeded at an "unreasonable speed."[3]

The vice officers followed the Pathfinder to a different intersection, where it was surrounded by cars to its front, right, and rear. The officers boxed in the Pathfinder by pulling alongside its driver's side. Officer Soto then immediately exited his vehicle and approached the Pathfinder, identifying himself as a police officer. Officer Littlejohn followed a few steps behind.

Because the surrounding vehicles prevented Brown from pulling over, Officer Soto told Brown to place the Pathfinder in park. As he was speaking, Soto noticed that Whren was holding two large clear plastic bags that Soto suspected to contain cocaine. Upon seeing the bags, which Soto suspected but had no objective reason to believe contain cocaine, the officer yelled "C.S.A." to notify the other officers that he had observed a Controlled Substances Act violation.[4]

2.　Brief for Petitioners at 5, *Whren v. United States*, 517 U.S. 806 (Feb. 16, 1996) (No. 95-5841). Officers Soto and Littlejohn disagreed as to whether any cars were stopped behind the Pathfinder. Soto testified that at least one car was stopped behind the Pathfinder, but acknowledged that no car behind the Pathfinder honked or otherwise requested the Pathfinder to move. Officer Littlejohn testified that there were no vehicles waiting behind the Pathfinder. *Id.*

3.　*Id.* at 5–6.

4.　*Id.* at 8.

According to Officer Soto, as he reached for the driver's side door, Whren yelled "pull off, pull off."[5] Officer Soto then observed Whren pull the cover off a power window control panel in the passenger door and place one of the large bags into a hidden compartment. Officer Soto opened the driver's side door, dove across Brown, and grabbed the other bag from Whren's left hand. At the same moment, Officer Littlejohn pinned Brown to the driver's seat.

Multiple officers then arrested Brown and Whren and proceeded to search the Pathfinder. The officers recovered two tinfoil packets containing marijuana laced with PCP, a bag of chunky white rocks, a large white rock of crack cocaine, numerous unused Ziplock bags, a portable phone, and personal papers. Petitioners were charged in a four-count indictment for violating various federal drug laws, including 21 U.S.C. §§ 844(a) and 860(a).

II

At a pretrial suppression hearing, petitioners challenged the legality of the stop and the resulting seizure of the drugs. They argued that the officers lacked probable cause, or even reasonable suspicion, to believe that petitioners were engaged in illegal drug-dealing activity. Petitioners further argued that Officer Soto's asserted ground for approaching the vehicle was pretextual.

Petitioners advanced two separate pretext claims.

---

5. *Id.*

First, petitioners alleged that the stop was racially motivated—that is, the officers stopped petitioners because they were Black, not because they committed a traffic infraction. Second, Petitioners alleged that the officers' actual reasons for stopping them was investigatory—that is, the officers stopped petitioners to investigate whether they possessed drugs, not to enforce the vehicle code.

To support the foregoing claims, under normal circumstances, D.C. vice officers do not concern themselves with mundane traffic violations. According to the D.C. police regulations, plainclothes officers are permitted to make traffic stops "only in the case of a violation that is so grave as to pose an *immediate threat* to the safety of others."[6] Vice officers, on the other hand, have a mandate to "find narcotics activity going on."[7] Testifying at the District Court, Officer Soto elaborated:

"The only circumstances that I would issue tickets . . . is for just reckless, reckless driving, something that in my personal view would somehow endanger the safety of anybody who's walking around the street or even the occupants of a vehicle, maybe children or whoever."[8]

It appears clear that after Brown took a turn without signaling, the officers lacked any objective reason (probable cause or reasonable suspicion) to believe that Brown or Whren had done anything other than commit a minor traffic infraction. Nor is there any evi-

---

6. Metro. Police Dept., Wash., D.C., General Order 303.1, pt.1(A)(2)(a)(4) (Apr. 30, 1992)), *reprinted in* Brief for Petitioners, *supra* note 2, at Addendum.

7. Brief for Petitioners, *supra* note 2, at 4 (quoting the District Court transcript).

8. *Id.* at 7 (quoting the District Court transcript).

dence to suggest that the officers could have believed that the traffic infraction constituted "a violation that is so grave as to pose an immediate threat to the safety of others."[9]

When asked why he stopped the Pathfinder, Officer Soto testified that the driver was "not paying full time and attention to his driving."[10] Officer Soto made clear that he never intended to issue a ticket for any traffic infractions. Rather, he wished to stop the Pathfinder to inquire why it was obstructing traffic and why it sped off without signaling in a school area. When questioned, Officer Soto testified that the decision to stop the Pathfinder was not based upon the "racial profile" of Brown and Whren, but rather on the driver's behavior.[11]

The District Court denied petitioners' suppression motion. It concluded that "the facts of the stop were not controverted" and "[t]here was nothing to really demonstrate that the actions of the officers were contrary to a normal traffic stop."[12] Subsequently, the Petitioners were convicted of the subject counts.

The Court of Appeals for D.C. affirmed the convictions. The panel concluded that "regardless of whether a police officer subjectively believes that the occupants of an automobile may be engaging in some other illegal behavior, a traffic stop is permissible as long as a reasonable officer in the same circumstances *could have* stopped the car for the suspected traffic violation."[13] We granted certiorari.

---

9.   GENERAL ORDER 303.1, *supra* note 6.

10. Brief for Petitioners, *supra* note 2, at 5.

11. *Id.* at 10.

12. *Id.* at 9 (quoting the District Court opinion).

13. F.3d 371, 375 (D.C. Cir. 1995).

III

The Fourth Amendment to the United States Constitution guarantees "[t]he right of the people to be secure in their persons, houses, papers, and effects, against unreasonable searches and seizures." Where police temporarily detain an individual during an automobile stop, even if brief and for a limited purpose, it constitutes a "seizure" of "persons" under the Fourth Amendment.[14] Accordingly, such stops must be "reasonable" to pass constitutional scrutiny.[15] Under most circumstances, it is reasonable for the police to conduct such a stop if they have probable cause to believe that a traffic violation has occurred.[16] We hold today, however, that certain traffic stops remain unreasonable under the Fourth Amendment even where probable cause of a traffic infraction exists.

The petitioners concede that Officer Soto had probable cause to believe that they had violated various D.C. traffic codes.[17] They argue, however, that our Fourth Amendment jurisprudence does not—and should not—condone a rule that states that all traffic stops conducted with probable cause are *per se*

---

14. See *Delaware v. Prouse*, 440 U.S. 648, 653 (1979); *United States v. Martinez-Fuerte*, 428 U.S. 543, 556–58 (1976); *United States v. Brignoni-Ponce*, 422 U.S. 873, 878 (1975).

15. See *Terry v. Ohio*, 392 U.S. 1, 19 (1968).

16. See *Prouse*, 440 U.S. at 654 ("[T]he reasonableness standard usually requires, at a minimum, that the facts upon which an intrusion is based be capable of measurement against 'an objective standard,' whether this be probable cause or a less stringent test." (footnotes omitted)). See also *Pennsylvania v. Mimms*, 434 U.S. 106, 109 (1977) (per curiam).

17. See D.C. Mun. Regs. 18 Vehicles and Traffic §§ 2213.4 (1995) ("An operator shall . . . give full time and attention to the operation of the vehicle"); § 2204.3 ("No person shall turn any vehicle . . . without giving an appropriate signal"); 2200.3 ("No person shall drive a vehicle . . . at a speed greater than is reasonable and prudent under the conditions").

"reasonable." Specifically, the petitioners contend that "in the unique context of civil traffic regulations" probable cause is not always enough.[18]

Because automobile use is so heavily and minutely regulated that it is nearly impossible to comply with all traffic and safety rules all the time, the petitioners contend that a police officer could almost invariably catch a motorist in a technical violation. Accordingly, if evidence of a traffic infraction always satisfies constitutional requirements, police officers would enjoy a level of discretion that invites the sort of governmental abuses that the Fourth Amendment is designed to prevent.

Specifically, the petitioners allege that holding all such stops "reasonable" would provide cover for law enforcement officers to stop drivers for decidedly unreasonable reasons, such as the driver's race. Moreover, they suggest that such a rule would embolden police to conduct pretextual stops used to investigate unlawful conduct for which the officers have no reasonable suspicion or probable cause to believe has occurred. To avoid this danger, petitioners argue that the Fourth Amendment test for traffic stops should not simply ask if an officer had probable cause to justify a stop, but whether that stop is indeed reasonable.

We agree.

We first explain why enforcing traffic laws in a racially discriminatory manner is unreasonable under the Fourth Amendment—even if officers have probable cause that a traffic violation occurred. We then discuss why pretextual stops, whereby officers employ

---

18. *Whren v. United States*, 517 U.S. 806, 810 (1996).

traffic stops to investigate unrelated crimes for which they lack probable cause, are also unreasonable under the Fourth Amendment.

A

Racialized policing is one of the most pernicious forms of state-sanctioned racism and remains a core feature of this nation's history.[19] The formal policing of African Americans stretches back at least as far as the slave codes, which codified into law extreme deprivations of life and liberty, and lay a legal groundwork for slave patrols—themselves a state-sanctioned tool to suppress antislavery resistance.[20] In a 1904 essay on the topic, W. E. B. Du Bois detailed how slave patrols formed a critical part of slavery's overarching framework:

"[T]he private well-ordering and control of slaves called for careful co-operation among masters. The fear of insurrection was ever before the South . . . [and the] result was a system of rural police . . . whose work

---

19. Regrettably, this Court has long been complicit in various forms of racial inequality. See *Regents of Univ. of California v. Bakke*, 438 U.S. 265, 391 (1978) (Marshall, J., dissenting) (describing how soon after Reconstruction, "with the assistance of this Court, the Negro was rapidly stripped of his new civil rights"); *id.*, at 402 ("After the Civil War our Government started several 'affirmative action' programs. This Court in the *Civil Rights Cases* and *Plessy v. Ferguson* destroyed the movement toward complete equality. For almost a century no action was taken, and this nonaction was with the tacit approval of the courts. Then we had *Brown v. Board of Education* and the Civil Rights Acts of Congress, followed by numerous affirmative-action programs. *Now*, we have this Court again stepping in, this time to stop affirmative-action programs of the type used by the University of California.").

20. As one example, the State of Georgia framed the need for a 1757 law establishing and regulating slave patrols as follows: "Patrols should be established under the proper Regulations in the settled parts thereof, for the better keeping of Negroes and other Slaves in Order and prevention of any Cabals, Insurrections or other Irregularities amongst them." Philip L Reichel, *Southern Slave Patrols as a Transitional Police Type*, 7. Am. J. Police 51, 56 (1988).

it was to stop the nocturnal wandering and meeting of slaves. It was usually an effective organization, which terrorized the slaves, and to which all white men belong, and were liable to active detailed duty at regular intervals."[21]

It should go without saying that racially discriminatory policing has no place in our constitutional democracy. That is precisely why many of the procedural safeguards that undergird our modern constitutional criminal procedure—from *Brown v. Mississippi*, 297 U.S. 278 (1936) to *Miranda v. Arizona*, 384 U.S. 436 (1966)—were a response (at least in part) to racially selective policing.

We also recognize that this Court has, at times, favored police power over individual rights in ways that render communities of color—and the African American community in particular—vulnerable to police surveillance, discipline, and social control. Our decision in *Terry v. Ohio*, 392 U.S. 1 (1968), which permitted police officers to stop and frisk people on the thinnest of justification and without probable cause is one relevant example. Even so, concerns about racially discriminatory policing have long informed much of our constitutional criminal procedure. We refuse to jettison those concerns today.

B

In deciding whether racially selective traffic stops are a permissible law enforcement practice, even in the

---

21. W.E.B. Du Bois, Some Notes on Negro Crime, Particularly in Georgia 3 (Atlanta University Press 1904).

presence of probable cause of a traffic violation, we must balance the "intrusion on the individual's Fourth Amendment interests against [the] promotion of legitimate governmental interests."[22] Under the facts of this case, we find it quite clear that the individual's interests outweigh those of the Government.

Rightfully, the Government does not argue that it has an interest in performing race-based traffic stops. Instead, it identifies an interest in promoting public safety through the enforcement of its traffic laws. Although valid, this interest deserves minimal deference where, as occurred here, plainclothes officers contravened departmental policy to enforce a minor traffic infraction that posed a minimal risk to public safety.

In contrast, the individual's Fourth Amendment privacy interests in freedom from unreasonable searches and seizures are substantial. The Government implies that a traffic stop, even when racially motivated, "poses only a modest intrusion on the motorist's privacy interests."[23] This characterization misunderstands the qualitatively distinct intrusion caused by *racially selective* police conduct—traffic stop or otherwise, probable cause or not.

To begin, racially selective policing compromises privacy and dignity by rendering its targets public spectacles, "something exhibited to view; . . . a remarkable or noteworthy sight; an object of curiosity or contempt."[24] Exposure to this form of racial humiliation

---

22. Brief for Petitioners, *supra* note 2, at 39 (quoting *United States v. Villamonte-Marquez*, 462 U.S. 579, 588 (1983)).

23. Brief for the United States at 9, *Whren v. United States*, 517 U.S. 806 (Mar. 15, 1996) (No. 95-5841).

24. Webster's Third New Intern'l Dictionary 218 (3d ed. 1986).

undermines one's personal sense of security, rendering them insecure in their own "person."[25] Indeed, widespread accounts of racial profiling often highlight the stigma and humiliation that derive from what people experience as a form of public shaming.[26] The apparent ubiquity of racial profiling has engendered a pithy if demoralizing turn of phrase: "driving while Black."[27]

At its core, racial profiling is pernicious precisely because it legitimizes the idea that one racial group's privacy, dignity, and security may be sacrificed for the "greater good"—a sacrifice that others are never asked, nor expected, to bear. That sacrifice can only be considered the "greater" good if you do not account for those experiencing the harm.

In the present context, the greater good is the "war on drugs." Crude stereotypes link drug use, criminality, and violence to African-Americans—often fueled by racialized representations in media and public discourse. That, in turn, has fueled the the proliferation

---

25. U.S. Const. amend. IV; see also *Camara v. Mun. Ct. of San Francisco*, 387 U.S. 523, 528 (1967) (quoting Wolf v. People of Colorado, 338 U.S. 25, 27 (1949)) (observing that "[t]he basic purpose of [the Fourth] Amendment . . . is to safeguard the privacy and security of individuals against arbitrary invasions by governmental officials").

26. We note that our dissenting colleagues' common concern about the stigma and racial resentment sown from racial classifications does not appear to have entered their consideration of the racial profiling concerns at issue here. See, e.g., *City of Richmond v. J.A. Croson Co.*, 488 U.S. 469, 493 (1989) ("Classifications based on race carry a danger of stigmatic harm. Unless they are strictly reserved for remedial settings, they may in fact promote notions of racial inferiority and lead to a politics of racial hostility.").

27. Just last year, prominent scholar and Harvard University professor Henry Louis Gates reflected on this creature of contemporary America by remarking that "[t]here's a moving violation that many African-Americans know as D.W.B.: Driving While Black." Henry Louis Gates, *Thirteen Ways of Looking at a Black Man*, NEW YORKER Oct. 23, 1995, at 59. Washington Post columnist Michael A. Fletcher also recently documented the great lengths Black men will go to avoid being stopped for what some "sardonically call DWB – driving while black." Michael A. Fletcher, *Driven to Extremes*, WASH. POST, Mar. 29, 1996.

of "drug courier profiles" that explicitly and implicitly view Blackness as a proxy for suspicion.

Meanwhile, whites effectively enjoy a racial immunity from the drug war, despite evidence that all racial groups use drugs in roughly equal proportions.[28] This suggests that, in the name of public safety,[29] law enforcement departments across the country disproportionately stop and search African-Americans not because of their conduct or the content of their character, but because of the color of their skin.[30]

Furthermore, when the State condones racial profiling as a "rational" and legitimate law enforcement tactic, it does more than compromise the privacy interests of the individuals profiled. Racial profiling of this sort undermines the egalitarian principals enshrined in our Constitution—principals from which we have too often strayed—and furthers the perception of African-Americans as a criminally suspect group. When police officers use racial stereotypes to guide and justify

---

28. See Nanette Graham, *The Influence of Predictors on Adolescent Drug Use: An Examination of Individual Effects*, 28 YOUTH & SOC'Y 215, 217, 224-227 (1996) (noting that " . . . Blacks report less drug use than do Whites" and finding that " . . . Whites were found to be significantly higher than Blacks on cigarette, alcohol, and marijuana use . . . On the other hand, Blacks, although not significantly different, were found to be higher than Whites on cocaine and heroin use . . . "); Alison M. Trinkoff, Christian Ritter & James C. Anthony, *The Prevalence and Self-Reported Consequences of Cocaine Use: an Exploratory and Descriptive Analysis*, 26 DRUG & ALCOHOL DEPENDENCE 217, 219-220 (1990) (concluding that cocaine use is more prevalent among white people than black people); Dan Weikel, *War on Crack Targets Minorities Over Whites*, L.A. TIMES, May 21, 1995, at A1, A26.

29 Rarely do we question whose "public safety" we intend to protect.

30. Two years before the Los Angeles Uprisings that followed the Rodney King beating, *Los Angeles Times* reporter Ron Harris remarked that "[m]aybe no one planned it, maybe no one wanted it and certainly few saw it coming, but around the country, politicians, public officials and even many police officers and judges say, the nation's war on drugs has in effect become a war on black people." Ron Harris, *Blacks Feel Brunt of Drug War*, L.A. TIMES, Apr. 22, 1990, at A1.

their investigation practices, it reinforces the stereo-type's descriptive accuracy and moral acceptability: Police are more likely to engage African-Americans, and in turn the police and public are more likely to view African-Americans as criminally suspect. This reinforcing spiral lends moral credence to using ste-reotypes as a driver of public policy.

In addition, racially selective policing has resulted in racially-disparate collateral damage across all dimensions of our criminal justice system—from stops and arrests, to incarceration and sentencing.[31] This does not even begin to describe the collateral consequences—from potential disenfranchisement to exclusion for housing and employment—that follow individuals post-arrest and incarceration. Dispirit-ingly, the "logic" of racial profiling often goes unques-tioned, despite evidence that the growing disparities in our criminal justice system are not caused by actual differences between racial groups in criminality.[32]

Though we have thus far focused our attention on Black Americans, they are far from the only racially vulnerable group to face state-sanctioned racial profil-ing in the name of public safety and national security.

---

31. See MICHAEL TONRY, MALIGN NEGLECT: RACE, CRIME, AND PUNISHMENT IN AMERICA 3–4 (1995).

32. Justice Stevens recently made this point, gesturing to a 1995 Special Report to Congress that contained the following noteworthy facts. In 1993, although 65% of persons who had used crack are white, whites represented only 4% of federal offend-ers convicted of trafficking crack; 88% of those convicted were Black. Justice Stevens's observations find additional support in a Bureau of Justice Statistics study that sug-gests that sentencing disparities grew dramatically after the implementation of the Sentencing Guidelines. These "presumably reliable," as Chief Justice Rehnquist put it, statistics belie any suggestion that disparities in arrest, conviction, or sentencing naturally and reasonably reflect disparities in criminality. To the contrary, they re-flect "troubling racial patterns of enforcement." *United States v. Armstrong*, 517 U.S. 456, 479–80 (1996) (Stevens, J., dissenting).

In the 1940s, drawing upon wartime "hysteria,"[33] the United States Government—including this Court—took us into "the ugly abyss of racism" when it incarcerated Japanese Americans on the racial assumption that they were, or were likely to be, disloyal.[34] Americans of German and Italian ancestry, in contrast, remained free from such unindividuated treatment, notwithstanding that Germany and Italy also constituted wartime adversaries.

Under the guise of "strictly scrutinizing" Japanese internment, this Court did not simply acquiesce, but affirmatively defended anti-Japanese racism. Forty years later in *Brignoni-Ponce,* we revived this ignoble tradition by holding that the government may employ a person's "apparent Mexican ancestry" as one factor among many in determining whether that person is, to use the dehumanizing term, an "*'illegal'* alien."[35] Without even applying strict scrutiny, our decision expressly incorporated racial discrimination into Fourth Amendment law. We see no compelling reason—indeed, not even a rational one—to compound those errors here.

The dissent, for its part, describes the underlying traffic stop as "run-of-the-mine"—a phrase apparently intended to capture its supposed reasonableness and banal character. Yet if true, this only proves our point: Racial profiling has become so ingrained in the fabric of American policing that it is rendered ordinary,

---

33. THE COMMISSION ON WARTIME RELOCATION AND INTERNMENT OF CIVILIANS, PERSONAL JUST. DENIED 18 (1983) ("The broad historical causes which shaped these decisions were race prejudice, war hysteria and a failure of political leadership.").

34. See *Korematsu v. United States*, 323 U.S. 214, 233 (1944) (Murphy, J., dissenting).

35. *United States v. Brignoni-Ponce*, 422 U.S. 873, 877, 883 (1975) (emphasis added).

and therefore constitutionally reasonable, in the eyes of Supreme Court justices. Tragically, this is not the first time members of this Court have cited racism's ordinary and everyday nature to justify its constitutionalization.[36] Whether ordinary or not, racial profiling constitutes the antithesis of "evenhanded law enforcement."[37]

It seems plain wrong that the Fourth Amendment, which is intended to ensure that police conduct is *reasonable*, would invite, let alone permit a rule that inoculates protect racially discriminatory policing—including discrimination rooted in racial animus—from constitutional scrutiny. At least since *Brown v. Board of Education*, 347 U.S. 483 (1954), we would not have thought it necessary nor controversial to assert that racism is, by definition, unreasonable.[38] Racial discrimination does not become reasonable just because the officer possesses probable cause of a traffic infraction. Indeed, we have repeatedly struck down laws or policies as unreasonable because they discriminated based on race.[39] Accordingly, we find it

---

36. See, e.g., *Plessy v. Ferguson*, 163 U.S. 537, 542-43 (1896) (quoting *Civil Rights Cases*, 109 U.S. 3 (1883)) ("[T]he act of a mere individual, the owner of an inn, a public conveyance or place of amusement, refusing accommodations to colored people, cannot be justly regarded as imposing any badge of slavery or servitude upon the applicant, but only as involving an ordinary civil injury, properly cognizable by the laws of the state, and presumably subject to redress by those laws until the contrary appears.").

37. Brief for the United States, *supra* note 23, at 14 (quoting *Horton v. California*, 496 U.S. 128, 138 (1990)).

38. But, apparently, we must make this point explicit, particularly given the array of law enforcement officials, politicians, and academics who profess that racially discriminatory policies and practices are both rational and constitutionally reasonable.

39. See, e.g., *McLaughlin v. Florida*, 379 U.S. 184, 190 (1964) (quoting *Gulf, Colo. & Santa Fé Ry. v. Ellis*, 165 U.S. 150, 155 (1897)) ("Classification 'must always rest upon some difference which bears a reasonable and just relation to the act in respect to which the classification is proposed, and can never be made arbitrarily, and without any such basis.'").

untenable to adopt a rule that would make racial discrimination constitutionally reasonable.

The dissent disagrees, apparently. It insists that it is not asking us to ignore our constitutional commitment to racial equality. Rather, it argues that the proper constitutional provision to contest racially discriminatory policing is the Fourteenth Amendment—not the Fourth.[40]

We agree that a claim of racial discrimination is colorable under the Fourteenth Amendment's Equal Protection Clause. But conduct impermissible under one Amendment is not therefore permissible under another. Any instance of police misconduct could potentially give rise to multiple constitutional claims, arising under distinct constitutional provisions. This is particularly true in the realm of constitutional criminal procedure, which rests on multiple constitutional anchors. Consider a criminal defendant, who could appropriately seek to suppress the same incriminating statement under the Fourth, Fifth, Sixth, or Fourteenth Amendments.

Petitioners need not cede their Fourth Amendment protections simply because they may find recourse under the Fourteenth Amendment. Indeed, we find it hard to understand how police conduct that would violate the Fourteenth Amendment would be considered

---

40. As a preliminary matter, it is not clear to us how the Fourteenth Amendment applies to this case, since the Government conduct in question does not implicate a state, but rather the Metropolitan Police Department. The relevant constitutional provision would be the Fifth Amendment's Due Process Clause, which itself incorporates the equal protection guarantees contained in the Fourteenth Amendment. Nonetheless, for purposes of this opinion we assume that the Equal Protection Clause applies, as it would to most of the criminal procedure cases before this Court.

reasonable under the Fourth. If anything, the fact that racially discriminatory policing raises a cognizable Fourteenth Amendment claim suggests the opposite.

First, we have historically interpreted the Constitution as a unified document, rather than as a series of disaggregated provisions.[41] On this view, by rendering racially discriminatory stops reasonable, notwithstanding the clear Fourteenth Amendment violation, we would untether the Fourth Amendment from the rest of the constitutional fabric. Such a conclusion would signal that the Fourth Amendment is neither concerned with, nor informed by, other constitutional safeguards.

Second, the Fourteenth Amendment's equal protection concerns are particularly applicable to our interpretation of the Fourth Amendment—perhaps far more than other constitutional provisions.[42] Whatever the Fourth Amendment's initial scope, the Fourteenth Amendment infused it with an equality dimension—one acutely attentive to America's disgraceful treatment of Black Americans—that informs

---

41. See, e.g., *United States v. U.S. Dist. Ct. for E.D. Mich.*, 407 U.S. 297, 313 (1972) ("National security cases, moreover, often reflect a convergence of First and Fourth Amendment values not present in cases of 'ordinary' crime."); *Mapp v. Ohio*, 367 U.S. 643, 662 (1961) (Black, J., concurring) ("[T]his has led me to conclude that when the Fourth Amendment's ban against unreasonable searches and seizures is considered together with the Fifth Amendment's ban against compelled self-incrimination, a constitutional basis emerges which not only justifies but actually requires the exclusionary rule.").

42. It is worth noting that a reasonableness inquiry commonly anchors our equal protection analysis. See, e.g., *San Antonio Indep. Sch. Dist. v. Rodriguez*, 411 U.S. 1, 47 (1973) (rejecting the District Court's conclusion that Texas had failed to "establish a reasonable basis for a system that results in different levels of per-pupil expenditure"). And across bodies of law that transcend the Constitution, reasonableness has historically been understood in terms of whether conduct is otherwise lawful or constitutional. See, e.g., *Kansas City S. R. Co. v. Carl*, 227 U.S. 639, 650 (1913) (employing reasonableness analysis to assess the lawfulness of a shipping contract).

our contemporary reasonableness inquiry.[43] A holistic reading of these two amendments suggests that, at minimum, one subset of unreasonable searches and seizures are those conducted in a racially discriminatory manner.

Third, the Fourth Amendment is applicable to the states through the Fourteenth Amendment's Due Process Clause, which—similar to the Fifth Amendment's Due Process Clause—contains an antidiscrimination dimension.[44] Time and again, we have reiterated that racial discrimination violates due process. For example, in *Cooper v. Aaron*, 358 U.S. 1 (1958), which principally concerned the Fourteenth Amendment's equal protection guarantee, we remarked that "[t]he right of a student not to be segregated on racial grounds . . . is indeed so fundamental and pervasive that it is embraced in the concept of due process of law."[45] *Cooper* is but one example of our well-established understanding that due process and equal protection are distinct yet overlapping and intertwined principles rooted in "our American ideal of fairness."[46]

The dissent's approach, however, would effectively

---

43. Professor Ely has remarked that "the Fourth Amendment can be seen as another harbinger of the Equal Protection Clause, concerned with avoiding indefensible inequities in treatment." JOHN HART ELY, DEMOCRACY OR DISTRUST: A THEORY OF JUDICIAL REVIEW 97 (1980). This is not to suggest that racial discrimination was not previously a concern of the Fourth Amendment. Rather, it is to mark that the Fourteenth Amendment's passage reinvigorated the Fourth Amendment with a normative commitment that compels our rejection of a jurisprudence that views racial discrimination as constitutionally reasonable.

44. See *Gibson v. Mississippi*, 162 U.S. 565, 591 (1896) ("The guaranties of life, liberty, and property are for all persons, within the jurisdiction of the United States, or of any state, without discrimination against any because of their race.").

45. *Cooper v. Aaron*, 358 U.S. 1, 19 (1958).

46. *Bolling v. Sharpe*, 347 U.S. 497, 499 (1954).

"incorporate" racism into the Due Process Clause and put the Fourteenth Amendment at war with itself, pitting its Equal Protection Clause against its Due Process Clause.[47] Perhaps this explains why our dissenting colleagues never state explicitly that racially targeted stops are constitutionally reasonable if conducted under the guise of enforcing traffic laws. Not once does the dissent utter the words "racial discrimination," "racialized policing," "racism," or "white supremacy." Instead, the dissent sanitizes its approach and obscures how it would constitutionally internalize racial discrimination by speaking in terms of "actual motivations," "ulterior motives," "subjective intentions," and "probable cause."

Consider the dissent's own reasoning:

"Here the District Court found that the officers had probable cause to believe that petitioners had violated the traffic code. That rendered the stop reasonable under the Fourth Amendment, the evidence thereby discovered admissible, and the upholding of the convictions by the Court of Appeals for the District of Columbia Circuit correct."

On its face, race is absent from the dissent's proposed rule. But make no mistake, this approach would endorse racial profiling: If a police officer observes A and B committing the same traffic infraction (and therefore has probable cause to enforce the infraction), and the officer decides to target B *because* B is Black, the dissent would find the stop reasonable

---

47. We see no good reason nor need to generate such tension. Doing so would uplift a vision of the Fourth Amendment inconsistent with our Constitution's unambiguous mandate that its rights and protections flow equally to all, irrespective of one's race.

under the Fourth Amendment. Furthermore, so long as there was probable cause of a traffic infraction, the dissent would approve of the stop—even if the officer had no intention of enforcing the traffic infraction, and was solely motivated by overt racism or an intent to harass B. This approach transforms probable cause from a shield that protects the public from arbitrary police intrusions into a sword police officers can wield to racially discriminate.[48]

That this sword is not colorblind raises broader constitutional concerns. This Court has long embraced the notion that "[o]ur Constitution is colorblind, and neither knows nor tolerates classes among citizens."[49] When Justice Harlan offered that rebuke in *Plessy*, he did not add a proviso: "except with respect to the Fourth Amendment."[50]

We recognize that our distinguished colleagues vary in how precisely they might adhere to our constitutional commitment to colorblindness. Competing positions, for instance, are reflected in the *Bakke*

---

48. We worry as well that were the dissent to have its day, we would open the door to arguments that the government may formally use race as a basis for the existence of probable cause. Our concern is not far-fetched. Two decades ago, in *Brignoni-Ponce*, this Court held that the government may take "apparent Mexican ancestry" into account in determining whether there is reasonable suspicion that a person has formal legal status in the United States. 422 U.S. 873, 885–87 (1975). The Court did so without even subjecting its reasoning to a strict scrutiny analysis—the very analysis we apply to remedial uses of race. It is bad enough that racially-inflected presumptions about who is, and is not, American have been folded into our reasonable suspicion framework. We will not facilitate the incorporation of racist lay theories into determinations of probable cause as well.

49. *Plessy v. Ferguson*, 163 U.S. 537, 559 (1896) (Harlan, J., dissenting).

50. As we have noted throughout, there is no reason to restrict racial discrimination claims to one constitutional provision. Just as multiple constitutional vehicles regulate when and how police officers can question us, so does the Constitution provide multiple checks against racial discrimination.

opinions authored by Justices Powell and Brennan.[51] Justice Powell, writing alone for the Court, invoked colorblindness to insist both that affirmative action must satisfy strict scrutiny, the highest level of judicial review, and that remedying societal discrimination was not a compelling interest sufficient to justify such a policy.

In contrast, Justice Brennan argued that affirmative action should receive intermediate scrutiny because it was a benign use of race to further remedial ends. From his perspective: "[W]e cannot . . . let color blindness become myopia which masks the reality that many 'created equal' have been treated within our lifetimes as inferior both by the law and by their fellow citizens."[52]

We are sympathetic to Justice Brennan's descriptive and normative account. Nevertheless, as the law currently stands, any express use of race is constitutionally suspect—even for benign or remedial purposes—and triggers the most exacting judicial scrutiny.[53] Indeed, Justice Scalia, who authors the dissent, has been one of the most forceful proponents of this hardline approach. Yet, here, he abandons such colorblind sensibilities in the face of racially discriminatory policing, instead relegating them to equal protection doctrine alone. If ever there were a context to uphold the line that our Constitution is colorblind, we think racially selective law enforcement is it.

---

51. *Regents of Univ. Cal. v. Bakke*, 438 U.S. 265 (1978).

52. *Id.* at 327 (Brennan, J., dissenting).

53. See *City of Richmond v. J.A. Croson Co.*, 488 U.S. 469, 493 (1989).

Accordingly, we hold that it is unreasonable for an officer to make a traffic stop because of a motorist's race. This is true even if the officer has probable cause of a traffic violation.

In articulating this "because of race" standard, Fourth Amendment litigants need not prove conscious racial motivation, the intent standard that applies in the Fourteenth Amendment context.[54] Scholars have roundly criticized that standard for reasons with which we largely agree.[55] While evidence of conscious intent to discriminate or explicit racial animus would certainly meet the "because of race" test we set forth here, the absence of that showing should not preclude the finding of a Fourth Amendment violation.

In this sense, our holding is narrow: We do not decide whether petitioners in this case were stopped because of their race. The District Court did not make a factual finding on this issue, and the record is insufficient for us to do so here. Accordingly, we remand to

---

54. See *Washington v. Davis*, 426 U.S. 229 (1976); *Arlington Heights v. Metropolitan Housing Dev. Corp.*, 429 U.S. 252 (1977); *Pers. Adm'r of Massachusetts v. Feeney*, 442 U.S. 256 (1979).

55. See, e.g., Charles R. Lawrence III, *The Id, the Ego, and Equal Protection: Reckoning with Unconscious Racism*, 39 STAN L. REV. 317, 324–25 (1987) ("By insisting that a blameworthy perpetrator be found before the existence of racial discrimination can be acknowledged, the Court creates an imaginary world where discrimination does not exist unless it was consciously intended."); Kimberlé Williams Crenshaw, *Race, Reform, and Retrenchment: Transformation and Legitimation in Antidiscrimination Law*, 101 HARV. L. REV. 1331 (1988); Alan David Freeman, *Legitimizing Racial Discrimination Through Antidiscrimination Law: A Critical Review of Supreme Court Doctrine*, 62 MINN. L. REV. 1049, 1053 (1978) (contrasting antidiscrimination law's prevailing "perpetrator" conception of racial discrimination—which requires litigants to identify a "blameworthy" individual who has engaged in "intentional" discrimination—with a "victim" conception which suggests that the problem of racial discrimination "will not be solved until the conditions associated with it have been eliminated").

the District Court so that it may take up petitioners' racial profiling claim in the first instance. In doing so, we urge the District Court to press the parties on the following counterfactual: Would the officers have stopped petitioners had they been white? In answering that question, the District Court should consider, among other factors (1) whether the officer's conduct violated departmental policy, (2) whether civilians have registered any complaints of racial bias or discrimination against the officer, (3) whether the officer employed racially-inflected language during the interaction, and (4) whether there is evidence of racial disparities in the rate at which officers in the department stop people for traffic infractions. We express no view as to how courts should weigh these factors. Nor do we present them as exhaustive. We simply note that each is relevant to the "because of race" test we have described.

B

We now turn to petitioners' pretext argument.

In recent years, this Court has examined several cases involving officers searching an impounded vehicle while taking inventory of the vehicle's contents. Just six years ago, in *Florida v. Wells,* 495 U.S. 1, 4 (1990), we stated that "an inventory search must not be a ruse for a general rummaging in order to discover incriminating evidence," and that "[t]he individual police officer must not be allowed so much latitude that inventory searches are turned into a 'purposeful and general means of discovering evidence of crime.'" That passage quoted Justice Blackmun's concurrence in *Colorado v. Bertine*, 479 U.S. 367 (1987), which we decided just three years earlier. In approving the inventory search in *Bertine*, we thought it significant that there was "no showing that the police, who were following standardized procedures, acted in bad faith or for the sole purpose of investigation." *Id.*, at 372.

That same year we upheld the constitutionality of a warrantless administrative inspection in *New York v. Burger*, 482 U.S. 691, 716–717 n. 27 (1987). We observed that New York was not employing the underlying administrative scheme "as a 'pretext' to enable law enforcement . . . [to investigate] penal violations." And there was no "reason to believe that the instant inspection was actually a 'pretext' for obtaining evidence of respondent's violation of the penal laws." *Ibid.*[56]

In each of the preceding cases we either explicitly or implicitly recognized that pretextual searches could violate the Fourth Amendment. Our dissenting colleagues do not quarrel with that conclusion. Instead, they perceive what they believe is an important distinction: in those cases, unlike here, the government lacked any probable cause. According to the dissent, this distinction makes all the difference:

"[O]nly an undiscerning reader would regard [the inventory] cases as endorsing the principle that ulterior motives can invalidate police conduct that is justifiable on the basis of probable cause to believe that

---

56. *New York v. Burger*, 482 U.S. 691, 716–717 n. 27 (1987). See also *South Dakota v. Opperman*, 428 U.S. 364, 376 (1976) (upholding an inventory search of an impounded car because "there is no suggestion whatever that this . . . was a pretext concealing an investigatory police motive").

a violation of law has occurred. In each case we were addressing the validity of a search conducted in the *absence* of probable cause. Our quoted statements simply explain that the exemption from the need for probable cause (and warrant), which is accorded to searches made for the purpose of inventory or administrative regulation, is not accorded to searches that are *not* made for those purposes."

Formally, the dissent is entirely right. Unlike the inventory or administrative search cases in which the government typically lack probable cause, the D.C. vice officers undisputedly had probable cause to believe that petitioners committed multiple traffic infractions. Substantively, however, the dissent identifies a distinction without a difference.

Given the catalogue of traffic code regulations in any given city, it is virtually impossible to drive a car without committing some infraction.[57] The D.C. traffic code, as the following regulations reflect, is no exception:

- The driver of a vehicle shall not follow another vehicle more closely than is reasonable and prudent, having due regard for the speed of the vehicles and the traffic upon and the condition of the roadway;
- Both the approach for a right turn and a right turn shall be made as close as practicable to the right-hand curb or edge or the roadway;

---

57. Justice Scalia has previously acknowledged the breath of common traffic laws, having noted that "[w]e know that no local police force can strictly enforce the traffic laws, or it would arrest half the driving population on any given morning." *Morrison v. Olson*, 487 U.S. 654, 727–28 (1988) (Scalia, J., dissenting).

- No person shall start a vehicle which is stopped, standing, or parked unless and until the movement can be made with reasonable safety;
- An operator shall, when operating a vehicle, give full time and attention to the operation of the vehicle;
- A signal of intention to turn right or left when required shall be given continuously during not less than the last one hundred feet (100 ft.) traveled by the vehicle before turning;
- No vehicle operated on the highways of the District shall have any object attached to or suspended from the rearview mirror or rearview mirror bracket.[58]

Considering the sprawling traffic codes in D.C. and elsewhere, only in the most formalistic sense does a probable cause requirement constrain a police officer's power to stop a motorist. Thus, while inventory searches are suspicion-less police intrusions in a *de jure* sense (police officers need no objective suspicion to conduct inventory searches), traffic stops are suspicion-less police intrusions in a *de facto* sense (the formal probable cause requirement does not, in practice, constrain an officer's authority to conduct a traffic stop).[59] For this reason, the inventory cases and their

---

58. D.C. Mun. Reg. 18 Vehicles & Traffic §§ 2201.9; 2203.3; 2206.1; 2213.4; 2204.4; 2213.7 (1995).

59. Nearly 25 years ago, Justice Marshall articulated similar concerns about pretextual stops. *United States v. Robinson*, 414 U.S. 218, 248 (1973) (Marshall, J., dissenting) ("There is always the possibility that a police officer, lacking probable cause to obtain a search warrant, will use a traffic arrest as a pretext to conduct a search. I suggest this possibility not to impugn the integrity of our police, but merely to point out that case-by-case adjudication will always be necessary to determine whether a full arrest was effected for purely legitimate reasons or, rather, as a pretext for searching the arrestee. 'An arrest may not be used as a pretext to search for evidence.'" (citations omitted)).

pretext analyses are more relevant to the present case than the dissent suggests. Critically, not a single one of the forgoing decisions confined our concerns about pretextual police intrusions only to those instances where officers lacked probable cause, or only to the inventory and administrative search context.[60]

Accordingly, we find that our inventory and investigatory precedents are relevant to the question at hand. We do not suggest, however, that our decision is underpinned by these cases alone. In addition to this body of law, the Fourth Amendment's requirement that we balance parties' interests—the government's law enforcement interests against people's interest in privacy and security—weighs against pretextual stops.

As we noted above, probable cause is *often* sufficient to establish that a stop or search is reasonable. The Government proposes that probable cause is *always* sufficient. As attractive as this proposed rule may be to the Government, it contravenes our Fourth Amendment precedent and principles. Specifically, it conflicts with our prior command that, in determining whether a search or seizure is reasonable, we consider "all

---

60. See *Steagald v. United States*, 451 U.S. 204, 215 (1981) (noting that an arrest warrant for one party is not a surrogate to search a third party's home and that a warrant may not serve as a "pretext for entering a home in which the police have a suspicion, but not probable cause to believe that illegal activity is taking place"); *United States v. Lefkowitz*, 285 U.S. 452, 467 (1932) (arrest warrant "may not be used as a pretext to search for evidence"); *Jones v. United States*, 357 U.S. 493, 500 (1958) (suppressing evidence where "testimony of the federal officers makes clear beyond dispute that their purpose in entering was to search . . . not to arrest"); *New York v. Class*, 475 U.S. 106, 122 n. (1986) (Powell, J., concurring) (police officer may enter car to obtain VIN, but "an officer may not use VIN inspection as a pretext for searching a vehicle for contraband or weapons"); *Texas v. Brown*, 460 U.S. 730, 743 (1983) (upholding evidence obtained at a roadblock where "the circumstances of this meeting . . . give no suggestion that the roadblock was a pretext whereby evidence of narcotics violation might be uncovered").

of the circumstances surrounding the search or seizure and the nature of the search or seizure itself."[61]
Even where probable cause exists, we must balance
the "intrusion on the individual's Fourth Amendment
interests against [the] promotion of legitimate governmental interests."[62]

As with racially selective stops, the Government
does not claim to possess an affirmative interest in
pretextual stops. Instead, it again describes its interest as promoting public safety through the enforcement of its traffic laws. This interest is legitimate.

We think it beyond dispute, however, that the public
safety interest is only minimally advanced by having
plainclothes officers in unmarked vehicles investigate
minor traffic infractions. Indeed, the Metropolitan
Police Department's own regulations prohibit such
a practice except where the underlying conduct is "so
grave as to pose an immediate threat to the safety of
others."[63] It may in fact hinder the underlying public
safety goals by producing motorist confusion and alarm.

In contrast to the Government' legitimate but limited interest, the individual burden is significant. The
Fourth Amendment "guarantees the privacy, dignity,
and security of persons against certain arbitrary and
invasive acts by officers of the Government or those
acting at their direction."[64] Even ordinary traffic

---

61. *United States v. Montoya de Hernandez*, 473 U.S. 531, 537 (1985) (citation omitted). See also Cooper v. California, 386 U.S. 58, 59 (1967) ("[W]hether a search and
seizure is unreasonable within the meaning of the Fourth Amendment depends upon
the facts and circumstances of each case. . . .").

62. *Montoya de Hernandez*, 473 U.S. at 537 (quoting *United States v.
Villamonte-Marquez*, 462 U.S. 579, 588 (1983)).

63. General Order 303.1, *supra* note 6.

stops entail "a possibly unsettling show of authority."[65] At best, traffic stops "interfere with freedom of movement, are inconvenient, and consume time."[66] At worst, they "create substantial anxiety" and can, in the most unfortunate circumstances, lead to injury or even death.[67] Such anxieties are no doubt more pronounced when a stop is conducted by plainclothes officers in unmarked cars. Under such circumstances, we find it reasonable for a driver—let alone a jury—to suspect that a stop was motivated by something other than a simple traffic infraction.

Our dissenting colleagues would have us refrain from balancing the parties' interests altogether. They contend that "[w]ith rare exceptions not applicable here . . . the result of [Fourth Amendment] balancing is not in doubt where the search or seizure is based upon probable cause." Those "rare exceptions," they say, concern searches or seizures conducted in an "extraordinary manner." Specifically, the dissent reads our case law as follows:

"Where probable cause has existed, the only cases in which we have found it necessary actually to perform the "balancing" analysis involved searches or seizures conducted in an extraordinary manner, unusually harmful to an individual's privacy or even physical interests—such as, for example, seizure by means of deadly force, see *Tennessee v. Garner*, 471 U.S. 1 (1985),

---

64. *Skinner v. Ry. Labor Executives' Ass'n*, 489 U.S. 602, 613–14 (1989) (citations omitted).

65. *Delaware v. Prouse*, 440 U.S. 648, 657 (1979).

66. *Id.*

67. *Id.*

unannounced entry into a home, see *Wilson v. Arkansas*, 514 U.S. 927 (1995), entry into a home without a warrant, see *Welsh v. Wisconsin*, 466 U.S. 740 (1984), or physical penetration of the body, see *Winston v. Lee*, 470 U.S. 753 (1985). The making of a traffic stop out of uniform does not remotely qualify as such an extreme practice, and so is governed by the usual rule that probable cause to believe the law has been broken "outbalances" private interest in avoiding police contact."

We do not read our precedent so narrowly. To begin, we have never suggested that balancing is relevant only in the absence of probable cause, and we decline to do so here. Nor have we ever articulated, much less adopted, the dissent's "extraordinary manner" standard as a basis for determining when balancing is necessary or appropriate. It is true that we have not previously performed balancing in a case quite like this. But that simply reflects that in several relevant respects, this case presents a matter of first impression. And as such, we see no reason to retreat from the view that "the balancing of competing interests" is a "key principle of the Fourth Amendment."[68]

Even if we apply the dissent's newly devised standard, we find that this case is "extraordinary." The question presented implicates critical issues of police power and discretion: Is it reasonable under the Fourth Amendment for officers to stop a person to investigate a crime for which they do not have probable cause (or, as discussed above, to engage in racial profiling), so long as they have probable cause that the person committed a traffic violation? Answering this question by balancing the parties' interests is not only appropri-

---

68. *Michigan v. Summers*, 452 U.S. 692, 700 n.12 (1981) (citation omitted).

ate, but necessary to address the intersecting privacy, dignitary, and security harms present in pretextual and racially predicated stops.

We find ourselves compelled to remind our colleagues that concerns about abuse of discretion and police authority are not throwaway lines in our Fourth Amendment jurisprudence. To the contrary, they anchor this body of law. Specifically, we have stated that "persons in automobiles on public roadways may not for that reason alone have their travel and privacy interfered with at the unbridled discretion of police officers."[69] This statement echoes our historic understanding that the Fourth Amendment is skeptical of unbridled law enforcement discretion.[70]

We are unable to see how a regime that permits pretextual traffic stops under the veil of probable cause aligns with these basic principles. Given the ubiquity of traffic infractions, the Government's proposed rule would afford officers discretion to single out and stop whomever they wish, whenever they wish, wherever they wish.[71] If unchecked, such discretion would invite

---

69. *Prouse*, 440 U.S. at 663.

70. See *id*. at 661 ("This kind of standardless and unconstrained discretion is the evil the Court has discerned when in previous cases it has insisted that the discretion of the official in the field be circumscribed, at least to some extent.").

71. The dissent contends that "we are aware of no principle that would allow us to decide at what point a code of law becomes so expansive and so commonly violated that infraction itself can no longer be the ordinary measure of the lawfulness of enforcement. And even if we could identify such exorbitant codes, we do not know by what standard (or what right) we would decide, as petitioners would have us do, which particular provisions are sufficiently important to merit enforcement." *Whren v. United States*, 517 U.S. 806, 818–19 (1996). The dissent would make this case harder than it is. Nothing in our opinion alters the authority of police to enforce the full breath of the traffic and vehicle regulations within their jurisdiction. We merely hold that in so doing, the Fourth Amendment prohibits police officers from weaponizing probable cause of a traffic infraction into pretext to investigate a crime for which probable cause is lacking.

arbitrary and capricious decisions, including racially selective ones, about whom to stop—affording officers the very "unconstrained discretion" that the Fourth Amendment is designed to prevent.[72] We decline to adopt a standard that would doctrinally sanction such an abuse of police power.

Reaching the contrary conclusion would come dangerously close to legitimizing the precise kind of suspicion-less traffic stop that we declared unconstitutional in *Prouse*. There, we cautioned that "were the individual subject to unfettered governmental intrusion every time he entered an automobile, the security guaranteed by the Fourth Amendment would be seriously circumscribed."[73] To put it finely, permitting law enforcement to perform pretextual stops risks subjecting every driver to "unfettered governmental intrusion every time" they drive.[74]

What, then, is our standard for determining whether an officer has employed a traffic stop pretextually? We think that the appropriate inquiry asks whether, under the totality of the circumstances, a reasonable police officer would have conducted the traffic stop. This is consistent both with our preceding race discrimination analysis and this Court's Fourth Amendment jurisprudence more broadly.

The dissent contends that this reasonableness inquiry is unmanageable because it would require us

---

72. *Prouse*, 440 U.S. at 663.

73. *Id.* at 662–63. Of course, there are distinctions between *Prouse* and the case before us. Unlike in Prouse, we assume that the officers here possessed probable cause to stop petitioners. But as we have explained, police officers will almost always possess probable cause in the traffic stop context. For this reason, *Prouse's* core logic extends to this case.

"to plumb the collective consciousness of law enforcement."[75] To the extent that is true, our test is no less manageable than the numerous totality of the circumstances frameworks scattered across our jurisprudence, including earlier Fourth Amendment decisions.[76] For example, to determine whether a person was seized, courts must ask whether, under the totality of the circumstances, a reasonable person would feel free to leave or otherwise terminate the encounter.[77] We have applied variations of this standard for

---

74. *Id.* We parenthetically note one additional reason to conclude that pretextual stops are unreasonable under Fourth Amendment law. Pretextual stops contravene our Fourth Amendment concerns about scope. Consider the following. Whereas reasonable suspicion that a person is armed and dangerous would permit an officer to frisk that person for weapons, reasonable suspicion does not permit that same officer to conduct an exploratory search into that person's pocket for drugs. See *Terry v. Ohio*, 392 U.S. 1 (1968); *Coolidge v. New Hampshire*, 403 U.S. 443 (1971). Similarly, while probable cause of criminal activity is generally sufficient to justify an arrest, probable cause does not justify seizing a person by shooting them dead. See Tennessee v. Garner, 471 U.S. 1 (1985). See also *Graham v. Connor*, 490 U.S. 386, 394 (1989); *City of Oklahoma City v. Tuttle*, 471 U.S. 808, 817 (1985). And while a warrant might afford an officer the right to search every room in a house for a stolen television, that same warrant may not justify an exploratory search of cabinets for drugs. See *Coolidge*, 403 U.S. at 466–67. In this case, the Government is effectively asking this Court to permit police officers to broaden the scope of the *purpose* for a particular seizure—a traffic stop—without broadening the underlying *justification*. Under the Government's rule, probable cause of a traffic infraction would permit an officer to stop a motorist to investigate a wholly unrelated reason for which no objective suspicion exists. Probable cause that a driver violated traffic laws authorizes the police to conduct a stop for that—but not some other—purpose. Stopping the person for an unrelated reason, and one that lacks the predicate level of objective suspicion, shares material traits with an officer who looks through medicine cabinets when the warrant authorizes a search for a television, or conducts a full search of a person when that officer has only reasonable suspicion that the person is armed and dangerous. In each instance, the officer has exceeded the scope justified by the objective evidence.

75. *Whren*, 517 U.S. at 815.

76. The search inquiry is also, effectively, a totality of the circumstances analysis in which we ask whether the government intrudes upon an expectation of privacy that society deems legitimate. See *Katz v. United States*, 389 U.S. 347 (1967).

77. See *INS v. Delgado*, 466 U.S. 210 (1984); *Florida v. Bostick*, 501 U.S. 429 (1991).

more than a decade, and not once has any justice on this Court criticized the "free to leave" framework for requiring us "to plumb the collective consciousness" of lay people. Moreover, it is worth noting that several lower courts have already applied our proposed standard—seemingly without issue.[78]

The facts of this case—including Officer Soto's admission that he never intended to issue a traffic ticket to the petitioners—leave significant doubt that a reasonable officer would have stopped petitioners for the identified traffic violations except as a pretext for investigating drugs. We have seen no evidence that plainclothes vice officers would have stopped the vehicle; the violations were minor; there was no identified threat to public safety; and the stop itself contravened departmental policy.

Nevertheless, we refrain from deciding whether a pretextual stop occurred in this case. The District Court made no finding on this issue and the Court of Appeals rested its decision on the view that petitioners' pretext claim is not cognizable under the Fourth Amendment. On remand, the District Court should evaluate the pretext question, along with the question of racially selective stops, consistent with the standard articulated herein.

It is so ordered.

---

78. See, e.g., *United States v. Guzman*, 864 F.2d 1512, 1517 (10th Cir. 1988) (applying "would have" test where defendant was stopped for not wearing seatbelt and charged with possession of cocaine); *United States v. Smith*, 799 F.2d 704 (11th Cir. 1986) (applying "would have" test where defendant was stopped for weaving based on officer's hunch that vehicle was carrying drugs).

Acknowledgments

This book did not begin as a book. Against the backdrop of the Ferguson uprisings, I decided to return my scholarship to the area of race and policing. I wrote a draft article, presented it to my colleagues at UCLA in the context of a faculty workshop, and comment after comment went something like: "Devon, what you have here is not an article; it's a book." I can't say that immediately thereafter I endeavored to write a book. I didn't. But after completing two articles on race and policing, I came to the realization that my colleagues were right. I did indeed have a book, though I was still uncertain as to its scope. It took me a few more years, and a few more articles, to figure that out.

Though the book does not track those prior articles in precise content or analytical style, the following works materially informed the project: *From Stop and Frisk to Shoot and Kill: Terry v. Ohio's Pathway to Police Violence*, 64 UCLA Law Review 1508 (2017); *Predatory Policing*, 85 UMKC Law Review 548 (2017); *From Stopping Black People to Killing Black People: The Fourth Amendment Pathways to Police Violence*, 105 California Law Review 125 (2017); and *Blue-on-Black Violence: A Provisional Model of Some of the Causes*, 104 Georgetown Law Journal 1479 (2016).

There are many people who have shaped my thinking about the book, directly or indirectly, including: Tendayi Achiume, Asli Bali, Mario Barnes, Khiara Bridges, Bennet Capers, Ann Carlson, Jennifer Chacon, Gabriel Chin, Beth Colgan, Guy Uriel Charles, Sumi Cho, Frank Rudy Cooper, Scott Cummings, Ingrid Eagly,

Jonathan Feingold, Rachel Godsil, Laura Gómez, Danny HoSang, Angela Harris, David Harris, Luke Charles Harris, Tanya Hernandez, Emily Hough, Charles Lawrence, Cynthia Lee, Robin Lenhardt, George Lipsitz, Ian Haney López, Mari Matsuda, Tracey Maclin, Eric Miller, Joel Modiri, Hiroshi Motomura, Jennifer Mnookin, Melissa Murray, Priscilla Ocen, Angela Onwuachi-Willig, Sunita Patel, Richard Re, Song Richardson, Dorothy Roberts, Russell Robinson, Adam Samaha, David Simson, Joanna Schwartz, David Sklansky, Stephanie Robinson, Ronald Sullivan, Sherod Thaxton, Anthony Thompson, Leti Volpp, Patricia Williams, Donald Weis, and Noah Zatz. There are far too many others to name. You know who you are.

Paul Butler, Kimberlé Crenshaw, Jerry Kang, Cheryl Harris, and Mitu Gulati in particular have been my "go to" interlocutors.

Participants at workshops or conferences at the following law schools provided terrific feedback on various pieces of the book: Berkeley, Boston University, Columbia, Georgetown, George Washington University, Loyola, Los Angeles, Michigan University, NYU, UCLA, and Wayne State University.

Numerous research assistants worked on the book or the articles on which it is based, including Hope Bentley, Jazmine Buckley, Sandra Hudson, Adé Jackson, Alanna Kane, Antonio Kizzie, Alison Korgan, Emmanuel Mauleón, Flinn Milligan, Will Pilon, Charlie Pollard-Durodola, Evelyn Rangel-Medina, Patrick Rock, Alicia Virani, Ashleigh Washington, and Sari Zureiqat. I thank them enormously for their input. The Hugh and Hazel Darling Law Library under the leadership of Kevin Gerson at UCLA provided extraordinary assistance, in particular the following people in their capacity (then or now) as research librarians: Stephanie Anayah, Scott Dewey, Cheryl Kelly Fischer, and Elyse Meyers. The role Serafin Canchola played helping me to translate my ideas into visual imagery was invaluable.

I am thankful as well for the various sources of funding I received for the book and/or for research and travel grants that helped to advance the project. Support from the UCLA School of Law Dean's Fund was particularly helpful. I am also grateful for support from the Atlantic Fellowship for Racial Equity, the American Bar Foundation, and the African American Policy Forum.

My agent, Tanya McKinnon, played an important role getting this project from proposal to book. Indeed, she saw the full vision of and potential for the book before I articulated it. My editor, Marc Favreau, was similarly instrumental. He read several drafts, offered insightful comments along the way, and signaled—at every turn—the importance of the ideas I was attempting to communicate. I should also thank the production team at The New Press for both their patience and the care and attention they evidenced getting the book to press.

Just prior to submitting the manuscript, I called upon two people to give it a careful read—Kwame J. Granderson and Emmanuel Mauleón. Their comments and suggestions helped me finally let go.

As with all my writing projects, Giovanna Tringali, Asmara Carbado, and Nyala Carbado have been my bedrock of support and encouragement. This book would not have been possible without them.

Notes

Prologue

1. *See* Martin L. King, Jr., *Letter from Birmingham Jail*, Christian Century: An Ecumenical Weekly, June 12, 1963, at 767-73, 768, http://www.christiancentury.org/sites/default/files/downloads/resources/mlk-letter.pdf [https://perma.cc/UPE2-XAL7] ("For years now I have heard the word 'Wait!' It rings in the ear of every Negro with piercing familiarity. This 'Wait' has almost always meant 'Never.'")

2. Devon W. Carbado, *(E)racing the Fourth Amendment*, 100 Mich. L. Rev. 946 (2002).

3. *See, e.g.*, Regina G. Lawrence, The Politics of Force: Media and the Construction of Police Brutality (2000) (employing the term "contempt of cop" and citing to its use as far back as 1969).

4. I am not using this term in the Rawslian sense. For a discussion of the theory of the veil of ignorance, see John Rawls, A Theory of Justice (1971).

5. *Cf* W.E.B. Du Bois, Souls of Black Folk (Candace Ward, 1994).

6. Nikki Jones, *"The Regular Routine": Proactive Policing and Adolescent Development Among Young, Poor Black Men*, 2014 New Directions Child & Adolescent Dev. 33 (2014).

7. Devon W. Carbado, *Strictly Scrutinizing the Black Body*, UCLA L. Rev. (forthcoming 2022).

8. For a broader understanding of the working identity phenomenon and the theory of racial palatability, see Devon W. Carbado & Mitu Gulati, *Working Identity*, 85 Cornell L. Rev. 1259 and Devon W. Carbado & Mitu Gulati, Acting White: Rethinking Race in Post-Racial America (2013).

9. Garnette Cadogan, *Black and Blue, in* Freeman's Arrival 133–34 (John Freeman ed., 2015).

10. *Id.* at 133.

11. *See* Paul Butler, Chokehold: Policing Black Men (2017).

12. Dorothy Roberts, Killing the Black Body: Race, Reproduction, and the Meaning of Liberty (1997); Priscilla A. Ocen, *Birthing*

Injustice: Pregnancy as a Status Offense, 85 GEO. WASH. L. REV. 1163 (2017); KAARYN GUSTAFSON, CHEATING WELFARE: PUBLIC ASSISTANCE THE CRIMINALIZATION OF POVERTY (2011).

13. *See* KELLY LYTLE HERNANDEZ, CITY OF INMATES: CONQUEST, REBELLION, AND THE RISE OF HUMAN CAGING IN LOS ANGELES, 1771-1965 (2017).

14. Monica C. Bell, *Police Reform and the Dismantling of Legal Estrangement*, 126 YALE L.J. 2054, 2104 (2017) (defining "vicarious marginalization" as "the marginalizing effect of police maltreatment that is targeted toward others.").

15. *See* BESSEL VAN DER KOLK, THE BODY KEEPS THE SCORE: BRAIN, MIND, AND BODY IN THE HEALING OF TRAUMA (2015).

Introduction

1. U.S. CONST. amend. V.

2. U.S. CONST. amend. VI ("In all criminal prosecutions, the accused shall enjoy the right to . . . have the Assistance of Counsel for his defence.").

3. U.S. CONST. amend. XIV § 1 ("[N]or shall any State deprive any person of life, liberty, or property, without due process of law; nor deny to any person within its jurisdiction the equal protection of the laws.").

4. *See, e.g.*, Bernard E. Harcourt & Jens Ludwig, *Broken Windows: New Evidence from New York City and a Five-City Social Experiment*, 73 U. CHI. L. REV. 271, 271 (2006). Moreover, at least some scholars argue that the costs of broken windows policing outweigh its benefits.

5. *See* Reed Collins, *Strolling While Poor: How Broken-Windows Policing Created a New Crime in Baltimore*, 14 GEO. J. ON POVERTY L. & POL'Y 419, 426 (2007) ("When police departments do adopt aggressive arrest policies to combat disorder . . . the group most affected by those strategies is the poor. The Baltimore City Council acknowledged as much in a report on arrest rates, stating that the 'unintended consequence' of vigorous policing in the city is 'the disproportionate arrest of both African Americans and the poor.'") (footnote omitted); Tracey Meares, *Broken Windows, Neighborhoods, and the Legitimacy of Law Enforcement or Why I Fell in and out of Love with Zimbardo*, J. RES. CRIME & DELINQ. 1 (2015) (finding that broken windows policing results in greater police stops of African Americans).

6. Over the past few years, legal scholars have increasingly drawn from social psychology to explain the relationship between racial profiling and police violence, on the one hand, and racial stereotypes and racial biases, on the other. *See* L. Song Richardson, *Cognitive Bias, Police Character, and the Fourth Amendment*, 44 ARIZ. ST. L.J. 267, 279–82 (2012); L. Song Richardson & Phillip Atiba Goff, *Interrogating Racial Violence*, 12 OHIO ST. J. CRIM. L. 115, 124–31 (2014) (also discussing stereotype threat); L. Song Richardson, *Police Racial Violence: Lessons from Social Psychology*, 83 FORDHAM L. REV. 2961, 2970 (2015); *see also* Cynthia Lee, *"But I Thought He Had a Gun": Race*

and Police Use of Deadly Force, 2 HASTINGS RACE & POVERTY L.J. 1, 24 n.108 (2004); Jerry Kang et al., *Implicit Bias in the Courtroom*, 59 UCLA L. REV. 1124 (2012). One of the best studies on the ways in which Blackness signals criminality remains Jennifer L. Eberhardt et al., *Seeing Black: Race, Crime, and Visual Processing*, 87 J. PERSONALITY & SOC. PSYCH. 876, 878 (2004).

7. Bennett Capers, *Policing, Race, and Place*, 44 HARV. C.R.-C.L. L. REV. 43, 66 n.148 (2009).

8. David Brooks, *The Culture of Policing is Broken*, ATLANTIC (June 16, 2020), https://www.theatlantic.com/ideas/archive/2020/06/how-police-brutality-gets-made/613030/ ("A cultural regime of dehumanization has been constructed in many police departments. In that fertile ground, racial biases can spread and become entrenched."); Barbara Amacost, *The Organizational Reasons Police Departments Don't Change*, HARV. BUS. REV. (Aug. 19, 2016) https://hbr.org/2016/08/the-organizational-reasons-police-departments-dont-change ("Repeated brutality that is not addressed by higher-ups is a systemic problem, not a problem of rogue individuals. It means that the organizational message being conveyed, whether or not explicit, is that some level of abusive behavior is okay.").

9. Curtis Gilbert, *Not Trained Not to Kill*, APM REPORTS (May 5, 2017), https://www.apmreports.org/story/2017/05/05/police-de-escalation-training (explaining that training is usually left up to local agencies and most do not conduct de-escalation training).

10. *See generally* Seth Soughton, *Law Enforcement's "Warrior" Problem*, 128 HARV. L. REV. F. 225 (2015).

11. Aaron Bekemeyer, *The Long Tie Between Police Unions and Police Violence – and What to Do About It*, WASH. POST (June 9, 2020), https://www.washingtonpost.com/outlook/2020/06/09/limits-when-police-can-use-force-is-better-solution-than-banning-police-unions/ (explaining how police unions display "a proud willingness to defend even the worst agents of police violence at any cost, and to gum up investigations and lawsuits and prevent penalties when abuse occurs").

12. *See, e.g.*, ALLISON COLLINS, ET AL., INTERNAL AFFAIRS UNITS, SHIELDED FROM JUSTICE: POLICE BRUTALITY AND ACCOUNTABILITY IN THE UNITED STATES, HUMAN RIGHTS WATCH (Cynthia Brown ed., 1998), https://www.ojp.gov/ncjrs/virtual-library/abstracts/shielded-justice-police-brutality-and-accountability-united-states.

13. *See, e.g.*, Safford Unified Sch. Dist. #1 v. Redding, 557 U.S. 364, 378 (2009).

14. Joanna C. Schwartz, *Suing Police for Abuse is Nearly Impossible. The Supreme Court Can Fix that*, WASH. POST (June 3, 2020), https://www.washingtonpost.com/outlook/2020/06/03/police-abuse-misconduct-supreme-court-immunity/.

15. *Id.*

16. Consider the case of *Stanton v. Sims*, where an officer had probable

cause to believe that a person committed a misdemeanor and chased that person into Drendolyn Sims's backyard. 571 U.S. 3, 5 (2013) (per curiam). The officer did not know Sims was in the backyard at the time and injured her as he "kick[ed]" open the gate." *Id.* Sims then sued the officer on the view that the officer needed more than probable cause to enter her backyard, but a warrant or reason to believe that there was an emergency that justified not having one. The Supreme Court sidestepped the question of whether the officer's conduct violated the Constitution, simply ruling that there was no "clearly established law" indicating that he had. *Id.* Punting on this question means that in a subsequent case, an officer who engages in similar conduct—that is, enters a backyard to arrest someone without a warrant or exigent circumstances—will argue that they should benefit from qualified immunity because there was no case that "clearly established" law that the conduct violates the Constitution.

17. *See* Joanna C. Schwartz, *Qualified Immunity's Boldest Lie,* 88 U. Chi. L. Rev. 605 (2021).

18. *Id.*

19. Ashcroft v. al-Kidd, 563 U.S. 731, 743–44 (2011) (quoting Malley v. Briggs, 475 U.S. 335, 341 (1986)).

20. Without getting into the particulars, you should know that advocates across the ideological spectrum routinely criticize qualified immunity for erecting too high a bar for holding police officers accountable for their acts of violence. *See, e.g.,* Jay Schweikert, *Qualified Immunity: A Legal, Practical, and Moral Failure,* CATO INSTITUTE (Sept. 14, 2020), https://www.cato.org/policy-analysis/qualified-immunity-legal-practical-moral-failure; Joanna C. Schwartz, *How Qualified Immunity Fails,* 127 YALE L.J. 2 (2017). For example, since 2018, the libertarian Cato Institute has engaged in concerted efforts "to abolish qualified immunity," an abolitionist sentiment that one also sees on display on progressive protest signs in marches against police violence. *End Qualified Immunity,* CATO INSTITUTE, https://www.cato.org/qualified-immunity.

21. Joanna C. Schwartz, *Police Indemnification,* 89 N.Y.U. L. Rev. 885, 890 (2014). At least one study "concluded that officers who initiated aggressive behaviors do not seem to be deterred to any substantial extent by concerns about liability and that, contrary to assumptions about lawsuits' deterrent effects, officers who had previously been sued were more aggressive than officers who had not." *Id.* at 942–43.

22. Monell v. Dep't of Soc. Servs., 436 U.S. 658, 694 (1978).

23. Sunita Patel, *Jumping Hurdles to Sue the Police,* 104 MINN. L. Rev. 2257 (2020) (discussing instances in which plaintiffs have met that burden).

24. Osagie K. Obasogie & Zachary Newman, *The Endogenous Fourth Amendment: An Empirical Assessment of How Police Understandings of Excessive Force Become Constitutional Law,* 104 CORNELL L. Rev. 1281 (2019).

25. Devon W. Carbado, *Predatory Policing*, 83 UMKC L. Rev. 545, 547 (2017).

26. Patricia J. Williams, The Alchemy of Race and Rights: Diary of a Law Professor (1992).

27. In the legal scholarship context, for example, arguments about carceral abolitionism are on the rise. *See* Dorothy Roberts, *Abolition Constitutionalism*, 133 Harv. L. Rev. 1 (2019). For other articulations, see Allegra M. McLeod, *Prison Abolition and Grounded Justice*, 62 UCLA L. Rev. 1156 (2015); Amna A. Akbar, *An Abolitionist Horizon for (Police) Reform*, 108 Cal. L. Rev. 1781 (2020); University of California Television, *Prison Abolition, and a Mule with Paul Butler*, YouTube (Dec. 4, 2019) https://www.youtube.com/watch?v=Mo3uEldhjUU.

28. Máximo Langer has engaged a version of this question with respect to arguments about criminal law minimalism. Máximo Langer, *Penal Abolitionism and Criminal Law Minimalism: Here and There, Now and Then*, 134 Harv. L. Rev. F. 42 (2020).

29. U.S. Const. amend. IV.

30. *See* Erwin Chemerinsky, Presumed Guilty: How The Supreme Court Empowered the Police and Subverted Civil Rights 41-43 (2021).

31. Saidiya V, Hartman, Scenes of Subjection: Terror, Slavery, and Self-Making in Nineteenth-Century America 96 (1997).

32. *See* Ronald S. Sullivan Jr., *Classical Racialism, Justice Story, and Margaret Morgan's Journey from Freedom to Slavery: The Story of* Prigg v. Pennsylvania, *in* Race Law Stories 59, 65 (Rachel E. Moran & Devon W. Carbado eds., 2008).

33. Prigg v. Pennsylvania, 41 U.S. 539, 561 (1842).

34. Sullivan, *supra* note 32, at 60.

35. *Prigg*, 41 U.S. at 540.

36. *Id.* at 627.

37. *Id.* at 540.

38. Dred Scott v. Sandford, 60 U.S. 393–403 (1857).

39. *See* Robert M. Cover, *Violence and the Word*, 95 Yale L. J. 1601, 1601 (observing that, "[l]egal interpretation takes place in a field of pain and death.").

40. *Dred Scott*, 60 U.S. at 411.

41. *Id.* at 407.

42. U.S. Const. amend. XIII § 1.

43. U.S. Const. amend. XIV § 1.

44. U.S. Const. amend. XV § 1.

45. This is central idea in Critical Race Theory. For a classic articulation of the idea, see Kimberlé Williams Crenshaw, *Race, Reform, and Retrenchment: Transformation and Legitimation in Antidiscrimination Law*, 101 HARV. L. REV. 1331 (1988). *See also* Devon W. Carbado, *Critical What What?*, 43 CON. L. REV. 1593 (2011).

46. Plessy v. Ferguson, 163 U.S. 537 (1896).

47. Brown v. Bd. of Educ. of Topeka, 347 U.S. 483, 495 (1954).

48. *Id.*

49. Loving v. Virginia, 388 U.S. 1 (1967).

50. Whren v. United States, 517 U.S. 806 (1996).

51. U.S. CONST. amend. IV.

52. Academics will want to know whether I am arguing that the Fourth Amendment causes the police to target Black people. Sometimes I'm asked that question in something like the following way: What if there were no Fourth Amendment? Would Black people be better off? The truth is, I don't know. It would depend on what other legal regimes are in place. But I am not interested in thinking about a world without the Fourth Amendment. I am interested in telling a story about how the Fourth Amendment fails to constrain police power in this one. The absence of that constraint effectively empowers the police.

Academics also sometimes like to draw a distinction between prohibition and authorization. My contention is that, with respect to the Fourth Amendment law, that distinction is more formalistic than substantive. That is to say, every time the Supreme Court says that a particular form of police conduct is constitutional, it is, for purposes of the Fourth Amendment law, authorizes that conduct. As I explain further along in this introduction, other legal institutions, like state courts, could interpret their own state constitutions to effectuate greater restraints on the scope of police power. Indeed, one of the reasons I wrote this book is to encourage such bodies to do just that.

53. *See, e.g.*, Carbado, *(E)racing the Fourth Amendment*, *supra* Prologue note 2, at 1030–31 (2002); David A. Harris, *The Stories, the Statistics, and the Law: Why "Driving While Black" Matters*, 84 MINN. L. REV. 265 (1999); Anthony E. Mucchetti, *Driving While Brown: A Proposal for Ending Racial Profiling in Emerging Latino Communities*, 8 HARV. LATINO L. REV. 1 (2005); Katheryn K. Russell, *"Driving While Black": Corollary Phenomena and Collateral Consequences*, 40 B.C. L. REV. 717 (1999); Wesley Lowery et al., *Even Before Michael Brown's Slaying In Ferguson, Racial Questions Hung Over Police Force*, WASH. POST, Aug. 13, 2014, at A1 ("It has been 'very hostile' for years, said Anthony Ross . . . 'Everybody in this city has been a victim of DWB [driving while black].'"); Adero S. Jernigan, *Driving While Black: Racial Profiling in America*, 24 L. & PSYCH. REV. 127 (2000); Andrea F. Siegel, *Victory for NAACP in Racial-Profiling Case; Maryland State Police Must Release Records on "Driving While Black"*, WASH. POST, Feb. 3, 2010, at B5; Victoria Bekiempis, *Driving While Black in Ferguson*, NEWSWEEK

(Aug. 15, 2014), http://www.newsweek.com/ferguson-profiling-police-courts-shooting-264744 [perma.cc/54XC-UQSN]; *Tell Me More: 'Driving While Brown'* (NPR radio broadcast Aug. 20, 2009).

54. Terry v. Ohio, 392 U.S. 1, 21 (1968). As I will explain in the chapter, Justice Warren's holding was slightly more nuanced in that he did not actually decide precisely what standard of justification would govern stops in which a person was not actually frisked.

55. WILLIAMS, *supra* note 26, at 163.

56. Crenshaw, *supra* note 45, at 1335.

57. Dorothy Roberts, *Foreword: Abolition Constitutionalism*, 133 HARV. L. REV. 1, 10 (2019).

58. Douglas NeJaime, *Winning Through Losing*, 96 Iowa Law Review (2011).

59. Scott L. Cummings, *Law and Social Movements: Reimagining the Progressive Canon*, 2018 Wisconsin Law Review 441 (2018).

60. Utah v. Strieff, 136 S.Ct. 2056, 2070 (2016).

61. MARK V. TUSHNET, I DISSENT: GREAT OPPOSING OPINIONS IN LANDMARK SUPREME COURT CASES XIII (2008).

62. *See* BARRY FRIEDMAN'S UNWARRANTED: POLICING WITHOUT PERMISSION (2017) (problematizing policing in relationship to concerns about democratic legitimacy).

Chapter One: Pedestrian Checks

1. *See, e.g.*, MICHAEL C. DAWSON, BEHIND THE MULE (1995).

2. *See, e.g.*, Washington v. Davis, 426 U.S. 229 (1976) (reasoning that the discriminatory intent of a policy is a relevant factor to determining its constitutionality).

3. *See* Florida v. Royer, 460 U.S. 491, 498 (1983) (suggesting that while police officers may approach an individual without reasonable suspicion or probable cause, that individual is free to ignore the police). The Court has also addressed whether police following people in public places constitutes a search and answered that question in the negative. *See, e.g.*, United States v. Knotts, 460 U.S. 276, 285 (1983).

4. Florida v. Bostick, 501 U.S. 429, 434 (1990) (declaring that "a seizure does not occur simply because a police officer approaches an individual").

5. *Id.*

6. *Id.* at 436.

7. *Id.* at 434; *see also* Florida v. Royer, 460 U.S. 491 (1983); INS v. Delgado, 466 U.S. 210 (1984).

8. 501 U.S. at 434.

9. *Id.* at 446 (Marshall, J., dissenting).

10. *Id.* at 431, 433–34.

11. *Id.* at 434.

12. *Id.*

13. *Id.*

14. *Id.* at 437.

15. *Id.*

16. 536 U.S. 194 (2002).

17. *Id.* at 194.

18. United States v. Drayton, 231 F.3d 787, 790–91 (11th Cir. 2000).

19. *Drayton*, 536 U.S. at 195; *Bostick*, 501 U.S. at 434.

20. These dynamics would affect Latinx people who are not Black. I include them here to disrupt the tendency of framing Blackness outside of the Latinx experience.

21. INS v. Delgado, 466 U.S. 210, 220 (1984) (holding that "factory sweep" questioning of workers by immigration officers with additional officers positioned at exits did not constitute seizure under the Fourth Amendment).

22. *See* Hiroshi Motomura, *The Rights of Others: Legal Claims and Immigration Outside of Law*, 59 DUKE L.J. 1723, 1747-49 (2011) (discussing how workplace raids affect employee rights).

23. *Delgado*, 466 U.S. at 212.

24. *Id.* at 220.

25. *Id.* at 219–20.

26. *Id.* at 220–21.

27. *Id.* at 212.

28. Brief for Respondents at 17, INS v. Delgado, 466 U.S. 210 (1984) (No. 82-1271).

29. 466 U.S. at 217.

30. Brief for Respondents, *supra* note 28, at 18.

31. *Id.* at 20.

32. *Delgado*, 466 U.S. at 229 (Brennan, J., dissenting).

33. *Id.* at 226 (Brennan, J., dissenting).

34. *Id.* at 216.

35. *Id.* at 218.

36. *Id.* In its brief, the government advanced a similar argument:

Preliminarily, we note that it is only in a theoretical sense that the work force here, or in any typical factory survey, can be characterized as having a "freedom to leave" that is restrained by the appearance of the INS. The factory surveys in this case were conducted entirely during normal working hours. At such times the employees presumably were obligated to their employer to be present at their work stations performing their employment duties; accordingly, quite apart from the appearance of the INS agents, the employees were not "free to leave" the factory in any real sense.

Brief for Petitioners at 22–23, INS v. Delgado, 466 U.S. 210 (1984) (No. 82-1271).

37. *See* Tracey Maclin, *The Decline of the Right of Locomotion: The Fourth Amendment on the Streets*, 75 CORNELL L. REV. 1258, 1305 (1990) (drawing on the totality of the circumstances test to argue that the Court should incorporate race into the seizure analysis).

38. *Id.* at 1306.

39. It is also important to note that at urban work sites such as the facilities raided in *Delgado*, as opposed to farming or ranching operations, there is a greater likelihood that citizens and legal residents work alongside illegal aliens. Asian immigrants also make up a substantial percentage of the labor force at factories subject to INS raids. In 1995, federal and state authorities raided a garment factory in El Monte, California where 72 Thai nationals were forced to work 18-hour days, seven days a week. The facility was surrounded by barbed wire to prevent escapes. *See Slavery's Long Gone? Don't Bet on It,* L.A. TIMES, Aug. 4, 1995, at B8.

40. *See* Schneckloth v. Bustamonte, 412 U.S. 218, 248–49 (1973).

41. Florida v. Bostick, 501 U.S. 429, 429 (1991).

42. *Schneckloth*, 412 U.S.

43. *Id.* at 220.

44. *Id.*

45. *Id.*

46. *Id.*

47. *Id.*

48. *Id.*

49. *Id.* at 222.

50. *Id.* at 220.

51. *Id.* at 227-28.

52. 536 U.S. 194 (2002).

53. United States v. Drayton, 231 F.3d 787, 789 (11th Cir. 2000), *rev'd,* 536 U.S. 194 (2002).

54. Brief for Petitioner at 21-22, Schneckloth v. Bustamonte, 412 U.S. 218 (1973) (No. 71-732).

55. 412 U.S. at 231 (arguing that "it would be thoroughly impractical to impose on the normal consent search the detailed requirements of an effective warning").

56. Brief for Petitioner, *supra* note 54, at 22.

57. *See* DAVID COLE, NO EQUAL JUSTICE: RACE AND CLASS IN THE AMERICAN CRIMINAL JUSTICE SYSTEM 30 (1999).

58. *See, e.g.*, United States v. Ambrose, 668 F.3d 943, 956–59 (7th Cir. 2012) (relatively restrictive security requirements at FBI building did not transform noncustodial voluntary interview into a custodial interview).

59. *See* Tracey Maclin, *"Voluntary" Interviews and Airport Searches of Middle Eastern Men: The Fourth Amendment in a Time of Terror*, 73 MISS. L.J. 471, 479–510 (2003) (explaining that people perceived to be Arab, Muslim, or Middle Eastern may not experience "voluntary" interviews as consensual).

60. *See, e.g.*, Whren v. United States, 517 U.S. 806, 813 (1996) ("Subjective intentions play no role in ordinary, probable-cause Fourth Amendment analysis.").

61. *See, e.g.*, United States v. Mendenhall, 446 U.S. 544, 554 (1980) ("We conclude that a person has been 'seized' within the meaning of the Fourth Amendment only if, in view of all of the circumstances surrounding the incident, a reasonable person would have believed that he was not free to leave.").

62. *See, e.g.*, Emmanuel Mauleón, *Black Twice: Policing Black Muslim Identities*, 65 UCLA L. REV. 1326, 1370–82 (2018) (describing Black Muslims' dual exposure to policing strategies targeting their racial identity, and counterterrorism programs targeting their religious identity).

63. Korematsu v. U.S., 323 U.S. 214 (1944).

64. *Id.* at 219.

65. *See* Roxane Ellis Rodriguez Assaf, *In Event of Another 9/11, Says Bush Appointee, "Forget Civil Rights in This Country,"* 21 WASH. REP. ON MIDDLE E. AFF. 64 (2002); Margaret Chon & Donna E. Arzt, *Walking While Muslim*, 68 LAW & CONTEMP. PROBS. 215 (2005); Abu B. Bah, *Racial Profiling and the War on Terror: Changing Trends and Perspectives*, 29 ETHNIC STUD. REV. 76 (2006); David A Harris, *On the Contemporary Meaning of* Korematsu: *"Liberty Lies in the Hearts of Men and Women,"* 76 MO. L. REV. 1 (2011); Craig Green, *Ending the* Korematsu *Era: An Early View from the War on Terror Cases*, 105 NW. U.L. REV. 983 (2011).

66. *See* United States v. Mendenhall, 446 U.S. 544 (1980) (taking the defendant's race and gender into account in the context of conducting the seizure analysis).

67. Carbado, *(E)racing the Fourth Amendment, supra* Prologue note 2, at 968 (arguing that the Court applies the Fourth Amendment with an assumption of race neutrality, that neither the way police engage people nor the way people interact with the police are shaped by race, and that race only becomes doctrinally relevant when an officer is overtly racist in her actions). *See also* Mauleón, *supra* note 62, at 545 (observing that race is "not

irrelevant" to whether a person has been seized).

68. *See* Florida v. Bostick, 501 U.S. 429, 437 (describing the seizure analysis as a totality of the circumstances test).

69. Tracey Maclin, *"Black and Blue Encounters"—Some Preliminary Thoughts About Fourth Amendment Seizures: Should Race Matter?*, 26 VAL. U. L. REV. 243, 250 (1991).

70. Carbado, *Strictly Scrutinizing the Black Body, supra* Prologue note 7.

71. *See, e.g.*, J.D.B. v. North Carolina, 564 U.S. 261, 271-72 (2011).

72. Cynthia Lee, *Reasonableness with Teeth: The Future of Fourth Amendment Reasonableness Analysis*, 81 MISS. L.J. 1133, 1152 (2012).

73. *See* Paul Butler, *The White Fourth Amendment*, 43 TEX. TECH. L. REV. 245, 250 (2010).

74. Patricia Williams employs the language of "spirit murder" to capture a version of what I am describing. WILLIAMS, *supra* Introduction note 26, at 73.

75. *J.D.B.*, 564 U.S. at 261 (internal citations omitted).

76. *See generally* Russell K. Robinson, *Perceptual Segregation*, 108 COLUM. L. REV. 1093 (2008) (discussing how race creates different common-sense understandings for black and white Americans).

77. Carbado, *(E)racing the Fourth Amendment, supra* Prologue note 2, at 966; Devon W. Carbado, *From Stopping Black People to Killing Black People: The Fourth Amendment Pathways to Police Violence*, 105 CAL. L. REV. 125, 142 (2017). The concurrence by Judge Rosenbaum also scholarship by David K. Kessler, Bennett Capers, and Tracey Maclin.

78. United States v. Knights, 989 F.3d 1281 (11th Cir. 2021).

79. *Id.* at 1289.

80. *See* Payton v. New York, 445 U.S. 573, 586 (1980) ("It is a 'basic principle of Fourth Amendment law' that searches and seizures inside a home without a warrant are presumptively unreasonable.").

81. *See, e.g.*, Michigan v. Fisher, 558 U.S. 45, 47-49 (2009) (holding that officer's warrantless entry was reasonable under the "emergency aid" exception); Brigham City v. Stuart, 547 U.S. 398, 403 (2006) (stating that "law enforcement officers may enter a home without a warrant to render emergency assistance to an injured occupant or to protect an occupant from imminent injury"); Mincey v. Arizona, 437 U.S. 385, 393-94 (1978) (noting that "warrants are generally required to search a person's home . . . unless 'the exigencies of the situation' make the needs of law enforcement so compelling that the warrantless search is objectively reasonable under the Fourth amendment.") *See also* DAVID S. RUDSTEIN, C. PETER ERLINDER & DAVID C. THOMAS, CRIMINAL CONSTITUTIONAL LAW § 3.02, Exigent Circumstances (2021).

82. Meghan Finnerty, *Fight to Remain Silent: People Often Waive*

Miranda Rights, Experts Say, CRONKITE NEWS AZ. PBS (Aug. 9, 2016), https://cronkitenews.azpbs.org/2016/08/09/fight-remain-silent-people -often-waive-miranda-rights-experts-say/.

83. *See* Berkemer v. McCarty, 468 U.S. 420, 429 (1984).

84. *See id.* at 441–42.

85. *See generally* Rinat Kitai-Sangero, *Respecting the Privilege against Self-Incrimination: A Call for Providing* Miranda *Warnings in Non-Custodial Interrogations,* 42 N.M. L. REV. 203 (2012). *See also* Megan A. Fairlie, Miranda *and Its (More Rights-Protective) International Counterparts,* 20 U.C. DAVIS J. INT'L L. & POL'Y 1, 12-19 (2013); Emily Bretz, Note, *Don't Answer the Door:* Montejo v. Louisiana *Relaxes Police Restrictions for Questioning Non-Custodial Defendants,* 109 MICH. L. REV. 221, 237-240, 246, 255-56 (2010). For a discussion of "custody" from a psychological perspective, see generally Fabiana Alceste, Different Strokes for Different but Reasonable Folks: Comparison of Legally Relevant Observers' Perceptions of Custody (2019) (Ph.D. dissertation, City University of New York) (ProQuest). *See also* Fabiana Alceste, Timothy J. Luke & Saul M. Kassin, *Holding Yourself Captive: Perceptions of Custody During Interviews and Interrogations,* 6 J. APPLIED RSCH. MEMORY & COGNITION 387 (2018) (study finding that perceptions of "custody" are not objective).

86. *See* Miranda v. Arizona, 384 U.S. 436 (1966). The opinion is grounded in the Fifth Amendment prohibition against compelled self-incrimination. *See id.* at 439–42, 457–58, 467–74.

87. *See* Massiah v. United States, 377 U.S. 201, 204–06 (1964).

88. To bring a due process claim, Tanya would have to argue that government's conduct was "overreaching," "oppressive," and "coercive." Colorado v. Connelly, 479 U.S. 157, 163–64, 167 (1986).

89. California v. Hodari D., 499 U.S. 621 (1991).

90. *See* Butler, *supra* note 73, at 254 ("The police have more power in high-crime neighborhoods than in low-crime neighborhoods."). *See also* Andrew Guthrie Ferguson, *Crime Mapping and the Fourth Amendment: Redrawing "High-Crime Areas,"* 63 HASTINGS L.J. 179, 183 (2011); Margaret Raymond, *Down on the Corner, out in the Street: Considering the Character of the Neighborhood in Evaluating Reasonable Suspicion,* 60 OHIO ST. L.J. 99 (1999).

91. Illinois v. Wardlow, 528 U.S. 119 (2000). Importantly, *Wardlow* does not say expressly that fleeing in a high crime area equals reasonable suspicion, but it comes pretty close.

92. Commonwealth v. Warren, 475 Mass. 530, 539 (2016). An FIO is a "field interrogation observation," in which an officer approaches a person and asks why they are in a particular area. *Id.* at 532 n.5.

93. *Hodari D.,* 499 U.S. at 621.

94. As with the point about Latinos, clearly Muslims who are not Black

would experience the dynamics I describe. I frame the hypothetical this way to make clear that Muslim identity is one of the categories through which Blackness is interpolated.

95. *See* United States v. White, 401 U.S. 745, 753 (1971) (holding that conversations with wired government informant are not protected by the Fourth Amendment).

96. *Id.* at 752.

97. Hoffa v. United States, 385 U.S. 293, 302 (1966).

98. On Lee v. United States, 343 U.S. 747, 757 (1952).

99. *White*, 401 U.S. at 751.

100. Amna Akbar, *Policing "Radicalization,"* 3 U.C. Irvine L. Rev. 809, 862 (2013).

101. *See* Amna Akbar, *National Security's Broken Windows,* 62 UCLA L. Rev. 834 (2015); Khaled Beydoun, *'Muslim Bans' and the (Re)Making of Political Islamophobia,* 27 U. Ill. L. Rev. 1733 (2017); Khaled Beydoun, *Acting Muslim,* 53 Harv. C.R.-C.L. L. Rev. 1 (2018).

102. *See, e.g.,* Bryce Covert, *The Myth of the Welfare Queen,* New Republic (July 2, 2019). https://newrepublic.com/article/154404/myth-welfare-queen ("As Ronald Reagan and other politicians ginned up anti-government and anti-poor resentment in the 1970s and '80s, the welfare queen stood in for the idea that black people were too lazy to work, instead relying on public benefits to get by, paid for by the rest of us upstanding citizens.").

103. Griffin v. Wisconsin, 483 U.S. 868, 872–76 (1987) (warrantless search of probationer's home comes under "special needs" exception to Fourth Amendment); Wyman v. James, 400 U.S. 309, 317–19 (1971) (mandatory home visit by welfare workers was not a Fourth Amendment search, and even if it were, it would have been reasonable); Sanchez v. San Diego, 464 F.3d 916, 920–26 (9th Cir. 2006) (applying both *Wyman* and *Griffin* to San Diego County welfare verification program).

104. *See, e.g.,* People v. Thomas, 38 Cal. App. 4th 1331, 1335 (1995) ("[A] person who occupies a temporary shelter on public property without permission and in violation of an ordinance prohibiting sidewalk blockages is a trespasser subject to immediate ejectment and, therefore, a person without a reasonable expectation that his shelter will remain undisturbed."); United States v. Ruckman, 806 F.2d 1471, 1472–74 (10th Cir. 1986) (no reasonable expectation of privacy in dwelling built in a cave on federal land); State v. Tegland, 269 Or. App. 1, 10–11 (2015) ("[W]here erecting a structure in the public space is illegal and the person has been so informed and told that the structure must be removed, there is no 'reasonable expectation of privacy' associated with the space."); People v. Nishi, 207 Cal. App. 4th 954, 962–63 (2012) (repeated removal by law enforcement from campsite occupied illegally tends to negate legitimate expectation of privacy in that location).

105. Toni Morrison, *On the Backs of Blacks,* Time (Dec. 2, 1993).

106. This is another moment to remind the reader that I am not suggesting that Black people are the only racial group who are impacted by the Court's seizure analysis. Note, for example, that the case establishing the idea that law enforcement may question a person about their immigration status without implicating the Fourth Amendment involved Latina/os litigants.

Chapter Two: Traffic Stops

1. CHARLES R. EPP ET AL., PULLED OVER: HOW POLICE STOPS DEFINE RACE AND CITIZENSHIP 66–68 (2014).

2. *Id.*

3. *Id.* at 67.

4. *Id.* at 68.

5. Michael S. Schmidt & Matt Apuzzo, *South Carolina Officer Is Charged with Murder of Walter Scott*, N.Y. TIMES (Apr. 7, 2015), http://www.nytimes .com/2015/04/08/us/south-carolina-officer-is-charged-with-murder-in -black-mans-death.html [https://perma.cc/KQX2-V4R6].

6. *Id.*

7. David Zucchino, *'Reason I Stopped You Is Your Brake Light Is Out,'* L.A. TIMES (Apr. 9, 2015), http://www.latimes.com/nation/la-na-south-carolina -dash-cam-20150409-story.html [https://perma.cc/J3X8-PHBS].

8. Schmidt & Apuzzo, *supra* note 5.

9. For two earlier efforts at describing what one might call the total effects of traffic stops, see David A. Sklansky, *Traffic Stops, Minority Motorists, and the Future of the Fourth Amendment*, 1997 SUP. CT. REV. 271 and Wayne R. LaFave, *The "Routine Traffic Stop" from Start to Finish: Too Much "Routine," Not Enough Fourth Amendment*, 102 MICH. L. REV. 1843 (2004).

10. *See* Delaware v. Prouse, 440 U.S. 648, 653 (1979) ("[S]topping an automobile and detaining its occupants constitute a 'seizure' within the meaning of [the Fourth and Fourteenth] Amendments. . . .").

11. *See* Whren v. United States, 517 U.S. 806 (1996) (holding that officer's racial motivations are irrelevant when officer has probable cause to stop a car for a traffic infraction).

12. *See id.*

13. Heien v. North Carolina, 574 U.S. 54 (2014) (holding that an officer's reasonable mistake of law does not render a traffic stop seizure unconstitutional).

14. *See id.*

15. *See* Utah v. Streiff, 136 S. Ct. 2056 (2016); Maryland v. Garrison, 480 U.S. 79 (1987).

16. *See Whren*, 517 U.S. at 806 (holding that when police officers have

probable cause to stop vehicles for traffic infractions, it is irrelevant whether they do so for pretextual reasons).

17. Elizabeth E. Joh, *Discretionless Policing: Technology and the Fourth Amendment*, 95 CAL. L. REV. 199, 209 (2007) (suggesting that pretextual stops occur "when the justification offered for the detention is legally sufficient, but is not the actual reason for the stop").

18. *See* Alberto B. Lopez, *$10 and a Denim Jacket? A Model Statute for Compensating the Wrongly Convicted*, 36 GA. L. REV. 665, 691–92 (2002) ("Unfortunately the probable cause standard is so low that proving its absence is nearly impossible."); Michael Mello, *"Is a Puzzlement!" An Overview of the Fourth Amendment*, 44 CRIM. L. BULL. 1 (2008) ("Probable cause, as defined by the U.S. Supreme Court, is a very low threshold."); Sadiq Reza, *Privacy and the Criminal Arrestee or Suspect: In Search of a Right, in Need of a Rule*, 64 MD. L. REV. 755, 796–97 (2005) ("A finding of probable cause—facts and circumstances that indicate a reasonable probability that a crime has been committed; a relatively low standard that falls somewhere below a prima facie showing of guilt—by a judge or magistrate is required to issue an arrest or search warrant.").

19. Ira Glasser, *American Drug Laws: The New Jim Crow*, 63 ALB. L. REV. 703, 708 (2000) ("We are talking about a national policy which is training police all over this country to use traffic violations, which everyone commits the minute you get into your car, as an excuse to stop and search people with dark skin."); John Dwight Ingram, *Racial and Ethnic Profiling*, 29 T. MARSHALL L. REV. 55, 79 (2003) ("Since almost everyone commits some traffic violation some time, the police are free to choose the drivers they will stop, and the choice may be made partly or solely on the basis of race or ethnicity."); Sklansky, *supra* note 9, at 271 ("Most Americans have never been arrested or had their homes searched by police, but almost everyone has been pulled over.").

20. N.Y. VEH. & TRAF. LAW § 375(2)(b).

21. *Id.* § 375(1)(a).

22. CAL. VEH. CODE § 22400.

23. N.Y. VEH. & TRAF. LAW § 1180(a).

24. FLA. STAT. ANN. § 316.0895.

25. MICH. COMP. LAWS ANN. § 257.639.

26. ARIZ. REV. STAT. § 28-751(1).

27. MICH. COMP. LAWS ANN. § 257.647(1)(b).

28. CAL. VEH. CODE § 22108.

29. OHIO REV. CODE ANN. § 4511.712(a).

30. N.Y. VEH. & TRAF. LAW § 1145.

31. OHIO REV. CODE ANN. § 4511.44.

32. For other racial critiques of traffic stop jurisprudence, see scholarship

on the intersection of race and routine traffic stops. *See* Lewis R. Katz, *'Lonesome Road': Driving Without the Fourth Amendment*, 36 SEATTLE U. L. REV. 1413 (2013); LaFave, *supra* note 9, at 1848; Jordan Blair Woods, *Decriminalization, Police Authority, and Routine Traffic Stops*, 62 UCLA L. REV. 672 (2015). *See generally* Carbado, *(E)racing the Fourth Amendment, supra* Prologue note 2; Devon W. Carbado & Cheryl Harris, *Undocumented Criminal Procedure*, 58 UCLA L. REV. 1543 (2011); Angela J. Davis, *Race, Cops, and Traffic Stops*, 51 U. MIAMI L. REV. 425 (1997); Samuel R. Gross & Katherine Y. Barnes, *Road Work: Racial Profiling and Drug Interdiction on the Highway*, 101 MICH. L. REV. 651 (2003); David A. Harris, *"Driving While Black" and All Other Traffic Offenses: The Supreme Court and Pretextual Stops*, 87 J. CRIM. L. & CRIMINOLOGY 544 (1997); Kevin R. Johnson, *How Racial Profiling in America Became the Law of the Land: United States v. Brignoni-Ponce and Whren v. United States and the Need for Truly Rebellious Lawyering*, 98 GEO. L.J. 1005 (2010); Nancy Leong, *The Open Road and the Traffic Stop: Narratives and Counter-Narratives of the American Dream*, 64 FLA. L. REV. 305 (2012); Tracey Maclin, *Race and the Fourth Amendment*, 51 VAND. L. REV. 331 (1998).

33. Gary Webb, *Driving While Black: Tracking Unspoken Law-Enforcement Racism*, ESQUIRE (Jan. 29, 2007), http://www.esquire.com/news-politics /a1223/driving-while-black-0499 [https://perma.cc/5E9R-EKUX].

34. EPP ET AL., *supra* note 1, at 36.

35. *Id.* (footnote omitted).

36. *Id.*

37. LaFave, *supra* note 9, at 1875 (footnotes omitted).

38. *See, e.g.*, United States v. Montoya de Hernandez, 473 U.S. 531, 541 (1985) ("The 'reasonable suspicion' standard has been applied in a number of contexts and effects a needed balance between private and public interests when law enforcement officials must make a limited intrusion on less than probable cause."); United States v. Cortez, 449 U.S. 411, 417–18 (1981) ("Based upon th[e] whole picture the detaining officers must have a particularized and objective basis for suspecting the particular person stopped of criminal activity."); United States v. Berber-Tinoco, 510 F.3d 1083, 1087 (9th Cir. 2007) ("[E]ven when factors considered in isolation from each other are susceptible to an innocent explanation, they may collectively amount to a reasonable suspicion.").

39. United States v. Brignoni-Ponce, 422 U.S. 873, 884–87 (1975).

40. Pennsylvania v. Mimms, 434 U.S. 106, 111 (1977) (requiring driver to exit car is at most a de minimis intrusion on driver's personal liberty).

41. Maryland v. Wilson, 519 U.S. 408, 414–15 (1997).

42. Michigan v. Long, 463 U.S. 1032, 1047–50 (1983) (finding that the *Terry* regime applies to vehicular stops and limited searches).

43. *See* Adams v. Williams, 407 U.S. 143 (1972) (holding that an anony-

mous tip that a man was in a nearby car in a high crime area with narcotics and a gun supported reasonable suspicion for search).

44. *See, e.g.,* Andrew Guthrie Ferguson & Damien Bernache, *The "High-Crime Area" Question: Requiring Verifiable and Quantifiable Evidence for Fourth Amendment Reasonable Suspicion Analysis,* 57 Am. U. L. Rev. 1587, 1609 (2008).

45. *See, e.g.,* Illinois v. Caballes, 543 U.S. 405, 406–08 (2005). This does not mean that there are no constraints on police officers' ability to employ drug-detection dogs. "A seizure that is justified solely by the interest in issuing a warning ticket to the driver can become unlawful if it is prolonged beyond the time reasonably required to complete that mission." *Id.* at 407; *see also* Rodriguez v. United States, 575 U.S. 348 (2015) (holding that the Fourth Amendment tolerates certain unrelated investigations that do not lengthen the roadside detentions).

46. As you will learn further along in this book, unlike criminal forfeiture, civil forfeiture does not necessarily entail the prosecution of a person. The subject of the lawsuit is the property itself.

47. In other words, Tanya may believe that if she refuses consent, the officer will (illegally) arrest her. *See, e.g.,* United States v. Freeman, 479 F.3d 743, 749 (10th Cir. 2007) ("Refusal to consent to a search—even agitated refusal—is not grounds for reasonable suspicion.").

48. State v. Robinette, 73 Ohio St. 3d 650, 645-55 (1995).

49. Ohio v. Robinette, 519 U.S. 33, 48 (1996) (Stevens, J., dissenting) (citation omitted).

50. Barry Friedman & Cynthia Benin Stein, *Redefining What's "Reasonable": The Protections for Policing,* 84 Geo. Wash. L. Rev. 281, 301 (2016) (citing study).

51. *See, e.g.,* Nw. Univ. Ctr. for Pub. Safety, Illinois Traffic Stops Statistics Study: 2007 Annual Report 11 (2007), http://www.dot .state.il.us/Assets/uploads/files/Transportation-System/Reports/Safety /Traffic-Stop-Studies/2007/2007%20Illinois%C20Traffic%C20Stop%20 Summary.pdf [https://perma.cc/594S-HVPT] (finding that, in Illinois, people of color are subject to consent searches at twice the rate of whites); *see also* Friedman & Stein, *supra* note 50, at 302 n.103 (discussing other studies).

52. *See* Atwater v. City of Lago Vista, 532 U.S. 318, 339–40, 345, 354 (2001) (discussing various reasons why custodial arrests even for very minor criminal offenses do not violate the Fourth Amendment).

53. *See id.* at 323–24.

54. *Id.*

55. *Id.* at 324.

56. *Id.* at 326.

57. *Id.* at 344–46.

58. *Id.*

59. The majority, after an extensive historical review, rejected Atwater's claim that "'founding-era common-law rules' forbade peace officers to make warrantless misdemeanor arrests except in cases of 'breach of the peace'." *Id.* at 37 (citations omitted). The Court also declined to adopt a "modern arrest rule," suggested by Atwater, which would bar custodial arrests for offenses that, upon conviction, could not result in incarceration. *Id.* at 346.

60. *Id.* at 360 (O'Connor, J., dissenting).

61. *Id.* at 372.

62. Florida v. Bostick, 501 U.S. 429, 436 (1991).

63. *Id.*

64. *Id.* at 437.

65. *Id.* at 432.

66. *Id.*

67. *Id.* at 446 (Marshall, J., dissenting) (citations omitted).

68. *Id.* at 450.

69. *Id.* at 438.

70. In the early 1990s, in the aftermath of the Rodney King beating incident, the NAACP held a series of hearings in cities across the nation to discuss police conduct in minority communities. CHARLES J. OGLETREE ET AL., BEYOND THE RODNEY KING STORY 4–9 (1995). Based on those hearings, the NAACP concluded that many minority citizens with valid grievances do not file formal complaints against police officers. *Id.* at 52–65. According to witnesses who testified at the hearings, such citizens often are actively discouraged from filing complaints by police, and many fear police reprisal. *Id.* at 52, 55. Others are uninformed about complaint procedures, which are often poorly publicized, or are skeptical that such complaints will be taken seriously. *Id.* at 54–55, 60–67.

71. Atwater v. City of Lago Vista, 532 U.S. 318, 369–70 (O'Connor, J., dissenting) (citations omitted).

72. *See* Virginia v. Moore, 553 U.S. 164, 177 (2008) (noting that the Fourth Amendment does not require exclusion of evidence obtained incident to an arrest that violated state law so long as the arrest was not itself unconstitutional).

73. *See* United States v. Robinson, 414 U.S. 218, 235–36 (1973) (noting that "the fact of [the] custodial arrest . . . gives rise to the authority to search" and that an arrest "being lawful, a search incident to the arrest requires no additional justification").

74. Arizona v. Gant, 556 U.S. 332, 346 (2009) (permitting police officers to "conduct a vehicle search when an arrestee is within reaching distance of the vehicle or it is reasonable to believe the vehicle contains evidence of the offense of arrest").

75. For a discussion of why we should pay far more attention to the costs of arrests, see Rachel A. Harmon, *Federal Programs and the Real Costs of Policing*, 90 N.Y.U. L. REV. 870 (2015).

76. 569 U.S. 435, 465–66 (2013).

77. *Id.* at 481 (Scalia, J., dissenting) (citation omitted).

78. *See, e.g.*, George M. Dery III, *Opening One's Mouth "For Royal Inspection": The Supreme Court Allows Collection of DNA from Felony Arrestees in* Maryland v. King, 2 VA. J. CRIM. L. 116, 155 (2014).

79. *See* Florence v. Bd. of Chosen Freeholders, 566 U.S. 318, 339 (2012).

80. *See id.* at 334.

81. *See, e.g.*, George M. Dery III, Florence *and the Machine: The Supreme Court Upholds Suspicionless Strip Searches Resulting from Computer Error*, 40 AM. J. CRIM. L. 173, 173 (2013).

Chapter Three: Stop-and-Frisk

1. Floyd v. City of New York, 959 F. Supp. 2d 540, 649 (S.D.N.Y. 2013).

2. *Id.*

3. *Id.* at 649–650.

4. *Id.* at 650.

5. *Id.*

6. *Id.* at 649.

7. *Id.* at 650.

8. *Id.*

9. Jamilah King, *Meet David Floyd, the Man at the Center of NYPD's Stop-and-Frisk Trial*, COLORLINES (Mar. 19, 2013), https://www.colorlines .com/articles/meet-david-floyd-man-center-nypds-stop-and-frisk-trial.

10. Seth Freed Wessler, *Video Exclusive: David Floyd on Why He Sued the NYPD*, COLORLINES (Mar. 25, 2013), http://www.colorlines.com/articles /video-exclusive-david-floyd-why-he-sued-nypd.

11. *Floyd*, 959 F. Supp. 2d at 650.

12. *Id.* at 651.

13. *Id. See also* Joseph Goldstein, *Trial to Start on Class Suit on Stop-and-Frisk Tactic*, N.Y. TIMES (Mar. 17 2013), http://www.nytimes.com/2013/03 /18/nyregion/stop-and-frisk-trial-to-open-this-week-in-federal-court.html.

14. *Floyd*, 959 F. Supp. 2d at 651.

15. *Id.*

16. Matt Sledge, *David Floyd, Lead Stop and Frisk Plaintiff, Takes Stand in First Day of Trial*, HUFF. POST (MAR. 19, 2013), http://www.huffingtonpost .com/2013/03/18/david-floyd-stop-and-frisk-trial_n_2903682.html.

17. Devon W. Carbado, *From Stop and Frisk to Shoot and Kill: Terry v. Ohio's Pathway to Police Violence*, 64 UCLA L. REV. 1508, 1547 (2017).

18. It should be noted that separating out "Black" and "Hispanic" (or Latinx) into mutually exclusive groups glosses over the very real and complicated ways in which these two identities intersect. Yet, the expert testimony and evidence subject to the court's analysis in this case were separated into these two distinct categories, making it difficult for us to retroactively assess the intersectional identities of the "Hispanic" group. Interestingly enough, the NYPD's own UF-250 forms used to track stops separated "Hispanic" into two categories—"black Hispanic" and "white Hispanic." Ligon v. City of New York, 925 F. Supp. 2d 478, 550 (S.D.N.Y. 2013).

19. *Floyd*, 959 F. Supp. 2d at 560.

20. *Id.* at 572.

21. *Id.* at 558–60, 574, 583–84; *see also* CTR. FOR CONSTITUTIONAL RIGHTS, STOP-AND-FRISK: FAGAN REPORT SUMMARY (2010), https://ccrjustice.org /sites/default/files/assets/Fagan%20Report%20Summary%20Final.pdf [https://perma.cc/858M-WR63]; *Stop and Frisk in Other Cities*, ACLU ILL., http://www.aclu-il.org/stop-and-frisk-in-other-cities [https://perma .cc/PU3X-L5H3].

22. The literature criticizing the programmatic nature of contemporary usage of stop and-frisk is growing. *See, e.g.*, Friedman & Stein, *supra* Chapter 2 note 50, at 286–87; Tracey L. Meares, *Programming Errors: Understanding the Constitutionality of Stop-and-Frisk as a Program, Not an Incident*, 82 U. CHI. L. REV. 159, 164 (2016); Kami Chavis Simmons, *The Legacy of Stop and Frisk: Addressing the Vestiges of A Violent Police Culture*, 49 WAKE FOREST L. REV. 849, 865–68 (2014).

23. *See* Carbado & Harris, *supra* Chapter 2 note 32, at 1565.

24. *See* John Q. Barrett, Terry v. Ohio: *The Fourth Amendment Reasonableness of Police Stops and Frisks Based on Less than Probable Cause*, in CRIMINAL PROCEDURE STORIES 295, 300 (Carol Steiker ed., 2006).

25. *See id.*

26. Tracey L. Meares, *The Law and Social Science of Stop and Frisk*, 10 ANN. REV. L. & SOC. SCI. 335, 337 (2014).

27. *See* JOHN ROBERT GREENE, AMERICA IN THE SIXTIES 82–83 (2010).

28. KERNER COMM'N, REPORT OF THE NATIONAL ADVISORY COMMISSION ON CIVIL DISORDERS 206, 299–305 (1968).

29. 392 U.S. 1 (1968).

30. *Id.* at 5.

31. *Id.*

32. *Id.* at 6.

33. *Id.* at 6–7.

34. *Id.* at 7.

35. *Id.* at 4.

36. *Id.* at 10.

37. "[T]he invasion of a constitutionally protected area by federal authorities is, as the Court has long held, presumptively unreasonable in the absence of a search warrant." Katz v. United States, 389 U.S. 347, 361 (1967) (Harlan, J., concurring).

38. *See* Dunaway v. New York, 442 U.S. 200, 207–08 (1979) ("Before *Terry v. Ohio*, the Fourth Amendment's guarantee against unreasonable seizures of persons was analyzed in terms of arrest, probable cause for arrest, and warrants based on such probable cause.") (citation omitted).

39. Probable cause is a "reasonable ground to suspect that a person has committed or is committing a crime" and "amounts to more than a bare suspicion but less than evidence that would justify a conviction." *Probable Cause*, BLACK'S LAW DICTIONARY (11th ed. 2019).

40. *Terry*, 392 U.S. at 15 (emphasis added).

41. *Id.* at 33 (Harlan, J., concurring).

42. *Id.* at 22 (majority opinion).

43. For a list of states that had stop-and-question statutes in 1967, see Brief of American Civil Liberties Union, American Civil Liberties Union of Ohio, and New York Civil Liberties Union, Amici Curiae at 8 n.6, Terry v. Ohio, 392 U.S. 1 (1968) (No. 67), which lists New Hampshire, Rhode Island, Delaware, Hawaii, Massachusetts, and the city of Miami, Florida. Also see the Uniform Arrest Act, printed in Sam Warner, *The Uniform Arrest Act*, 28 VA. L. REV. 315, 343–47 (1942), which authorized police officers to detain and question suspects on less than probable cause. For a recent list of states with stop-and-frisk statutes, see ACLU ILL., *supra* note 21, and Aziz Z. Huq, *The Consequences of Disparate Policing: Evaluating Stop and Frisk as a Modality of Urban Policing*, 101 MINN. L. REV. 2397 (2017).

44. 392 U.S. 40 (1968).

45. *Id.* at 43 (quoting N.Y. CRIM. PROC. LAW § 180-a (McKinney Supp. 1966) (currently codified at N.Y. CRIM. PROC. LAW § 140.15 (McKinney 2004))).

46. *See id.* at 70 (Harlan, J., concurring).

47. *Id.* at 71.

48. *See* Brief of National District Attorneys Ass'n at 9, Terry v. Ohio, 392 U.S. 1 (No. 67) ("Granting the police the right of temporary field detention and protective patdown on a standard less than probable cause to arrest is the only effective way to meet 'the challenge of crime in a free society.'" (quoting NICHOLAS DEB. KATZENBACH ET AL., PRESIDENT'S COMM'N ON LAW ENF'T & ADMIN. OF JUSTICE, THE CHALLENGE OF CRIME IN A FREE SOCIETY (1967)); Brief of Americans for Effective Law Enforcement, as

Amicus Curiae at 13, Terry v. Ohio, 392 U.S. 1 (No. 67) ("[T]here may be a concept of *variable* probable cause which applies to pre-arrest investigatory procedures such as field interrogation, and that the true test is the *balancing* of the degree of interference with personal liberty against the information possessed by the officer which impelled him to act."); Brief of Attorney General of the State of New York as Amicus Curiae in Support of Appellees at 3, 4, Terry v. Ohio, 392 U.S. 1 (1968) (No. 67) (discussing "the common law right of a police officer to question any individual in a public place where there is a reasonable suspicion that a crime has been committed or is about to be committed" and arguing that "[t]his power to question is a necessary element in crime prevention"); Brief for the United States as Amicus Curiae at 2, Terry v. Ohio 392 U.S. 1 (1968) (No. 67) ("[A] lesser showing will meet the constitutional test of reasonableness in the case of a brief detention on the street [as compared to] the case of a conventional arrest.").

49. United States v. Brignoni-Ponce, 422 U.S. 899 (1975) (ruling that the government may employ reasonable suspicion as a basis for stopping and questioning a person about their immigration status).

50. *See* Jeffrey Fagan, Terry's *Original Sin*, 2016 U. CHI. LEGAL F. 43, 56; *see also* Carbado & Harris, *supra* Chapter 2 note 32, at 1568–78 (discussing the extension of *Terry* to the immigration enforcement context).

51. *See* WILLIAM E. RINGEL, SEARCHES & SEIZURES, ARRESTS & CONFESSIONS §13:3 (2nd ed. 2020).

52. David A. Harris, *Factors for Reasonable Suspicion: When Black and Poor Means Stopped and Frisked*, 69 IND. L.J. 659, 660 (1994).

53. Illinois v. Wardlow, 528 U.S. 119 (2000).

54. *Id.* at 124.

55. California v. Hodari D., 499 U.S. 621, 623 n.1 (1991) ("[T]he wicked flee when no man pursueth.") (quoting Proverbs 28:1).

56. *Wardlow*, 528 U.S. at 124. *See* Butler, *supra* Chapter 1 note 73, at 254 ("The police have more power in high-crime neighborhoods than low-crime neighborhoods."); *see also* Raymond, *supra* Chapter 1 note 90.

57. *Wardlow*, 528 U.S. at 124.

58. *Id.* at 125.

59. Ferguson, *supra* Chapter 1 note 90, at 183. One could argue that the Court's analysis included the fact that the defendant was holding an opaque bag and the officers' sense of the neighborhood vis-à-vis drug distribution. "Just as a man with a hammer sees every problem as a nail, so a man with a badge may see every corner of his beat as a high crime area." United States v. Montero-Camargo, 208 F.3d 1122, 1143 (9th Cir. 2000) (Kozinkski, J., concurring).

60. *See, e.g.*, Ferguson & Bernache, *supra* Chapter 2 note 44, at 1590–91 (discussing the failure of courts to offer guidance on what constitutes a "high crime area").

61. *See* Donald F. Tibbs, *From Black Power to Hip Hop: Discussing Race, Policing, and the Fourth Amendment Through the "War on" Paradigm*, 15 J. GENDER RACE & JUST. 47, 67 (2012) (suggesting that *Wardlow's* use of "'high crime neighborhood' is code for poor Black ghetto"); *see also* Tovah Renee Calderón, *Race-Based Policing From Terry to Wardlow: Steps Down the Totalitarian Path*, 44 HOW. L.J. 73, 93 (2000) (noting how "when officers claim they are patrolling a 'high crime area' they are often speaking in 'code' about a poor, black urban neighborhood," and further suggesting how *Wardlow* substantiates this "code").

62. *See* Butler *supra* Chapter 1 note 73, at 250–52; I. Bennett Capers, *Policing, Race, and Place*, 44 HARV. C.R.-C.L. L. REV. 43 (2009); Ferguson & Bernache, *supra* Chapter 2 note 44, at 1609; Ferguson, *supra* Chapter 1 note 90; Raymond, *supra* Chapter 1 note 90.

63. Report of Plaintiffs' Expert Dr. Jeffrey Fagan, PhD at 17, 51 tbl.11, Floyd v. City of New York, 959 F. Supp. 2d 540 (S.D.N.Y. 2013) (No. 08 Civ. 1034).

64. *See* Ben Grunwald & Jeffrey Fagan, *The End of Intuition-Based High-Crime Areas*, 107 CALIF. L. REV. 345, 388–89 (2019).

65. *Id.* at 383–384 (2019).

66. Floyd v. City of New York, 959 F. Supp. 2d 540, 581 (S.D.N.Y. 2013).

67. *Id.* at 558 ("Between January 2004 and June 2012, the NYPD conducted over 4.4 million *Terry* stops. . . . 52% of all stops were followed by a protective frisk for weapon. A weapon was found after 1.5% of these frisks. In other words, in 98.5% of the 2.3 million frisks, no weapon was found.").

68. *Id.*

69. For a list of states that have enacted "stop and identify" statutes, see *Hiibel v. Sixth Judicial Dist. Court of Nevada, Humboldt Cnty.*, 542 U.S. 177, 182 (2004).

70. *See* Florida v. Bostick, 501 U.S. 429, 436 (1990).

71. *See* Illinois v. Wardlow, 528 U.S. 119, 124 (2000).

72. *See, e.g.*, Ornelas v. United States, 517 U.S. 690, 700 (1996) (relying on the officer's past narcotic experience to conclude that his search was reasonable).

73. For a discussion of how implicit biases, including stereotypes, affect various dimensions of policing, see L. Song Richardson, *Police Efficiency and the Fourth Amendment*, 87 IND. L.J. 1143 (2012) and Cynthia Lee, *Making Race Salient: Trayvon Martin and Implicit Bias in a Not Yet Post-Racial Society*, 91 N.C. L. REV. 1555 (2013).

74. *See, e.g.*, Toussaint Cummings, *I Thought He Had a Gun: Amending New York's Justification Statute to Prevent Police Officers from Mistakenly Shooting Unarmed Black Men*, 12 CARDOZO PUB. L. POL'Y & ETHICS J. 781, 785–86 (2014); Jennifer L. Eberhardt et al., *Seeing Black: Race, Crime, and Visual Processing*, 87 J. PERSONALITY & SOC. PSYCHOL. 876, 878 (2004);

Jessica J. Sim et al., *Understanding Police and Expert Performance: When Training Attenuates (vs. Exacerbates) Stereotypic Bias in the Decision to Shoot*, 39 PERSONALITY & SOC. PSYCHOL. BULL. 291, 292 (2013).

75. Jennifer Eberhardt et al., *supra* note 74.

76. *Id.* at 879.

77. *Id.*

78. *Id.* at 879 fig.1.

79. *Id.* at 880.

80. *Id.* at 878. The researchers hypothesized that seeing a Black face would serve as "a visual tuning effect, reducing the perceptual threshold for spontaneously recognizing guns and knives." *Id.*

81. *Id.* at 882.

82. *Id.* at 882–84.

83. For an account of how this science ought to impact our conceptions of reasonable suspicion and self-defense, see L. Song Richardson & Phillip Atiba Goff, *Self-Defense and the Suspicion Heuristic,* 98 IOWA L. REV. 293 (2012) (suggesting that cognitive biases lead police officers to perceive a need for self-defensive violence more often when dealing with racial minorities).

84. Jerry Kang, *Trojan Horses of Race,* 118 HARV. L. REV. 1489 (2005) (describing the real world consequences of implicit bias as social cognition research develops). For a discussion of the relevance of various literatures in social cognition to policing, see generally, Devon W. Carbado & Patrick Rock, *What Exposes African Americans to Police Violence?*, 51 HARV. C.R.-C.L. L. REV. 159 (2016).

85. L. Song Richardson, *Implicit Racial Bias and Racial Anxiety: Implications for Stops and Frisks,* 15 OHIO ST. J. CRIM. L. 73 (2017).

86. For a thoughtful discussion of whether Justice Warren should have anticipated where the *Terry* regime landed, see Carol S. Steiker, *Terry Unbound,* 82 MISS. L.J. 329 (2013), which argues that Justice Rehnquist played a critical role pushing the *Terry* standard well beyond the boundaries that Justice Warren articulated.

87. John Q. Barrett, *Deciding the Stop and Frisk Cases: A Look Inside the Supreme Court's Conference,* 72 ST. JOHN'S L. REV. 749, 826 (1998) (quoting Letter from Justice William J. Brennan, Jr. to Chief Justice Earl Warren 2 (Mar. 14, 1968) (on file with the Library of Congress)).

88. Brief for the N.A.A.C.P. Legal Defense and Educational Fund, Inc., as Amicus Curiae at 3, Terry v. Ohio, 392 U.S. 1 (No. 67).

89. *Id.*

90. *Id.* at 62.

91. *See* SEAN DENNIS CASHMAN, AFRICAN-AMERICANS AND THE QUEST FOR CIVIL RIGHTS, 1900–1990, 198 (1991); CIVIL RIGHTS AND THE

AMERICAN NEGRO: A DOCUMENTARY HISTORY 598 (Albert P. Blaustein & Robert L. Zangrando eds., 1968); THE ENCYCLOPEDIA OF CIVIL RIGHTS IN AMERICA 120 (David Bradley & Shelley Fisher Fishkin eds., 1998).

92. The Black Panther Party was founded in 1966. *See* CASHMAN, *supra* note 91, at 201; ENCYCLOPEDIA OF CIVIL RIGHTS IN AMERICA, *supra* note 91, at 118. As Paul Butler observes, when Black Panther members saw police officers harassing Black people, "they would approach and watch with their guns drawn." BUTLER, *supra* Prologue note 11, at 87.

93. Bloody Sunday occurred on March 7, 1965, and the Selma-to-Montgomery march was finally completed on the marchers' third attempt on March 21, 1965. *See* CASHMAN, *supra* note 91, at 189–90; ENCYCLOPEDIA OF CIVIL RIGHTS IN AMERICA, *supra* note 91, at 792–93; *see also* Richard H. King, *'How Long? Not Long'*: Selma, *Martin Luther King and Civil Rights Narratives*, 49 PATTERNS PREJUDICE 466 (2015).

94. *See* IAN HANEY LÓPEZ, DOG WHISTLE POLITICS: HOW CODED RACIAL APPEALS HAVE REINVENTED RACISM AND THE WRECKED MIDDLE CLASS (2014).

95. *See* DANIEL S. LUCKS, SELMA TO SAIGON: THE CIVIL RIGHTS MOVEMENT AND THE VIETNAM WAR 102–03 (2014).

96. President John F. Kennedy was assassinated on November 22, 1963. *See* ENCYCLOPEDIA OF THE COLD WAR: A POLITICAL, SOCIAL, AND MILITARY HISTORY 708 (Spencer C. Tucker ed., 2007). Malcolm X was assassinated on February 21, 1965. *See* CASHMAN, *supra* note 91, at 176; ENCYCLOPEDIA OF CIVIL RIGHTS IN AMERICA, *supra* note 91, at 560. Martin Luther King, Jr. was assassinated on April 4, 1968. *See* CASHMAN, *supra* note 91, at 210; ENCYCLOPEDIA OF CIVIL RIGHTS IN AMERICA, *supra* note 91, at 505; *see also* ROBERT COOK, SWEET LAND OF LIBERTY?: THE AFRICAN-AMERICAN STRUGGLE FOR CIVIL RIGHTS IN THE TWENTIETH CENTURY 212–13 (1998). Senator Robert F. Kennedy was assassinated on June 5, 1968. *See* ENCYCLOPEDIA OF AMERICAN CIVIL RIGHTS AND LIBERTIES 580 (Otis H. Stephens, Jr. et al. eds., 2006).

97. Bennett Capers, *Criminal Procedure and the Good Citizen*, 118 COLUM. L. REV. 653 (2018) (examining how policing shapes citizenship).

98. Terry v. Ohio, 392 U.S. 1, 14 n.11 (1968).

99. Nancy Leong, *Making Rights*, 92 B.U. L. REV. 405 (2012) (suggesting that courts give content to our Fourth Amendment rights in the context of cases in which defendants are seeking to suppress evidence).

100. *Terry*, 392 U.S. at 7–8, (discussing the defendant's motion to suppress the gun the officer found upon conducting a frisk); *id.* at 12–15 (describing the genesis and rationales for the exclusionary rule).

101. For an early articulation of the exclusionary rule, see *Boyd v. United States*, 116 U.S. 616 (1886). Initial justifications for the exclusionary rule sounded in the language of judicial integrity, the idea being that courts

should not sanction the illegal conduct of police officers. *See* Weeks v. United States, 232 U.S 383, 393 (1914); *see also* Elkins v. United States, 364 U.S. 206, 222–23 (1960), *cited in* Mapp v. Ohio, 367 U.S. 643, 659 (1961). Subsequently, the Court would rest the justification for the rule more squarely on arguments about deterrence. *See* Kit Kinports, *Culpability, Deterrence, and the Exclusionary Rule*, 21 WM. & MARY BILL RTS. J. 821 (2013).

102. *Terry*, 392 U.S. at 12.

103. *Id.*

104. *Elkins*, 364 U.S. at 217.

105. *Terry*, 392 U.S. at 14.

106. *Id.* at 15.

107. Thus the notion of "rational racism" or "rational discrimination." *See* David A. Harris, *The Stories, the Statistics, and the Law: Why "Driving While Black" Matters*, 84 MINN. L. REV. 265, 294 (1999); JODY DAVID ARMOUR, NEGROPHOBIA AND REASONABLE RACISM, THE HIDDEN COSTS OF BEING BLACK IN AMERICA (1997).

108. *See supra* note 75 (listing examples).

109. KHALIL GIBRAN MUHAMMAD, THE CONDEMNATION OF BLACKNESS: RACE, CRIME, AND THE MAKING OF MODERN URBAN AMERICA (2011).

110. *See* Floyd v. City of New York, 959 F. Supp. 2d 540, 596 (S.D.N.Y. 2013).

111. Kate Taylor, *Stop and Frisk Policy 'Saves Lives,' Mayor Tells Black Congregation*, N.Y. TIMES, June 11, 2012, at A14.

112. *Id.*

113. *Floyd*, 959 F. Supp. 2d at 606.

114. Philip V. McHarris, *Should Mike Bloomberg's stop-and-frisk record disqualify him?*, WASH. POST (Feb. 16, 2020), https://www.washingtonpost .com/outlook/2020/02/16/should-mike-bloombergs-stop-and-frisk-record -disqualify-him/.

115. For a thoughtful discussion of this issue, see Leong, *supra* note 99.

116. As the story goes, two women with a baby approach King Solomon, each woman claiming the baby is hers. Solomon asks for a sword and suggests cutting the living baby in half to share among the two. When one woman rejects this idea, insisting the other woman take the baby rather than allowing the baby to die, Solomon asserts that the woman who rejected 'splitting the baby' is the mother and hands her the child. *See* 1 *Kings* 3:16–27.

117. *See, e.g.*, Anthony C. Thompson, *Stopping the Usual Suspects: Race and the Fourth Amendment*, 74 N.Y.U. L. REV.956, 962–65; Tracey Maclin, *Terry v. Ohio's Fourth Amendment Legacy: Black Men and Police Discretion*, 72 ST. JOHN'S L. REV. 1271 (1998).

118. Frank Rudy Cooper, *The Spirit of 1968: Toward Abolishing* Terry

Doctrine, 31 N.Y.U. Rev. L. & Soc. Change 539 (2007).

119. Bennett Capers, *Re-thinking The Fourth Amendment: Race, Citizenship, and the Equality Principle*, 46 Harv. C.R.-C.L. L. Rev. 1, 32 (2011).

Chapter Four: Stop-and-Strip

1. *See e.g.*, United States v. Vega-Barvo, 729 F.2d 1341, 1345 (11th Cir. 1984).

2. Susan Ferriss, *'Shocked and Humiliated': Lawsuits Accuse Customs, Border Officers of Invasive Searches of Minors, Women*, Ctr. for Pub. Integrity (Sept. 12, 2018), https://publicintegrity.org/inequality-poverty-opportunity /immigration/shocked-and-humiliated-lawsuits-accuse-customs-border -officers-of-invasive-searches-of-minors-women/ [https://perma.cc/6LHB-JN4Y] (describing U.S. Customs and Border Protection officers performing a luggage and body cavity search of a Black woman at a New York airport as she was returning to the United States from Jamaica, performing body cavity searches of female minors at the Texas and San Diego borders, performing multiple body cavity searches of a woman returning to the United States from Mexico at a pedestrian port in San Diego, and performing body cavity searches and ordering hospital staff to conduct X-rays and CT scans of a Black woman seized at the Philadelphia airport as she was returning from the Dominican Republic, and of a Latinx woman entering the United States from a pedestrian port in El Paso).

3. For the classic articulation of intersectionality, see Kimberlé Crenshaw, *Demarginalizing the Intersection of Race and Sex: A Black Feminist Critique of Antidiscrimination Doctrine, Feminist Theory and Antiracist Politics*, 1989 Chi. Legal F. 139.

4. The preceding account draws on the accounts of stop-and-strip Black women provided on *Dateline NBC: Color Blind? Disproportionate Number of Black Women are Strip-Searched by U.S. Customs Agents* (NBC television broadcast Apr. 27, 1999).

5. United States v. Montoya de Hernandez, 473 U.S. 531, 536–39, 541 (1985) (holding that a strip search of a person at the border is justified at its inception if customs agents reasonably suspect that the traveler is smuggling contraband in her alimentary canal).

6. *See, e.g.*, Paul Butler, *Stop and Frisk and Torture-Lite: Police Terror of Minority Communities*, 12 Ohio St. J. Crim. L. 57, 57 (2014).

7. *Montoya de Hernandez*, 473 U.S. at 536.

8. *Id.* at 534.

9. *Id.* at 535.

10. *Id.*

11. *Id.* at 535–36.

12. *Id.* at 544.

13. *Id.* at 541–42.

14. U.S. Const. amend. IV ("The right of the people to be secure in their persons, houses, papers, and effects, against unreasonable searches and seizures, shall not be violated. . . .").

15. *Montoya de Hernandez*, 473 U.S. at 541–42.

16. *Id.*

17. *See* Wayne R. LaFave, Search and Seizure: A Treatise on the Fourth Amendment, § 9.2(g) (Place of detention limits); § 9.2(d) (Use of force; show of force); § 9.2(f) (Time and investigative method limits) (6th ed. 2020).

18. *Montoya de Hernandez*, 473 U.S. at 542–43.

19. *See id.*

20. *See id.*

21. *See id.* at 544.

22. *See id.*

23. *See id. See also* United States v. Flores-Montano, 541 U.S. 149, 152–53 (2004); United States v. Place, 462 U.S. 696, 703 (1983); United States v. Ramsey, 431 U.S. 606, 616 (1977) ("That searches made at the border, pursuant to the long-standing right of the sovereign to protect itself by stopping and examining persons and property crossing into this country, are reasonable simply by virtue of the fact that they occur at the border, should, by now, require no extended demonstration."); United States v. Martinez-Fuerte, 428 U.S. 543, 561–63 (1976); United States v. Brignoni-Ponce, 422 U.S 873, 881–82 (1975).

24. *Montoya de Hernandez*, 473 U.S. at 541.

25. *Id.*

26. *Id.*

27. *Id.* at 543.

28. *Id.*

29. Justice Rehnquist purports not to have decided whether reasonable suspicion is enough to justify strip searches. *Id.* at 541 n.4. That might well be, as a technical matter, for what Justice Rehnquist clearly did decide was that reasonable suspicion was enough to justify a seizure within which a strip search occurred.

30. *See* Tennessee v. Garner, 471 U.S. 1, 2 (1985).

31. *Montoya de Hernandez*, 473 U.S. at 545 (Brennan, J., dissenting) (footnote omitted).

32. *Id.* at 550.

33. *Id.* at 558–59.

34. *Id.* at 559.

35. *Id.* at 544 (majority opinion).

36. *See* Susan Ferriss, *In Horrifying Detail, Women Accuse U.S. Customs Officers of Invasive Body Searches*, WASH. POST (Aug. 19, 2018), https://www.washingtonpost.com/world/national-security/in-horrifying-detail-women-accuse-us-customs-officers-of-invasive-body-searches/2018/08/18/ad7b7d82-9b38-11e8-8d5e-c6c594024954_story.html [https://perma.cc/3EMS-6BPS].

37. U.S. GEN. ACCOUNTING OFFICE, GAO/GGD-00-38, U.S. CUSTOMS SERVICE: BETTER TARGETING OF AIRLINE PASSENGERS FOR PERSONAL SEARCHES COULD PRODUCE BETTER RESULTS 12 tbl.3 (2000).

38. Michael Higgins, *O'Hare Strip Search Suit Settled*, CHI. TRIB. (Feb. 5, 2006), https://www.chicagotribune.com/news/ct-xpm-2006-02-05-0602050279-story.html [https://perma.cc/94TP-Y3XN].

39. Ferriss, *supra* note 36; *accord* Higgins, *supra* note 38.

40. *Montoya de Hernandez*, 473 U.S. at 545 (Brennan, J., dissenting) (quoting United States v. Holtz, 479 F.2d 89, 94 (9th Cir. 1973) (Ely, J., dissenting)).

41. Complaint at 3, Catlin for C.R. v. United States, No. 3:18-cv-00322 (S.D. Cal. Feb. 9, 2018); Complaint at 7, Cervantes v. United States, No. 4:16-cv-00334 (D. Ariz. June 8, 2016); Complaint at 2, Ferguson v. United States, No. 2:14-cv-06807 (E.D. Pa. Dec. 1, 2014).

42. Complaint, *Ferguson, supra* note 41, at 2.

43. *Id.* at 8; Complaint, *Cervantes, supra* note 41, at 5.

44. Complaint at 8, Lovell v. United States, No. 1:18-cv-01867 (E.D.N.Y. Mar. 28, 2018); Complaint at 6, Doe v. El Paso Cty. Hospital Dist., No. 3:13-cv-00406 (W.D. Tex. Dec. 18, 2013).

45. Complaint, *Cervantes, supra* note 41, at 5; Complaint at 11, Lewis v. United States, No. 3:15-cv-02319 (S.D. Cal. Oct. 15, 2015). In *Lewis*, a white woman was strip-searched. She was mistaken by CBP for another woman, an African American, who had an outstanding warrant. *See id.*

46. Complaint, *Ferguson, supra* note 41, at 8.

47. Complaint, *Catlin for C.R., supra* note 41, at 3; Complaint, *Ferguson, supra* note 41, at 12; Complaint, *Doe, supra* note 44, at 5.

48. Complaint, *Lewis, supra* note 45, at 11.

49. Complaint, *Catlin for C.R., supra* note 41, at 3.

50. *Id.*; Complaint, *Lewis, supra* note 45, at 11.

51. Complaint, *Catlin for C.R., supra* note 41, at 3; Complaint, *Doe, supra* note 44, at 5; Complaint, *Ferguson, supra* note 41, at 13.

52. Complaint, *Doe, supra* note 44, at 6; Complaint, *Lovell, supra note* 44, at 6; Complaint, *Cervantes, supra* note 41, at 8.

53. Complaint, *Doe, supra* note 44, at 8; Complaint, *Lovell, supra note* 44, at 6; Complaint, *Cervantes, supra* note 41, at 8.

54. Complaint, *Doe, supra* note 44, at 8.

55. Complaint, *Lewis, supra* note 45, at 14.

56. Complaint, *Cervantes, supra* note 41, at 5.

57. Complaint, *Doe, supra* note 44, at 6; Complaint, *Ferguson, supra* note 41, at 2; Complaint, *Cervantes, supra* note 41, at 6.

58. Complaint, *Doe, supra* note 44, at 7.

59. *Id.*; Complaint, *Ferguson, supra* note 41, at 14.

60. Complaint, *Ferguson, supra* note 41, at 2.

61. Complaint, *Doe, supra* note 44, at 6; Complaint, *Cervantes, supra* note 41, at 8.

62. Complaint, *Ferguson, supra* note 41, at 2.

63. Complaint, *Doe, supra* note 44, at 9; Complaint, *Lewis, supra* note 45, at 11–13; Complaint, *Ferguson, supra* note 41, at 2; Complaint, *Cervantes, supra* note 41, at 8.

64. Complaint, *Lewis, supra* note 45, at 15–16.

65. Complaint, *Ferguson, supra* note 41, at 11.

66. Complaint, *Cervantes, supra* note 41, at 5–6.

67. SARAH HALEY, NO MERCY HERE: GENDER, PUNISHMENT, AND THE MAKING OF JIM CROW MODERNITY (2016).

68. *See, e.g.*, ANGELA Y. DAVIS, VIOLENCE AGAINST WOMEN AND THE ONGOING CHALLENGES TO RACISM (1985); Kimberlé Crenshaw, *Mapping the Margins: Intersectionality, Identity Politics, and Violence Against Women of Color*, 43 STAN. L. REV. 1241 (1991); HAZEL CARBY, RECONSTRUCTING WOMANHOOD: THE EMERGENCE OF THE AFRO-AMERICAN WOMAN NOVELIST (1987); Cheryl Harris, *Whiteness as Property*, 106 HARV. L. REV. 1707 (1993), Dorothy Roberts, *The Paradox of Silence and Display: Sexual Violation of Enslaved Women and Contemporary Contradictions in Black Female Sexuality, in* BEYOND SLAVERY: OVERCOMING ITS RELIGIOUS AND SEXUAL LEGACIES (Bernadette J. Brooten ed., 2000); Khiara Bridges, *When Pregnancy is an Injury: Rape, Law, and Culture*, 65 STAN. L. REV. 457 (2013); Priscilla Ocen, *Unshackling Intersectionality*, 10 DU BOIS REV.: SOC. SCI. RSCH. RACE 471 (2013); Hortense J. Spillers, *Mama's Baby, Papa's Maybe: An American Grammar Book*, 17 DIACRITS 64 (1987); Ruth Wilson Gilmore, *Race, Prisons and War: Scenes from the History of US Violence*, 45 SOCIALIST REGISTER 73 (2009).

69. To repeat: These are not the only prongs. Fundamentally, intersectionality is concerned with mapping how power works, including how power functions to produce overlapping social categories such as race, class, gender, and LGTQT+ statuses.

70. Crenshaw, *supra* note 3; *see also*, Devon W. Carbado, *Colorblind*

Intersectionality, 38 SIGNS: J. WOMEN IN CULTURE & SOC'Y 811 (2013).

71. According to a U.S. General Accounting Office report, Black women traveling internationally were nine times more likely than white women to be subjected to X-rays by U.S. Customs officials, even though they were less than half as likely to be carrying contraband, and more likely to be strip-searched than any other group of citizens. *See* U.S. GEN. ACCOUNTING OFFICE, *supra* note 37, at 2. *See also Black Women Searched More, Study Finds*, N.Y. TIMES, Apr. 10, 2000, at A17; Jennifer Loven, *Report: Black Women More Subject to Customs Searches*, LIMA NEWS, Apr. 10, 2000, at A4 (indicating that while Black women passing through U.S. Customs as they return home from overseas trips are more likely to be subjected to strip searches and X-rays, they are the least likely to be carrying drugs); David Johnston, *U.S. Changes Policy on Searching Suspected Drug Smugglers*, N.Y. TIMES (Aug. 12, 1999), https://www.nytimes.com/1999/08/12/us/us-changes-policy-on-searching-suspected-drug-smugglers.html [https://perma.cc/6X7J-ALWX] (describing policy changes limiting border agents' ability to search amid criticism of racial bias particularly against Black women).

72. Kimberlé Williams Crenshaw & Andrea J. Ritchie, *Say Her Name: Resisting Police Brutality Against Black Women*, AF. AMER. POL'Y F. (https://www.aapf.org/sayhername).

73. WESTLAW, westlaw.com (search: advanced: (Terry /p "race" "racial profile" "racial profiling") & "Terry v. Ohio", Jurisdictions: All States and All Federal (last visited Apr. 23, 2021)).

74. WESTLAW, westlaw.com (search: advanced: ("Montoya de Hernandez" /p "race" "racial profile" "racial profiling"), Jurisdictions: All States and All Federal (last visited Apr. 23, 2021)).

75. WESTLAW, westlaw.com (search: advanced: (Terry /p "black man" "African American man") & "Terry v. Ohio", Jurisdictions: All States and All Federal (last visited Apr. 23, 2021)).

76. WESTLAW, westlaw.com (search: advanced: ("Montoya de Hernandez" /p "black woman" "African American woman"), Jurisdictions: All States and All Federal (last visited Apr. 23, 2021)).

77. WESTLAW, westlaw.com (search: advanced: ("reasonable suspicion" /p "black man" "African American man"), Jurisdictions: All States and All Federal (last visited Apr. 23, 2021)).

78. WESTLAW, westlaw.com (search: advanced: ("reasonable suspicion" /p "black woman" "African American woman"), Jurisdictions: All States and All Federal (last visited Apr. 23, 2021)).

79. WESTLAW, westlaw.com (search advanced: (Terry /p "black man" "African American man") & "Terry v. Ohio", Jurisdictions: All States and All Federal (last visited Apr. 23, 2021)).

80. WESTLAW, westlaw.com (search: advanced: (Terry /p "black woman" "African American woman") & "Terry v. Ohio", Jurisdictions: All States and

All Federal (last visited Apr. 23, 2021)).

81. *Cf.* BUTLER, *supra* Prologue note 11 (deconstructing the ways the criminal justice system holds Black men in a chokehold).

82. *See* ANGELA J. DAVIS, POLICING THE BLACK MAN: ARREST, PROSECUTION, AND IMPRISONMENT (2017).

83. BUTLER, *supra* Prologue note 11.

84. WESTLAW, westlaw.com (search: advanced: ("Black wom*n + strip searches"), Jurisdictions: All States and All Federal (last visited Apr. 23, 2021)).

85. 446 U.S. 544 (1980).

86. *Id.* at 547 n.1.

87. *Id.* at 544.

88. *Id.* at 547 n.1.

89. *Id.* at 559–60.

90. *Id.*

91. WESTLAW, westlaw.com (search: advanced: United States v. Mendenhall, citing references, cases, secondary sources, Jurisdictions: All States and All Federal (last visited Apr.23, 2020)).

92. *Id.*

93. WESTLAW, westlaw.com (search: advanced: United States v. Mendenhall, citing references, cases: ("black wom*n"), Jurisdictions: All States and All Federal (last visited Apr.23, 2020)).

94. WESTLAW, westlaw.com (search: advanced: United States v. Mendenhall, citing references, cases: ("black wom*n" and "sexual violence"), Jurisdictions: All States and All Federal (last visited Apr.23, 2020)).

95. WESTLAW, westlaw.com (search: advanced: United States v. Mendenhall, citing references, cases: ("black wom*n" and "police violence"), Jurisdictions: All States and All Federal (last visited Apr. 23, 2020)).

96. *Mendenhall*, 446 U.S. at 558.

97. *Id.* at 545.

98. United States v. Brignoni-Pounce, 422 U.S. 873 (1975) (applying reasonable suspicion to the immigration enforcement detentions); Floyd v. City of New York, 959 F. Supp. 2d 540, 558, 566 (S.D.N.Y. 2013)., *aff'd in part*, 770 F.3d 1051, 1054–55 (2d Cir. 2014) (per curiam).

99. United States v. Place, 462 U.S. 696, 696 (1983).

100. United States v. Choudhry, 461 F.3d 1097, 1098 (9th Cir. 2006).

101. Arizona v. Johnson, 555 U.S. 323, 327 (2009).

102. Hiibel v. Sixth Judicial Dist. Ct. of Nev., Humboldt Cty., 542 U.S. 177, 188–89 (2004).

103. United States v. Stewart, 473 F.3d 1265, 1269 (10th Cir. 2007) (citing Muehler v. Mena, 544 U.S. 93, 101 (2005)). The only limitation is that ques-

tions cannot unduly prolong the stop. *See* United States v. Moore, 795 F.3d 1224, 1229 (10th Cir. 2015) ("[Officers] ask questions, whether or not related to the purpose of the stop, so long as they do not prolong the stop.").

104. Wilson v. Arkansas, 514 U.S. 927, 927 (1995).

105. Maryland v. Buie, 494 U.S. 325, 327 (1990).

106. United States v. Knights, 534 U.S. 112, 112 (2001).

107. Samson v. California, 547 U.S. 843, 843 (2006).

108. United States v. Brignoni-Ponce, 422 U.S. 873, 885–87 (1975).

109. *See* Ibrahim v. Dep't of Homeland Sec., 62 F. Supp. 3d 909, 918 (N.D. Cal. 2014) ("FBI agents and other government employees normally nominate individuals to the [Terrorist Screening Database (TSDB)] using a 'reasonable suspicion standard'. . . . [T]his 'reasonable suspicion' standard was adopted by internal Executive Branch policy and practice."); Elhady v. Kable, 391 F. Supp. 3d 562, 568 (E.D. Va. 2019) ("Nominated individuals are added to the TSDB if their nomination is based 'upon articulable intelligence or information which . . . creates a reasonable suspicion that the individual is engaged, has been engaged, or intends to engage, in . . . terrorism and/or terrorist activities.'") (citation omitted); Kashem v. Barr, 941 F.3d 358, 381 (9th Cir. 2019) (finding that the government's reasonable suspicion standard for placing individuals on the No Fly list satisfied procedural due process); Mohamed v. Holder, 995 F. Supp. 2d 520, 525 (E.D. Va. 2015) (citing to the Terrorist Screening Center and its maintenance of the TSDB, of which the No Fly List is a subset); Latif v. Holder, 28 F. Supp. 3d 1134, 1151–52 (D. Or. 2014). For an extended discussion of this particular extension of reasonable suspicion, see Shirin Sinnar, *Rule of Law Tropes in National Security*, 129 Harv. L. Rev. 1566, 1593–96 (2016). *See also* Jeffrey Kahn, *The Unreasonable Rise of Reasonable Suspicion: Terrorist Watchlists and* Terry v. Ohio, 26 Wm. & Mary Bill Rts. J. 383, 385–86 (2017).

110. United States v. Hensley, 469 U.S. 221, 227 (1985). *See also* State v. Spillner, 173 P.3d 498 (Haw. 2007) (finding that the officer's knowledge of the defendant's misconduct one to two weeks prior was enough to create reasonable suspicion). Further, the FBI's *About the Terrorist Screening Center* webpage explains that "[i]ndividuals are included in the [Terrorist Screening Database, commonly known as 'the watchlist'] when there is reasonable suspicion to believe that a person is a known or suspected terrorist." *Federal Bureau of Investigation, The Terrorist Screening Database,* FBI, https://www.fbi.gov/about/leadership-and-structure/national-security -branch/tsc [https://perma.cc/2HKJ-Q7AZ]. Additionally, Congressional Research Service Report R44678, "The Terrorist Screening Database and Preventing Terrorist Travel" discusses the reasonable suspicion standard for making it onto the TSDB: "Exceptions to the reasonable suspicion threshold exist, and some people are placed in the TSDB 'to support immigration and border screening by the Department of State and the Department of Homeland Security.'" Cong. Research Serv., R44678, The Terrorist

Screening Database and Preventing Terrorist Travel 6 n.30 (2016), https://crsreports.congress.gov/product/pdf/R/R44678 [https://perma.cc/CW6Y-PN5E] (citation omitted).

111. Adams v. Williams, 407 U.S. 143, 147 (1972).

112. Navarette v. California, 572 U.S. 393 (2014). In *Navarette*, there was no additional corroboration, except that the officer observed the vehicle in the vicinity where the tipster had indicated that the driver was driving erratically.

113. Illinois v. Wardlow, 528 U.S. 119, 124–25 (2000); Floyd v. City of New York, 959 F. Supp. 2d 540, 651 (S.D.N.Y. 2013).

114. United States v. Sokolow, 490 U.S. 1, 10 (1989).

115. Michigan v. Summers, 452 U.S. 692, 700 n.12 (1981) (describing investigative methods that can be used within a *Terry*-stop, including holding suspects to show them to witnesses) (citation omitted).

116. Hayes v. Florida, 470 U.S. 811, 816 (1985).

117. United States v. Sharpe, 470 U.S. 675, 686 (1985).

118. United States v. Ramdihall, 859 F.3d 80, 85, 95 (1st Cir. 2017).

119. Safford Unified Sch. Dist. No. 1 v. Redding, 557 U.S. 364, 376–77 (2009) (finding the search at issue unconstitutional because it was not based on reasonable suspicion).

120. O'Connor v. Ortega, 480 U.S. 709, 726 (1987).

121. United States v. Alfonso, 759 F.2d 728, 734 (9th Cir. 1985). The "extended border" can be quite extended. *See, e.g., id.* at 734–35 (describing search of boat 36 hours after it crossed the border); United States v. Martinez, 481 F.2d 214, 218–21 (5th Cir. 1973) (describing search conducted 150 miles from the border and 142 hours after a border crossing was an extended border search).

122. United States v. Cotterman, 709 F.3d 952, 957 (9th Cir. 2013) (en banc).

123. United States v. Ramsey, 431 U.S. 606, 606 (1977).

124. United States v. Vega-Barvo, 729 F.2d 1341, 1349–50 (11th Cir. 1984).

Chapter Five: Predatory Policing

1. U.S. Dep't of Justice, Investigation of the Ferguson Police Department (2015).

2. *Id.* at 4.

3. I use this term to trade on a practice with which many Americans are now familiar—predatory lending. *See History of Predatory Lending*, GeorgiaLegalAid.org (June 15, 2005), http://www.georgialegalaid.org/resource/history-of-predatory-lending [https://perma.cc/F5ZY-HZP6].

4. Mass criminalization, also called overcriminalization, has been docu-

mented for decades by scholars studying the growing volume of state and federal criminal laws and the impact this volume has, particularly on people from over-policed communities. *See* Sara Sun Beale, *The Many Faces of Overcriminalization: From Morals and Mattress Tags to Overfederalization*, 54 AM. U. L. REV. 747, 750–52 (2005); Jamie Michael Charles, Note, *"America's Lost Cause": The Unconstitutionality of Criminalizing Our Country's Homeless Population*, 18 PUB. INT. L.J. 315, 315–16 (2009); Erik Luna, *Principled Enforcement of Penal Codes*, 4 BUFF. CRIM. L. REV. 515, 528–29 (2000); Erik Luna, *The Overcriminalization Phenomenon*, 54 AM. U. L. REV. 703, 703–12 (2005); William J. Stuntz, *The Pathological Politics of Criminal Law*, 100 MICH. L. REV. 505, 515– 16 (2001); Eric S. Tars et al., *Can I Get Some Remedy?: Criminalization of Homelessness and the Obligation to Provide an Effective Remedy*, 45 COLUM. HUM. RTS. L. REV. 738, 739–40 (2014).

5. *See, e.g.*, VA. CODE ANN. § 18.2-322 (2004).

6. *See, e.g.*, ARIZ. REV. STAT. ANN. § 13-3415 (2000); FLA. STAT. § 893.145(8) (2001); MASS. GEN. LAWS ch. 94C, § 321 (2000). *See also* William J. Stuntz, *supra* note 4, at 516 n.51.

7. ARK. CODE ANN. § 5-71-213 (1997); CAL. PENAL CODE § 647(d) (West 1988). *See also* Pamela Sirkin, *The Evanescent Actus Reus Requirement: California Penal Codes 647(d)—Criminal Liability for "Loitering with Intent . . ."—Is Punishment for Merely Thinking Certain Thoughts While Loitering Constitutional?*, 19 SW. U. L. REV. 165, 165–66, 166 n.8 (1990). The Model Penal Code itself notably includes provisions against "disorderly conduct, public drunkenness or drug incapacitation, and loitering or prowling." Luna, *Principled Enforcement of Penal Codes, supra* note 4, at 528–29, 529 n.58 (citing Model Penal Code §§ 250.2 (disorderly conduct), 250.5 (public drunkenness and drug incapacitation), 250.6 (loitering or prowling) (A.L.I. Official Draft and Revised Comments 1985)).

8. NAT'L LAW CTR. ON HOMELESSNESS & POVERTY, NO SAFE PLACE: THE CRIMINALIZATION OF HOMELESSNESS IN U.S. CITIES 1, 8 (2011), https://www .nlchp.org/documents/No_Safe_Place.

9. *See, e.g.*, DALL., TEX., CITY CODE, vol. II, ch. 31 §31-13(a)(1) (1992).

10. NAT'L LAW CTR. ON HOMELESSNESS & POVERTY, *supra* note 8.

11. *See, e.g.*, LAWRENCE, KAN., CITY CODE, ch. XIV, art. IV, § 14-417(C)– (D) (2005); ORL., FLA., CITY CODE, tit. II, ch. 43, § 43.52(2) (2000); SARASOTA, FLA., CITY CODE, ch. 34, art. V, § 34-41(b) (2005); PORTLAND, OR., MUN. CODE, tit. 14, ch. 14A.50, § 14A.50.020(B) (2006); NAT'L LAW CTR. ON HOMELESSNESS & POVERTY, *supra* note 8, at 7.

12. NAT'L LAW CTR. ON HOMELESSNESS & POVERTY, *supra* note 8, at 8.

13. SANTA ANA, CAL., MUN. CODE, ch. 10, art. VIII, §§ 10-400–10-403 (1992); Tobe v. City of Santa Ana, 892 P.2d 1145, 1150–52, 1169 (Cal. 1995) (upholding Santa Ana ordinance against challenge for facial unconstitutional vagueness).

14. *Tobe*, 892 P.2d at 1151.

15. *Id.*

16. *Id.*

17. *Id.*

18. Alexandra Natapoff, *Misdemeanors*, 85 S. CAL. L. REV. 1313, 1315 n.8 (2012).

19. Alexandra Natapoff, *Misdemeanors*, 11 ANN. REV. L. & SOC. SCI. 255, 256 (2015).

20. *Id.*

21. *See* ALEXANDRA NATAPOFF, PUNISHMENT WITHOUT CRIME: OUR MASSIVE MISDEMEANOR SYSTEM TRAPS THE INNOCENT AND MAKES AMERICA MORE UNEQUAL (2018); ISSA KOHLER-HAUSMANN, MISDEMEAN-ORLAND: CRIMINAL COURTS AND SOCIAL CONTROL IN AN AGE OF BROKEN WINDOWS POLICING (2018).

22. Mass criminalization enables the police to arrest African Americans not only through the criminalization of non-serious conduct, but also through the diffusion of criminal justice officials, norms, and strategies into the structure and organization of the welfare state. Consider, for example, the school-to-prison pipeline. Devon W. Carbado, *Blue-on-Black Violence: A Provisional Model of Some of the Causes*, 104 GEO. L.J. 1479, 1490 (2016). Lawyers, scholars, and activists have long decried the ways in which school disciplinary policies and practices create a prison-like environment that facilitates the incarceration of Black youth. For general discussion of the school-to-prison pipeline, see, for example, *School-to-Prison Pipeline*, ACLU, https://www.aclu.org/issues/juvenile-justice/school-prison-pipeline?redirect=fact-sheet/what-school-prison-pipeline [https://perma.cc/63BL-F84G] (last visited Jan. 31, 2017); Editorial, *Stop the School-to-Prison Pipeline*, 26 RETHINKING SCH. (2011–12), http://www.rethinkingschools.org/archive/26_02/edit262.shtml [https://perma.cc/K79R-N72P] (last visited Apr. 3, 2017); Mary Ellen Flannery, *The School-to-Prison Pipeline: Time to Shut It Down*, NEATODAY (Jan. 5, 2015), http://neatoday.org/2015/01/05/school-prison-pipeline-time-shut/ [https://perma.cc/LC7Z-8EAU].

23. *See* Mary Murphy, Note, *Race and Civil Asset Forfeiture: A Disparate Impact Hypothesis*, 16 TEX. J. ON C.L. & C.R. 77, 80–83 (2010). *See also* DICK M. CARPENTER II, ET AL., INST. FOR JUST., POLICING FOR PROFIT: THE ABUSE OF CIVIL ASSET FORFEITURE 11–13, 16–20 (2d ed. 2015), https://ij.org/wp-content/uploads/2015/11/policing-for-profit-2nd-edition.pdf.

24. *See* Whren v. United States, 517 U.S. 806 (1996) (holding that so long as an officer has probable cause to believe that a person committed a traffic infraction, the officer may use that traffic infraction as a pretext to investigate crimes for which the officer may lack probable cause).

25. Schneckloth v. Bustamonte, 412 U.S. 218 (1973) (holding that police officers need not inform suspects of their right to refuse consent).

26. Unlike criminal forfeiture, civil forfeiture does not require an individual to be charged or convicted of a crime in order to have their property seized. The property itself becomes the subject of a lawsuit, such as *Commonwealth v. $9,000 U.S. Currency.* Commonwealth v. $9,000 U.S. Currency, 8 A.3d 379 (Pa. Cmmw. Ct. 2010); Sarah Stillman, The Rise of Civil Forfeiture: Taken, NEW YORKER (Aug. 12, 2013), http://www.newyorker.com /magazine/2013/08/12/taken; If the officer was particularly vindictive, he could impound Tanya's car or any other property found in the vehicle under expansive forfeiture laws. Often, property impounded through civil asset forfeiture will either be used by the police, or auctioned off to support discretionary police funds that may be used to fund anything from first-class flights to end-of-year bonuses. *Id.*

27. Stillman, *supra* note 26.

28. Michael Sallah et al., *Stop and Seize*, WASH. POST (Sept. 6, 2014), http: //www.washingtonpost.com/sf/investigative/2014/09/06/stop-and-seize/. In 2015, then Attorney General Eric H. Holder, Jr., issued an order which "eliminated most opportunities for state and local law enforcement . . . to avail themselves of federal forfeiture and related equitable sharing proceeds," which contributed to a reduction in the number of DEA cash seizures by over half. OFFICE OF THE INSPECTOR GENERAL, U.S. DEP'T OF JUST., REVIEW OF THE DEPARTMENT'S OVERSIGHT OF CASH SEIZURE AND FORFEITURE ACTIVITIES iv (Mar. 2017), https://oig.justice.gov/reports /2017/e1702.pdf. Various attorneys general under the Trump administration signaled support for civil asset forfeiture despite pushback from Congress. *Compare* George Will, *Does Anyone Besides Jeff Sessions Defend Today's Civil-Forfeiture Practices?*, NAT'L REV. (Dec. 24, 2016), http://www .nationalreview.com/article/443299/civil-forfeiture-jeff-sessions-defends -seizing-property-without-judicial-process, Christopher Ingraham, *Jeff Sessions's Justice Department Turns a $65 Million Asset Forfeiture Spigot Back On*, WASH. POST (July 19, 2017), https://www.washingtonpost.com/news /wonk/wp/2017/07/19/jeff-sessions-justice-department-turns-a-65-million -asset-forfeiture-spigot-back-on/, and Brian Tashman, *What We Learned From William Barr's Confirmation Hearing*, ACLU (Jan. 16, 2019), https: //www.aclu.org/blog/civil-liberties/executive-branch/what-we-learned -william-barrs-confirmation-hearing, *with* Nick Sibilla, *Rand Paul Introduces Bill to Abolish "Nonjudicial" Civil Forfeiture*, FORBES (June 30, 2020), https://www.forbes.com/sites/nicksibilla/2020/06/30/rand-paul-introduces -bill-to-abolish-nonjudicial-civil-forfeiture/.

29. Stillman, *supra* note 26.

30. *See* CARPENTER, *supra* note 23, at 152–67.

31. William H. Freivogel, *No Drugs, No Crime and Just Pennies for School: How Police Use Civil Asset Forfeiture*, PULITZER CTR. (Feb. 18, 2019), https: //pulitzercenter.org/reporting/no-drugs-no-crime-and-just-pennies-school -how-police-use-civil-asset-forfeiture.

32. ACLU OF PENN., GUILTY PROPERTY 7 (2015), https://www.aclupa.org /files/3214/3326/0426/Guilty_Property_Report_-_FINAL.pdf. The report highlighted several hurdles which those whose property is seized must overcome including lack of notice and procedural hoops to jump through. *Id.* at 5–7.

33. *See, e.g.*, Nick Sibilla, *Cops Use Traffic Stops to Seize Millions From Drivers Never Charged With a Crime*, FORBES (Mar. 12, 2014), https://www .forbes.com/sites/instituteforjustice/2014/03/12/cops-use-traffic-stops-to -seize-millions-from-drivers-never-charged-with-a-crime/.

34. *See* Stillman, *supra* note 26; Clifton Adcock, *Most Police Seizures of Cash Come from Blacks, Hispanics*, OKLA. WATCH (Oct. 7, 2015), http:// oklahomawatch.org/2015/10/07/most-police-seizures-of-cash-come-from -blacks-hispanics/ (finding that, in Oklahoma, nearly two-thirds of civil asset forfeitures came from Blacks, Hispanics, and other racial minorities); Howard Witt, *Highway Robbery? Texas Police Seize Black Motorists' Cash, Cars*, CHI. TRIB. (Mar. 10, 2009), http://www.chicagotribune.com/news /nationworld/chi-texas-profiling_wittmar10-story.html (reporting that civil rights attorneys fighting asset forfeitures in Tenaha, Texas refer to the practice as "highway robbery," "disproportionately targeted toward minorities"); Sallah, *supra* note 28 (finding that the majority of defendants in federal seizure cases were Black, Hispanic, or another ethnic minority); *See also* Murphy, *supra* note 23; GUILTY PROPERTY, *supra* note 32, at 10 (finding that Black Philadelphians were subject to 71 percent of forfeitures without convictions, despite only making up 44 percent of the population).

35. *See* Lynae Trista Turner, *Racial Disparity in the Development of the Drug Courier Profile and Civil Asset Forfeiture Provisions*, 3 HOW. SCROLL SOC. J. REV. 183 (1996).

36. THOMAS HARVEY ET AL., ARCHCITY DEFENDERS: MUNICIPAL COURTS WHITE PAPER (2014), http://www.archcitydefenders.org/wp-content /uploads/2014/11/ArchCity-Defenders-Municipal-Courts-Whitepaper.pdf; DEP'T OF JUST., *supra* note 1.

37. DEP'T OF JUST., *supra* note 1, at 2. *See also* Opinion, *Policing for Profit in St. Louis County*, N.Y. TIMES (Nov. 14, 2015), http://www.nytimes.com/2015 /11/15/opinion/sunday/policing-for-profit-in-st-louis-county.html [https:// perma.cc/3462-XC74] ("The Missouri Legislature has since set limits on how much of a city's revenue can come from traffic fines. But municipal creativity, at least in St. Louis County, seems boundless. An investigation by the St. Louis Post Dispatch this spring warned that towns in the county might start looking for cash in violations of building codes and neatness ordinances."). Michael Martinez et al., *Policing for Profit: How Ferguson's Fines Violated Rights of African-Americans*, CNN (Mar. 6, 2015), http://www.cnn.com/2015/03/06/us /ferguson-missouri-racism-tickets-fines/ [https://perma.cc/W6KN-GRDP] ("Just about every branch of Ferguson government—police, municipal court, city hall—participated in 'unlawful' targeting of African-American residents such as Hoskin for tickets and fines. . . .").

38. Dep't of Just., *supra* note 1, at 11–13.

39. *Id.*

40. *Id.* at 4–5, 62–63.

41. *Id.* at 4.

42. *Id.* at 4–5, 44–46.

43. *Id.* at 50–51.

44. *Id.* at 3. Harvey et al., *supra* note 36, at 36.

45. Dep't of Just., *supra* note 1, at 55.

46. *Id.* at 53; *see also* Harvey et al., *supra* note 36, at 37.

47. Dep't of Just., *supra* note 1, at 58.

48. *Id.* at 2 ("The City budgets for sizeable increases in municipal fines and fees each year, exhorts police and court staff to deliver those revenue increases, and closely monitors whether those increases are achieved.")

49. *Id.* at 13.

50. *Id.* at 10.

51. *Id.*

52. *Id.*

53. *Id.* at 11.

54. *Id.* at 42.

55. *Id.* at 11.

56. *Id.* ("Each month, the municipal court provides [Ferguson Police Department] supervisors with a list of the number of tickets issued by each officer and each squad. Supervisors have posted the list inside the police station, a tactic officers say is meant to push them to write more citations.").

57. *Id.* ("[Ferguson Police Department] supervisors and line officers have undertaken the aggressive code enforcement required to meet the City's revenue generation expectations. . . . Indeed, officers told us that some compete to see who can issue the largest number of citations during a single stop.").

58. *Id.* at 13.

59. Beth Colgan, *Lessons from Ferguson on Individual Defense Representation as a Tool of Systemic Reform,* 58 Wm. & Mary L. Rev. 1171, 1187 (2017).

60. *Id.* at 1187–88 (footnotes omitted).

61. *See* Stephen Bingham et al., Stopped, Fined, Arrested: Racial Bias in Policing and traffic Courts in California 1 (2016) ("Across the country, low-income people who commit minor offenses are saddled with fines, fees and penalties that pile up, driving them deeper into poverty. What's worse, they are arrested and jailed for nonpayment, increasing the risk of losing their jobs or their homes.").

62. For instance, residents in the approximately ninety municipali-

ties surrounding Ferguson report similar instances of predatory policing. Orlando de Guzman & Tim Pool, *The Policing of Black Bodies: Racial Profiling for Profit and the Killing of Ferguson's Mike Brown*, FUSION (Mar. 23, 2015), http://fusion.net/video/108471/ferguson-a-report-from-occupied -territory/ [https://perma.cc/Q2LM-KW9P] ("This problem, however, is not unique to Ferguson. St. Louis County is made of around 90 municipalities, each with their own police departments and courts. Residents report similar discriminatory treatment at the hands of law enforcement. And with so many different jurisdictions, a small infraction like an expired license plate can turn into dozens of fines and eventually warrants. Those in St. Louis who live below the poverty line are faced with the reality of buying food or paying fines."); *see* Editorial, *Policing for Profit Perverts Justice: Our View*, USA TODAY (Mar. 11, 2015), http://www.usatoday.com/story/opinion/2015/03/11 /ferguson-mo-police-traffic-tickets-justice-department-editorials-debates /70175690/ [https://perma.cc/26PE-P8QD] (asserting that "Ferguson, Mo. is not the only guilty municipality," and exploring similar practices in cities in Ohio, Alabama, and Mississippi).

63. Jag Davies, *Above the Law: New DPA Report Finds 'Policing for Profit' Gone Wild*, HUFF. POST (Apr. 29, 2015), http://www.huffingtonpost.com/jag -davies/civil-asset-forfeiture_b_7174238.html [https://perma.cc/VRH9- LHG5] (reporting on rampant "policing for profit" across the country including in Baltimore and multiple cities in Los Angeles County). *See also* BINGHAM ET AL., *supra* note 61, at 1.

64. Utah v. Strieff, 136 S. Ct. 2056 (2016) (declining to exclude evidence found when the officer discovers the defendant has an outstanding, valid arrest warrant during an unconstitutional stop).

65. Wong Sun v. United States, 371 U.S. 471, 484–88 (1963).

66. *Id.* at 488.

67. *See Strieff*, 136 S. Ct. at 2060. In *Strieff*, an officer stopped someone without reasonable suspicion, demanded their identification, ran that information through a warrant database, and subsequently arrested the person based on the discovery that the person had an outstanding warrant. *Id.* A search incident to arrest uncovered drugs. *Id.* The defendant moved to suppress the drugs on the ground that it was the fruit of an illegal seizure. *Id.* The Court concluded that suppression was not warranted because the officer's mistake as to reasonable suspicion was not flagrantly unlawful and because the discovery of the warrant acted as an intervening act between the illegal seizure and the discovery of the evidence. *Id.* at 2064. *See, e.g.*, Maryland v. Garrison, 480 U.S. 79 (1987) (finding reasonable an officer's mistake as to the existence of two apartments on the third floor of a building).

68. *Wong Sun, supra* note 65.

69. *Wong Sun, supra* note 65; *see Strieff*, 136 S. Ct. at 2056.

70. *See* Ben Fenwick & Alan Schwarz, In Rape Case of Oklahoma Officer, Victims Hope Conviction Will Aid Cause, N.Y. TIMES (Dec. 11, 2015),

http://www.nytimes.com/2015/12/12/us/daniel-holtzclaw-oklahoma-police
-rape-case.html [https://perma.cc/YDA9-RLGX]; see also Jacquellena Car-
rero, Oklahoma City Cop Daniel Holtzclaw Sentenced to 263 Years for
Rapes, NBC NEWS (Jan. 21, 2016), http://www.nbcnews.com/news/us-news
/oklahoma-city-cop-daniel-holtzclaw-sentenced-263-years-rapes-n501111
[https://perma.cc/YG3G-ATTZ]; Sarah Larimer, Disgraced Ex-Cop Daniel Holtzclaw Sentenced to 263 Years for On-Duty Rapes, Sexual Assaults,
WASH. POST (Jan. 22, 2016), https://www.washingtonpost.com/news
/post-nation/wp/2016/01/21/disgraced-ex-officer-daniel-holtzclaw-to-be
-sentenced-after-sex-crimes-conviction/ [https://perma.cc/9J7D-MLNP];
Eliott C. McLaughlin et al., Oklahoma City Cop Convicted of Rape Sentenced to 263 Years in Prison, CNN (Jan. 22, 2016), http://www.cnn.com
/2016/01/21/us/oklahoma-city-officer-daniel-holtzclaw-rape-sentencing/
[https://perma.cc/NDG6-RHVV]. He was convicted under several Oklahoma criminal statutes. State of Oklahoma v. Holtzclaw, OKLA. ST. CTS.
NETWORK http://www.oscn.net/dockets/GetCaseInformation.aspx?db
=oklahoma&cmid=3167778&number=CF-2014-5869 [https://perma.
cc/4EVB-SEF3] (last visited June 15, 2016). Holtzclaw's race is listed as "Asian
or Pacific Islander" in the Oklahoma State Courts Network. Party Record,
OKLA. ST. CTS. NETWORK, http://www.oscn.net/dockets/GetPartyRecord
.aspx?db=oklahoma&cn=CF-2014-5869&id=15801826 [https://perma
.cc/UH3R-WWSP] (last visited June 15, 2016). However, as Kirsten
West Savali points out, "[t]hat Holtzclaw's mother is reportedly of Japanese descent does not matter; once he put on that uniform, he became a
beneficiary of a racist system that devalues and destroys black people
as a matter of course and with impunity." Kirsten West Savali, If Daniel Holtzclaw's Victims Were White, Everyone Would Know His Name,
Root (Nov. 5, 2015), http://www.theroot.com/articles/news/2015/11/hate
_crime_if_daniel_holtzclaw_s_victims_were_white_everyone_would
_know.html [https://perma.cc/F5RL-D3TE].

71. McLaughlin et al., *supra* note 70.

72. *See* YOLANDE M. S. TOMLINSON, BLACK WOMEN'S BLUEPRINT, INVIS-
IBLE BETRAYAL: POLICE VIOLENCE AND THE RAPES OF BLACK WOMEN
IN THE UNITED STATES (2014) http://tbinternet.ohchr.org/Treaties/CAT
/Shared%20Documents/USA/INT_CAT_CSS_USA_18555_E.pdf [https://
perma.cc/9RQX-PTAQ]; see also NAT'L POLICE MISCONDUCT STATISTICS &
REPORTING PROJECT, CATO INST., 2010 ANNUAL REPORT (2010), http://www
.policemisconduct.net/statistics/2010-annual-report/ [https://perma.cc
/C84F-3KJN] (reporting that there were "618 officers involved in sexual
misconduct complaints [throughout 2010], 354 of which were involved in
complaints that involved forcible non-consensual sexual activity such as
sexual assault or sexual battery"); Amy Goodman, When Cops Rape: Daniel Holtzclaw & the Vulnerability of Black Women to Police Abuse, DEMOC-
RACY NOW! (Dec. 15, 2015), http://www.democracynow.org/2015/12/15
/daniel_holtzclaw_convicted_of_serial_rape [https://perma.cc/4HN6
-CKS8]; Letter on Policy and Oversight: Women of Color's Experiences of

Policing from Andrea J. Ritchie, Soros Justice Fellow, to President's Task Force on 21st Century Policing, U.S. Dep't of Justice 3 (Jan. 28, 2015), http://changethenypd.org/sites/default/files/docs/Women%27s%20Sign%20 Letter%20on%20to%20Presidential%20Task%20Force%20-%20Policy%20 and%20Oversight%20-%20FINAL.pdf [https://perma.cc/99RB-JHDN] (suggesting that police violence against women of color is endemic); Matt Sedensky & Nomaan Merchant, Hundreds of Officers Lose Licenses over Sex Misconduct, ASSOCIATED PRESS (Nov. 1, 2015), http://bigstory.ap.org/ article/fd1d4d05e561462a85abe50e7eaed4ec/ap-hundreds-officers-lose-licenses-over-sex-misconduct [https://perma.cc/SYE5-27KQ] ("In a year-long investigation of sexual misconduct by U.S. law enforcement, The Associated Press uncovered about 1,000 officers who lost their badges in a six-year period for rape, sodomy and other sexual assault; sex crimes that included possession of child pornography; or sexual misconduct such as propositioning citizens or having consensual but prohibited on-duty inter-course.").

73. Cameron Kimble, *Sexual Assault Remains Dramatically Underreported*, BRENNAN CTR. (Oct. 4, 2018), https://www.brennancenter.org/our-work /analysis-opinion/sexual-assault-remains-dramatically-underreported.

74. Kimberlé W. Crenshaw, *From Private Violence to Mass Incarcera-tion: Thinking Intersectionally About Women, Race, and Social Control*, 59 UCLA LAW REVIEW 1418 (2012); KIMBERLÉ CRENSHAW & ANDREA J. RITCHIE, AFR. AM. POL'Y F. & CTR. FOR INTERSECTIONALITY AND SOC. POL'Y STUD., SAY HER NAME: RESISTING POLICE BRUTALITY AGAINST BLACK WOMEN 1–5 (2015), http://static1.squarespace.com/static /53f20d90e4b0b80451158d8c/t/560c068ee4b0af26f72741df/144362868653 5/AAPF_SMN_Brief_Full_singles-min.pdf [https://perma.cc/HY5R -SHVF].

75. ANDREA RITCHIE, INVISIBLE NO MORE: POLICE VIOLENCE AGAINST BLACK WOMEN AND WOMEN OF COLOR 137–49 (2017).

76. *See* Goldie Taylor, *White Cop Convicted of Serial Rape of Black Women*, DAILY BEAST (Dec. 10, 2015), http://www.thedailybeast. com/articles/2015/12/10/the-most-horrific-cop-rape-case-you-ve -never-heard-of.html [https://perma.cc/U8PP-KQ24] ("[Holtzclaw] didn't go after doctors, lawyers, housewives, and schoolteachers in a white sub-urb. . . . Holtzclaw targeted and preyed on women he thought no one would believe, women who didn't have the power to push an investigation or to demand his arrest.").

77. McLaughlin et al., *supra* note 70.

78. Taylor, *supra* note 76.

79. *See* Jessica Testa, *The 13 Women Who Accused a Cop of Sexual Assault, in Their Own Words*, BUZZFEED (Dec. 10, 2015), http://www.buzzfeed.com /jtes/daniel-holtzclaw-women-in-their-ow#.ufX3Wg1nv [https://perma .cc/X4KW-EEUY].

80. For a discussion of the extent to which we might think of police inter-actions as bargaining zones, see Carbado, *(E)racing the Fourth Amendment, supra* Prologue note 2, at 1020.

81. Rachel A. Harmon, *Why Arrest*, 115 MICH. L. REV. 307, 313 n.14, 313 n.15 (2016).

82. *Id.* at 314.

83. Beth A. Colgan, *Fines, Fees, and Forfeitures*, 18 CRIMINOLOGY, CRIM. JUST. LAW & SOC'Y 22, 23 (2017).

84. MATTHEW MENENDEZ, MICHAEL F. CROWLEY, LAUREN-BROOKE EISEN & NOAH ATCHISON, THE STEEP COSTS OF CRIMINAL JUSTICE FEES AND FINES: A FISCAL ANALYSIS OF THREE STATES AND TEN COUNTIES 46 (2019).

85. Joseph Shapiro, *As Court Fees Rise, The Poor Are Paying the Price*, NPR (May 19, 2014), https://www.npr.org/2014/05/19/312158516/increasing-court-fees-punish-the-poor.

86. CHRIS MAI & MARIA RAFAEL, THE HIGH PRICE OF USING JUSTICE FINES AND FEES TO FUND GOVERNMENT IN FLORIDA 3 (2020).

87. HEATHER HUNT & GENE R. NICHOL JR., COURT FINES AND FEES: CRIMINALIZING POVERTY IN NORTH CAROLINA 5 (2017).

88. CHRISTIAN HENRICHSON ET. AL., THE COSTS AND CONSEQUENCES OF BAIL, FINES AND FEES IN NEW ORLEANS 21 (2017).

89. CHRIS MAI & MARIA RAFAEL, THE HIGH PRICE OF USING JUSTICE FINES AND FEES TO FUND GOVERNMENT IN NEW YORK 3 (2020).

90. Helen A. Anderson, *Penalizing Poverty: Making Criminal Defendants Pay for Their Court-Appointed Counsel through Recoupment and Contribu-tion*, 42 U. MICH. J.L. REFORM 323, 333 (2009).

91. Wayne A. Logan & Ronald F. Wright, *The Political Economy of Applica-tion Fees for Indigent Criminal Defense*, 47 WM. & MARY L. REV. 2045, 2053 (2006) (describing how trial judges can waive fees in some jurisdictions, oth-ers will condition appointment on future collection).

92. Anderson, *supra* note 90, at 329–30.

93. ALICIA BANNON, MITALI NAGRECHA & REBEKAH DILLER, CRIMINAL JUSTICE DEBT: A BARRIER TO REENTRY 7 (2010).

94. *Id.*

95. *Id.* at 7.

96. MENENDEZ, CROWLEY, EISEN & ATCHISON, *supra* note 84, at 34.

97. *Id.* at 40.

98. The following fines and fees could have been imposed on these women if they were arrested and convicted or subjected to deferred judgment in Oklahoma. The women could have potentially owed a $93 misdemeanor court filing fee, a $150 state mental health fee, a $150 lab fee, a minimum

$50 transportation/service fee, and up to $52 a day if incarcerated in county jail, among others. *A Journey Into Debt*, OKLA. WATCH (Feb. 4, 2020), https://oklahomawatch.org/2015/01/31/list-journey-into-debt/. Additionally, the women could have been subject to further fees in order to exercise their guaranteed rights, including $40 for "Indigent application for representation," $30 "Each time a jury is requested," $10 for a "Courthouse security fee," and $35 to file a bond, again, among others. *See* Order RE: Uniform Oklahoma Fee Schedule, No. SCAD-2019-89 (Okla. 2019).

All in all, if convicted and incarcerated, the women could have faced tens or hundreds of thousands of dollars in fines and fees. *See Prisoners of Debt: Justice System Imposes Steep Fines, Fees*, OKLA. WATCH (Oct. 28, 2019) https://oklahomawatch.org/2015/01/31/justice-system-steeps-many-offenders-in-debt/. And like other jurisdictions discussed above, Oklahoma issues "failure to pay" warrants if Oklahomans fail to keep up with payments on debts that collectively total hundreds of millions of dollars across the state. Damion Shade, *Reducing Oklahoma's Court Fines and Fees Is Police Reform*, OKLA. POL'Y INST. (Dec. 10, 2020)).

99. The women repeatedly stated they did not report the assaults they experienced because they would not be deemed believable. S.H., one of the survivors, stated: "I didn't think that no one would believe me." Another survivor, C.R., stated: "It was nobody there but just me and him, so to me, I just took it as my word against his." C.J., another survivor, stated: "Who are they going to believe? It's my word against his because I'm a woman and, you know, like I said, he's a police officer." Testa, *supra* note 79.

100. *Id.*

101. Savali, *supra* note 70.

102. Jessica Testa, *How Police Caught the Cop Who Allegedly Sexually Abused Black Women*, BUZZFEED (Sept. 5, 2014), https://www.buzzfeednews. com/article/jtes/daniel-holtzclaw-alleged-sexual-assault-oklahoma-city [https://perma.cc/HC4Q-2HBM] ("Holtzclaw's 'mistake' . . . was believing [Jannie Ligons] was similar to his other alleged victims: all black middle-aged women, but women of a lower social status and with reason to fear the authorities. . . . [whereas Jannie Ligons] had no criminal record to be held over her. She was driving through the neighborhood where the other women were confronted, but she didn't live there.").

103. *Id.*

104. Goodman, *supra* note 72 (Jannie Ligons also stated, "I was traumatized. I went to therapy. I had a stroke behind this. And I still live with this, day after day."); *see also* Testa, *supra* note 102 (noting that Holtzclaw got caught after "he profiled the wrong woman"); Carbado, Predatory Policing, *supra* Introduction note 25 (noting that predatory policing works in conjunction with mass criminalization to facilitate not only the surveillance, social control, and economic exploitation of African-Americans but also their arrest, incarceration, and exposure to police violence).

105. *See* Testa, *supra* note 102.

106. DEP'T OF JUST., *supra* note 1, at 62, 67.

107. *Id.* at 62.

108. Carbado, Predatory Policing, *supra* Introduction note 25.

109. For a judicial primer on quid pro quo harassment, see generally *Burlington Industries, Inc. v. Ellerth*, 524 U.S. 742, 752–754 (1998), which describes the academic origin of the quid pro quo theory of sexual harassment, and its applicability when evaluating claims of sexual harassment.

110. Testa, *supra* note 79 (recounting that Holtzclaw told a seventeen-year-old girl he was convicted of raping, "You got warrants. I don't want to have to take you to jail. . . . This is what you're going to have to do.").

111. *Id.* (documenting that Holtzclaw repeatedly told the women that he would be back).

112. *Id.* (T.B.'s story).

113. *See* CRENSHAW & RITCHIE, *supra* note 74, at 26 ("Black women are particularly vulnerable to sexual assault by police due to historically entrenched presumptions of promiscuity and sexual availability. Historically, the American legal system has not protected Black women from sexual assault, thereby creating opportunities for law enforcement officials to sexually abuse them with the knowledge that they are unlikely to suffer any penalties for their actions."). For a discussion of the ways the perceived respectability of an individual shapes whether that individual can function as a civil rights icon, see Devon W. Carbado, *Black Rights, Gay Rights, Civil Rights*, 47 UCLA L. REV. 1467 (2000). *See also* Jasmine Sankofa, *Mapping the Blank: Centering Black Women's Vulnerability to Police Sexual Violence to Upend Mainstream Police Reform*, 59 HOW. L.J. 651, 680 (2016) ("When activists in Oklahoma City reach[ed] out to Black churches, they were turned away because the survivors were not seen as 'sanctified,' rendering them 'throw away women.' Thus, our quest for 'respectable' survivors entrenches victim blaming and silences the experiences of vulnerable populations at the margins, such as Black transgender women." (footnotes omitted)).

114. DEP'T OF JUST., *supra* note 1, at 60.

115. Jocelyn Simonson, *Bail Nullification*, 115 MICH. L. REV. 585, 594–95 (2017).

Chapter Seven: Reasonable

1. I should be clear to note that this rewritten opinion limits its archive—the materials on which it formally relies—to sources that were available to the Court when the *Whren* case was litigated. I do not pretend that this citational practice fully avoids the pitfalls of presentistism. To be perfectly transparent about the matter, how I view *Whren* is very much informed by the broad literature that has emerged over the past two decades arguing that

the case was wrongly decided. Still, that I have limited our archive along the preceding lines helps us make the case that the Court could have reached a different conclusion—and within the boundaries of Fourth Amendment law—that centered the dignity and sanctity of Black lives.

Index

About the Author

Devon Carbado is the Honorable Harry Pregerson Professor of Law at UCLA School of Law. The author of numerous articles and edited volumes, he is also the co-author of *Acting White? Rethinking Race in "Post-Racial" America*. He lives in Los Angeles.

Publishing in the Public Interest

Thank you for reading this book published by The New Press. The New Press is a nonprofit, public interest publisher. New Press books and authors play a crucial role in sparking conversations about the key political and social issues of our day.

We hope you enjoyed this book and that you will stay in touch with The New Press. Here are a few ways to stay up to date with our books, events, and the issues we cover:

- Sign up at www.thenewpress.com/subscribe to receive updates on New Press authors and issues and to be notified about local events
- www.facebook.com/newpressbooks
- www.twitter.com/thenewpress
- www.instagram.com/thenewpress

Please consider buying New Press books for yourself; for friends and family; or to donate to schools, libraries, community centers, prison libraries, and other organizations involved with the issues our authors write about.

The New Press is a 501(c)(3) nonprofit organization. You can also support our work with a tax-deductible gift by visiting www.thenewpress.com/donate.